GLOBAL INEQUALITY AND AMERICAN FOREIGN POLICY IN THE 1970s

GLOBAL INEQUALITY AND AMERICAN FOREIGN POLICY IN THE 1970s

MICHAEL FRANCZAK

CORNELL UNIVERSITY PRESS

Ithaca and London

First published 2022 by Cornell University Press

Library of Congress Cataloging-in-Publication Data

Names: Franczak, Michael, 1990– author.
Title: Global inequality and American foreign policy in the 1970s / Michael Franczak.
Description: Ithaca [New York]: Cornell University Press, 2022. | Includes bibliographical references and index.
Identifiers: LCCN 2021036537 (print) | LCCN 2021036538 (ebook) | ISBN 9781501763915 (hardcover) | ISBN 9781501763922 (pdf) | ISBN 9781501763939 (epub)
Subjects: LCSH: Globalization—United States—History—20th century. | Globalization—Developing countries—History—20th century. | United States—Foreign economic relations—Developing countries—History—20th century. | United States—Foreign relations—Developing countries—History—20th century. | United States—Economic policy—History—20th century.
Classification: LCC HF1456.5.D44 F74 2022 (print) | LCC HF1456.5.D44 (ebook) | DDC 337.730172/4—dc23
LC record available at https://lccn.loc.gov/2021036537
LC ebook record available at https://lccn.loc.gov/2021036538

To my daughter, Lucy Noelle,
who was stillborn November 16, 2020.
"Sweet joy befall thee."

CONTENTS

ACKNOWLEDGMENTS

This book would have been impossible without the many friends, colleagues, and institutions that supported me along the way. Mentioned here are some that come to mind.

As an undergraduate at the University of Michigan, I was lucky to find good mentors early on. Tomoko Masuzawa took a chance on me as a freshman when I ended up in her graduate seminar on European intellectual history. William "Buzz" Alexander brought me down from the clouds through his Prison Creative Arts Project. Ronald Grigor Suny taught me the elements of my craft and giants of my field while supervising my senior thesis. In addition to recommending me for graduate study, Robert Franzese taught me methods in international relations and international political economy with great skill and patience.

At Boston College, I always found support in my PhD cohort: Allison Vander Broek, Joanna Kelly, and John Morton. Philipp Stelzel was a kind colleague and friend through tough times. Craig Gallagher and Janet Kay were always just a few doors down. James Cronin introduced me to the concept of contemporary history and showed me its value through his teaching, scholarship, and advising. Seth Jacobs refined my knowledge of US diplomatic history with care and wit. I especially gained from teaching for Sylvia Sellers-Garcia. Alan Rogers was a great squash partner, and I look forward to our next match.

I owe both thanks and apologies to many librarians and archivists. First among them is Anne Kenny at Boston College, who forgave so many Interlibrary Loan infractions and facilitated so much research. I also benefited from grants and assistance from many sources, including the Gerald Ford Presidential Library, the Jimmy Carter Presidential Library, Purdue University, University of Notre Dame, University of Pennsylvania, Yale University, the World Bank, and the Society for Historians of American Foreign Relations. The Clough Center for Constitutional Democracy at Boston College was a dedicated and generous source of support. Thanks to Vlad Perju and the other graduate and law fellows, the Clough Center was also an intellectual home. At Boston

College Law School, Frank Garcia was a generous reader and thoughtful interlocutor.

A postdoctoral fellowship in international security studies at Yale University gave me the space and support to revise the manuscript for this book. I benefited from a brilliant cohort of historians and political scientists whose advice improved the manuscript and whose friendship improved my life. They are Fritz Bartel, Jean-François Bélanger, Susan Colbourn, Matthias Frendem, Mayumi Fukushima, Louis Halewood, Michael Joseph, John Maurer, Brandon Merrell, Peter Slezkine, Emily Whalen, and Claire Yorke. Nuno Monteiro was an inspiring director, scholar, and friend to us all. His warmth and humor was unmatched, and he is sorely missed. Arne Westad, David Engerman, and Joanne Meyerowitz all provided valuable advice, feedback, and encouragement. Michael Brenes and Daniel Steinmetz-Jenkins became close friends and intellectual collaborators. Samuel Moyn joined the project in its early stages and convinced me that I was on to something. Sam's professional and intellectual generosity has been unwavering, and I am grateful for his mentorship and friendship.

A second postdoctoral fellowship at the University of Pennsylvania's Perry World House allowed me to complete the book. Special thanks to Michael Horowitz, Michael Weisberg, and LaShawn Jefferson for making PWH such an inviting and intellectually exciting place to be. My talented cohort has been supportive through some especially challenging times. They are Shae Frydenlund, Meg K. Guliford, Richard J. McAlexander, Francesca Parente, Lauren Pinson, and Andrea Restrepo-Mieth. Koko Warner, Zeid Ra'ad al Hussein, Melissa Lee, and Jesse Keenan influenced my thinking in different ways. A number of other faculty at Penn and across Philadelphia gave me crucial feedback on revisions and much more, especially Robert Vitalis, Erin Graham, Julia Gray, Orfeo Fioretos, Artemy Kalinovsky, and Richard Immerman.

I owe Guy Erb, Gordon Streeb, and Henry Nau for providing me with an inside view of US State Department and National Security Council decision making in the 1970s and early 1980s via oral interviews. Other scholars who lent their time and insights to the project include Paul Adler, Roham Alvandi, Daniel Bessner, Vivian Chang, Cindy Ewing, Giuliano Garavini, Michael de Groot, Verena Kröss, Piers Ludlow, Mario del Pero, Kathleen Rasmussen, Christian Ruth, Shaine Scarminach, Giles Scott-Smith, Debbie Sharnak, and Rasmus Sondergaard.

Daniel Sargent and Quinn Slobodian were ideal readers for the manuscript, and their thoughtful and comprehensive reports were essential for revisions. At Cornell University Press, I had a dedicated editorial team in Michael McGandy, who brought the manuscript to peer review, and Sarah Grossman and Ellen Labate, who carried it over the line and into print. I am also grateful to Michelle

Abbreviations

ACP	African, Caribbean, Pacific
BHN	basic human needs
CAP	Common Agricultural Policy
CDM	Coalition for a Democratic Majority
CERDS	Charter of Economic Rights and Duties of States
CIA	Central Intelligence Agency
CIEC	Conference on International Economic Cooperation
COMECON	Council for Mutual Economic Assistance
EC	European Community
ECLA	Economic Commission on Latin America
ECOSOC	UN Economic and Social Council
ECSC	European Coal and Steel Community
EEC	European Economic Community
EPB	Economic Policy Board
EPG	Economic Policy Group
FAO	UN Food and Agriculture Organization
FNLA	National Liberation Front of Angola
FSLN	Sandinista National Liberation Front
G-7	Group of 7
G-77	Group of 77
GATT	General Agreement on Tariffs and Trade
GDP	gross domestic product
GNP	gross national product
GSP	generalized system of preferences
IBRD	International Bank for Reconstruction and Development
IDA	International Development Association
IDCA	International Development Cooperation Authority
IEA	International Energy Agency
IFAD	International Fund for Agricultural Development
ILO	International Labor Organization
IMF	International Monetary Fund

IRB	International Resources Bank
ISI	import substitution industrialization
ISTC	Institute for Scientific and Technical Cooperation
IWC	International Wheat Council
LAFTA	Latin American Free Trade Association
LDC	less developed country
MOC	multinational oil company
MPLA	People's Movement for the Liberation of Angola
MSA	Most Seriously Affected
NAFTA	North American Free Trade Agreement
NATO	North Atlantic Treaty Organization
NIEO	New International Economic Order
NSC	National Security Council
OAS	Organization of American States
OAU	Organization of African Unity
ODC	Overseas Development Council
OECD	Organization for Economic Cooperation and Development
OEEC	Organization for European Economic Cooperation
OMB	Office of Management and Budget
OPEC	Organization of Petroleum Exporting Countries
OPIC	Overseas Private Investment Corporation
PRC	People's Republic of China
PRM	presidential review memorandum
SALT	Strategic Arms Limitation Talks
SELA	Latin American Economic System
UN	United Nations
UNCSTD	United Nations Conference on Science and Technology for Development
UNCTAD	United Nations Conference on Trade and Development
UNDP	United Nations Development Program
USAID	United States Agency for International Development
USDA	United States Department of Agriculture
WTO	World Trade Organization

Timeline of
Significant Events

NOTABLE NORTH-SOUTH DIALOGUE MEETINGS		US FOREIGN POLICY AT A GLANCE
	1971	Nixon's New Economic Policy devalues dollar and delinks from gold
UN Conference on Trade and Development (UNCTAD) III, Santiago, April–May 1972	**1972**	Nixon visits China, pursues détente with US-Soviet grain deal
	1973	Kissinger negotiates US withdrawal from Vietnam; World food security disintegrates amid oil crisis
UN Sixth Special Session on Raw Materials and Development, New York, April–May 1974	**1974**	Nixon resigns, Ford takes over
World Food Conference, Rome, November 1974		
UN Seventh Special Session on Development and International Economic Cooperation, New York, September 1975	**1975**	Last Americans leave South Vietnam as communists capture Saigon; East and West sign Helsinki Final Act, advancing detente
Conference on International Economic Cooperation, Paris, December 1975–January 1977		
UNCTAD IV, Nairobi, May 1976	**1976**	Carter defeats Ford; Mao Zedong dies
	1977	Carter signs Panama Canal treaty, pursues human rights in Latin America
	1978	Deng Xiaoping becomes China's paramount leader, begins economic reforms
UNCTAD V, Manila, May–June 1979	**1979**	Shah of Iran's fall and Soviet invasion prompt Carter Doctrine for Middle East
UN Conference on Science and Technology for Development, Vienna, August 1979		
	1980	Federal Reserve chief Volcker begins interest rate "shocks"; Reagan defeats Carter
International Meeting on Cooperation and Development, Cancún, October 1981	**1981**	Reagan makes good with Saudis in major arms deal
	1982	Mexico's default sparks regional debt crisis; Reagan begins rollback in Latin America

GLOBAL INEQUALITY AND AMERICAN
FOREIGN POLICY IN THE 1970s

Introduction

On May 22, 1977, Jimmy Carter delivered the first postelection articulation of his foreign policy to the graduating class of the University of Notre Dame. The speech was memorable for Carter's declaration that human rights are a "fundamental tenet" of US foreign policy. More radical, however, was his insistence that history had disproved the two most consistent elements of postwar US foreign relations: first, the "belief that Soviet expansion was almost inevitable but that it must be contained"; and second, "the corresponding belief in the importance of an almost exclusive alliance among non-Communist nations on both sides of the Atlantic." In contrast, Carter depicted a world divided not between a free West and an unfree East but between a rich North and a poor South. "We know a peaceful world cannot long exist one-third rich and two-thirds hungry," the new president declared.[1]

Carter had good reason to claim a relationship between global inequality and national security. In 1972 crop failures and the depletion of US grain reserves through a deal with the Soviet Union had launched the Third World into its most severe food crisis ever. In 1973, citing in part rising food prices charged by developed countries, members of the Organization of Petroleum Exporting Countries (OPEC) drove a price revolution that quadrupled the price of oil they sold to the West.

While Western leaders castigated OPEC for exacerbating the food crisis, the oil producers' show of strength was a catalyst to an emerging Third World

coalition in the United Nations whose members sought "economic decolonization" by establishing a "right to development" and other major changes in
global economic governance.² On May 1, 1974—International Workers' Day—
they presented their demand for a New International Economic Order (NIEO)
that would redistribute both economic resources and political power from the
North—that is, the United States, Canada, western Europe, and Australasia—
to the South—everyone else, with the exception of the Eastern Bloc. The goal
was to fundamentally transform the crumbling postwar economic order in
their favor through comprehensive economic negotiations; the weapon was
the newly established economic might of cash-flush OPEC members. "We do
understand that a collapse in the world economy brought about by serious
disagreements in the developed countries could mean a similar disaster for the
developing ones," declared Venezuelan president and OPEC leader Carlos Andrés Pérez. "What we aim, is to take advantage of this opportunity when raw
materials, and energy materials primarily, are worth just as much as capital
and technology, in order to reach agreements that will ensure fair and lasting
balances."³

The countries of the South did not achieve their goal of an NIEO, which is
why historians have long neglected it. However, in the last few years, interest
in the NIEO has exploded. New perspectives on its significance have been offered by scholars in a variety of disciplines.⁴ Still, these studies have generally
assumed the NIEO's defeat from the start; none have comprehensively addressed US foreign policy through the eight years of North-South dialogue
and negotiations that followed.

This book tracks US policy toward these unprecedented global negotiations
from their beginning in the early 1970s to their abrupt and unexpected end in
1982. US policymakers had an obvious interest in defeating the NIEO, or at
least rendering it toothless, but perception is reality, and the perception up until
1982 was that a breakdown in the dialogue could sabotage the West's fragile
post-1973 economic recovery. This book asks and answers two basic questions:
How did successive US administrations respond to the South's challenge, both
inside and outside the various economic forums in which the NIEO was debated? What was the North-South dialogue's legacy for US foreign policy as it
moved out of the crisis-ridden 1970s and toward a new era of neoliberal reform, intensive globalization, and eventually post–Cold War triumphalism?

Global Inequality argues that Third World solidarity around the NIEO forced
presidents from Richard Nixon to Ronald Reagan to defend, sometimes con-
cede, but ultimately consolidate US hegemony over an international economic
order that was under attack abroad and lacked support at home. Newly available sources from presidential libraries; the papers of cabinet members, am-

bassadors, and nongovernmental organizations; and personally conducted interviews with top government officials reveal how the NIEO brought global inequality to the forefront of US national security, with lasting and visible effects on US politics and power.

With virtually zero Soviet involvement or interest, the North-South dialogue upended fundamental assumptions about world order across the US foreign policy community. For successive US governments, the NIEO's major significance was not the threat of it actually being enacted lock, stock, and barrel but it is very real and immediate effects on US global leadership. The NIEO convinced realists in the Ford administration and liberal internationalists in the Carter administration of the necessity of North-South cooperation on energy, food, and other commodities, but it also galvanized neoliberals who sought to return international economics to the free market. The effort found sympathy among some US and European proponents of détente and arms control who saw the Cold War as having had largely destructive consequences for Third World development, but it faced opposition from a growing number of US neoconservatives who co-opted human rights language to delegitimize the regimes—and, by association, the economic grievances—of the NIEO's Third World proponents.

Global Inequality places the NIEO's significance within the larger context of US grand strategy through the 1970s. In doing so, it reveals how both Democratic and Republican administrations tried to pacify the countries of the South through new policies on everything from food, finance, and foreign aid to apartheid and the Panama Canal. Additionally, through a focus on the US domestic political economy, it argues that the NIEO and North-South dialogue became an inflection point for some of the greatest economic, political, and moral crises of the 1970s, including the end of golden age liberalism and the return of the market, the splintering of the Democratic Party and the building of the Reagan coalition, and the rise of human rights in US foreign policy in the wake of the Vietnam War. Although US foreign policy did not change the NIEO's character, the NIEO changed the character of US foreign policy. Policy debates and decisions in the North-South dialogue were pivotal moments in the histories of three ideological trends—neoliberalism, neoconservatism, and human rights—that would form the core of the United States' post–Cold War foreign policy.

Understanding the NIEO's significance for US foreign policy requires a brief explanation of its target. That is, what was the old international economic order? And why did representatives from Latin America, Africa, and Asia demand in the early 1970s not just its reform but its replacement?

A fitting starting point is July 1944, when 730 delegates from all forty-four Allied nations occupied a run-down, sweltering-hot hotel in rural Bretton Woods, New Hampshire, for the three-week-long United Nations Monetary and Financial Conference. Since 1941, the two conference leaders—Britain's economist-diplomat extraordinaire John Maynard Keynes and US assistant treasury secretary Harry Dexter White—had been crafting dueling yet similar plans for a new international monetary system. By providing emergency loans to distressed governments, a new international fund (the two believed) would prevent countries from turning to autarchy or worse during downturns. Neither man was known for his humility, but at Bretton Woods, they were particularly dismissive of the twenty-seven non-European delegations.[5] Keynes deemed their presence "the staging of a monkey house, in order that the [US] President [Franklin Roosevelt] can say that 44 nations have agreed on the [plans]"; according to White, the Cuban delegation's purpose was to "provide cigars."[6]

Keynes's and White's derision did not mean that delegates from poor nonwhite countries were silent. After almost seventy years of neglect, the release of the full Bretton Woods transcripts in 2012 demonstrated that delegates from Latin America, Africa, the Middle East, and Asia assailed the proposed International Monetary Fund (IMF) for its uneven voting powers, assumption of the dollar as the world's reserve currency, and lack of development content.[7] The International Bank for Reconstruction and Development was intended for war-torn Europe; only after Marshall Plan money began to flow in 1948 did it adopt the World Bank name and mission.

For poor countries, the most troubling aspect of the proposed order at Bretton Woods was rich countries' expectation of a fixed international division of labor that left poor nations stuck as suppliers of cheap commodities (and purchasers of expensive manufactured goods). Instead, delegates from Mexico, Egypt, China, and India argued that trade and development went hand in hand and that economic inequality between nations could be just as destructive as inequality within them.

A. D. Shroff was one such delegate. A director of Tata Sons Ltd., the major Indian conglomerate, Shroff was a liberal capitalist who would soon coauthor India's postindependence Bombay Plan. Expecting independence and knowing that India would need money and machinery from outside Britain's "sterling area"—particularly from the United States—Shroff was in favor of an open international economy. Yet he feared that the Americans were about to kick away the ladder for countries like India—by far the most populous at the conference, he reminded the other delegates—just as they were given permission to climb. As Shroff stated at a tense July 10 meeting for the IMF:

You want to facilitate the expansion and balance of international trade. You, incidentally, want to help build up a higher level of employment and income throughout the world as a whole. [US treasury secretary] Mr. [Henry] Morgenthau, in his very fine opening address, said poverty is a menace wherever it is found in the country. Do you expect to fulfill the main objectives of this [International Monetary] Fund if you allow large countries to be festered with this sort of poverty?[8]

As the Cold War took off, development aid to Third World countries became a major weapon in the United States' foreign policy arsenal. During the 1950s and 1960s economists and social scientists dedicated to modernization theory dominated Washington and the World Bank alike. By promising a speedy route to development through state-assisted capitalism and infrastructure spending, modernization theory's advocates also hoped to convince aid recipients of the dangers of Soviet aid.[9] This objective was neatly summarized in the title of a 1960 book—*The Stages of Economic Growth: A Non-Communist Manifesto*—by W. W. Rostow, its main proponent in the administrations of John F. Kennedy and Lyndon Johnson.[10]

Yet just as President Kennedy declared the 1960s the Development Decade, focused on achieving annual growth rates, poor countries began organizing for a more ambitious goal: global structural change. Two organizations of particular importance were OPEC, founded in 1960, and the United Nations Conference on Trade and Development (UNCTAD), founded in 1964.

The technocrats from Latin America and the Middle East who formed OPEC saw it not as a cartel (as the United States and others later called it) but as a new mechanism for the global South's commodity producers to improve their declining terms of trade with the North. One of its first resolutions declared: "It is no longer possible to live in peace in a world where the rich are getting richer and the poor are getting poorer. The problems of decreasing export values for the underdeveloped countries are not peculiar to petroleum."[11] These ideas were elaborated (and reached a larger audience) through UNCTAD. Under the leadership of famed Argentinean development economist Raúl Prebisch— "Latin America's Keynes," as the *Economist* eulogized him—UNCTAD functioned for the developing countries as a favorable counterbalance to the US-dominated General Agreement on Tariffs and Trade (GATT).[12] Like the UN General Assembly (and unlike the GATT, IMF, and World Bank), UNCTAD operated on a one-country, one-vote principle, giving developing countries a sound majority. There, the Group of 77 (G-77) could strategize on how to band together to change the rules of trade and finance in their favor—or at least get a better seat at the bargaining table.

A note on terminology is in order. Throughout the book I use the phrases *Third World*, *South*, *developing countries*, and *poor countries* to refer to the one hundred–plus members of the G-77 caucus that signed on to establish a NIEO in the 1970s. A critical reader might regard these terms with skepticism. Is it not highly reductive, or even insulting, to speak of a unified and coherent *South*, given those countries' immense political, cultural, and economic diversity? *Third World* is clearly a Cold War holdover, contrasting the "First World" of relatively wealthy industrial democracies (the West) and the Second World of relatively wealthy and heavily industrialized communist dictatorships of eastern Europe. That US and European newspapers and politicians still use this obvious anachronism, both as a geographic term and as a stand-in for any poor and politically dysfunctional country, is offensive and historically illiterate. Yet *poor countries* is also vexing, as there is no obvious reason why Mexico, a country with at least a century of industrialization under its belt, should identify or align politically with Sierra Leone or the Congo. One is now more likely to come across the term *global South* in a journal of postcolonial literary studies than in one of international relations or economics, suggesting its irrelevance for understanding global power and conflict today.

Why do I use these terms more or less interchangeably in my narrative if they are so analytically and politically fraught? The short answer is: because the agents of my narrative—US foreign policy elites and their counterparts in Europe and the South—did the same. Administrations from Nixon to Reagan recognized North-South relations as a new axis of international conflict and incorporated it into their statecraft—as did governments in Canada, Britain, France, West Germany, the Netherlands, and Scandinavia. At the United Nations, the North-South divide and the NIEO were inescapable, dominating the General Assembly (controlled by a Third World majority) year after year. "The 1970s was the great age of Third World rhetoric of common cause and common action," explains historian B. R. Tomlinson. "In retrospect, we can see that the UN resolutions of 1974 concerning the New International Economic Order marked a high point in the diplomatic solidarity of Third World governments . . . and in the rhetoric associated with the international economic relations of development."[13]

The longer answer is that what these countries shared was a lack of self-determination in global politics and the economy. The 1955 Bandung Conference marked the Third World's entrance on the diplomatic stage, where leaders adopted a common policy of nonalignment in the Cold War. Often, prominent figures in the Non-Aligned Movement, such as Egypt's Gamal

Abdel Nasser and India's Jawaharlal Nehru, took money from both the Americans and the Soviets, playing the two giants against each other to their own advantage.[14]

Decolonization became a reality in the 1960s, as some three dozen new African countries joined the United Nations. With few exceptions, European colonial governments had invested almost nothing in those countries' civil societies beyond what was necessary for defense and economic extraction. Most of Latin America had been independent since the nineteenth century, but British, French, and especially US governments and firms overcame such formalities through gunboat diplomacy. What countries in Latin America, Africa, and Asia shared was their integration into the global capitalist economy in a subservient (or dependent) role: as exporters of raw materials and importers of finished manufactured goods.

Whereas most Third World leaders promoted some form of socialism at home, in the form of state-owned industries and a welfare state, the countries behind the NIEO had no interest in international class struggle. Hence the conspicuous lack of influence from the world's largest developing country: the People's Republic of China. At the 1974 Sixth Special Session, paramount leader Mao Zedong's speech was delivered by his eventual successor Deng Xiaoping. In it, the chairman declared his country's support for OPEC's actions ("What was done in the oil battle should and can be done in the case of other raw materials") and the NIEO program.[15] According to historian Elizabeth Ingleson, the speech was the "first time a Chinese leader publicly articulated Mao's vision of an international society divided into Three Worlds," and it "reflected Mao's desire to position China, not the Soviet Union or the United States, as the leader of the developing world."[16] But it was too little, too late. In 1971, when the People's Republic began to represent China at the United Nations, it rejected the G-77's offer to join its caucus; for that reason, it was not listed among the ninety-nine developing countries on whose behalf the NIEO was introduced.[17] Lacking membership in the G-77, all China could do was spectate. In contrast, leaders and experts in the Soviet Union and other Eastern Bloc countries viewed the NIEO as "parochial" and "excessively utopian" (one wonders whether Moscow saw the irony). Instead, the Soviets held up the Eastern Bloc's Council for Mutual Economic Assistance as "a model of equitable economic integration" superior to the NIEO. The G-77 did not bite.[18]

According to several sources, the terms *North* and *South* were first used as geopolitical categories by British philosopher and diplomat Lord Oliver Franks.[19] Mostly forgotten by historians today, Franks first served as professor of philosophy at the University of Glasgow (1936–46) before joining Clement Attlee's Labour government. As his country's ambassador to Washington (1948–52), Franks was one of Britain's most important postwar diplomats, playing key roles in the success of the Marshall Plan, the North Atlantic Treaty Organization (NATO), and the Organization for Economic Cooperation and Development (OECD).

Franks's involvement in postwar European reconstruction and cooperation led to a new focus by the end of the 1950s. In 1959 Franks, then chairman of London's Lloyds Bank, undertook a tour of India and Pakistan at the request of World Bank president Eugene Black. Black himself had been prompted by a bipartisan resolution from US senators John F. Kennedy and John Sherman Cooper (the latter a Kentucky Republican who had served as Eisenhower's ambassador to India), recommending that members of the business and banking community visit these countries to gain a better understanding of their economic challenges. Shocked at the extent of poverty but impressed by the seriousness of both governments' development plans, Franks returned home convinced that Western governments' policies toward poor countries ranged from inadequate (not enough foreign aid) to actively harmful (barriers to trade).[20] In 1960 Franks toured the United States and warned audiences of an impending "North-South problem of equal importance" as the Soviet challenge. "If 12 years ago the balance of the world turned on the recovery of Western Europe," Franks insisted, "now it turns on a right relationship of the industrial north of the globe to the developing south."[21] This "founding father" of the Marshall Plan in Europe (as Franks's sole biographer called him) was now arguing that the United States and its OECD allies should make a commensurate effort toward the countries of the global South, and for the same reason: peace and security.[22]

The lectures made an impression on members of the new Kennedy administration, including development guru Walt Rostow, treasury secretary Douglas Dillion, and, especially, iconoclastic undersecretary of state George Ball.[23] In 1964 Ball led the US delegation to UNCTAD I, and when he returned home he went on his own lecture circuit to spread awareness of the "vertical division between the industrialized North and the impoverished South," as described in Franks's report.[24] Ball was well aware of the South's "wide diversity" as well as US foreign policy's "rather romantic" understanding of the Third World. Nevertheless, he recognized that the structural critique of international relations "bind[s] together disparate peoples who would otherwise have little in common." Third World alliances such as the "Afro-Asian bloc" (prominent at Bandung) were not just about anti-imperialism and political self-determination. "That banner, that slogan, has intense symbolic significance. It means much more than the dismantling of colonial empires," Ball explained to an audience at the University of North Carolina. "It is an amalgam of memories, resentments, and aspirations—the insistence on a place in the sun, the demand for equality, the hope for improvement in economic well-being."[25]

Although US policymakers were aware of the North-South framework in the 1960s, not until the 1973 oil crisis and the 1974 NIEO declaration did they begin to take it seriously. This was also the case for political scientists, especially those in the emerging subfield of international political economy. Pioneering scholars such as Joseph Nye, Susan Strange, Gerry Helleiner, John Ruggie, and Stephen Krasner began or made careers in the 1970s and early 1980s with books and articles analyzing the eruption of North-South conflict in international relations.[26] How else could one explain countries like Venezuela (with a gross domestic product surpassing West Germany's) and Saudi Arabia (which literally had more money than it could spend) aligning behind the same economic critique and remedy as the poorest ones? By the end of the 1970s, there was enough of a literature for Robert W. Cox to write a comprehensive review article for *International Organization*, still one of the field's premier journals.[27] Whether in or out of government, foreign policy analysts in the 1970s had to reckon with North and South as much as East and West.

As much as the United States was responsible for the creation of the Bretton Woods order, it was also responsible for its abrupt collapse. This book begins in 1971, a year of tremendous importance for US foreign policy and the global economy. On August 15 the Nixon administration unilaterally ended the Bretton Woods gold exchange standard by allowing the dollar to float. The administration's "New Economic Policy" suspended the dollar's convertibility into gold and imposed a ninety-day wage and price freeze, a 10 percent cut in foreign aid, and a 10 percent import surcharge.[28] Because oil was priced in dollars, the devaluation caused a major drop in OPEC members' real revenue. It was the "exorbitant privilege" exercised par excellence.

The dollar's devaluation was one reason for OPEC's policies during and after the 1973 Arab-Israeli war, which matched the Arab members' embargo with production cuts. A second, even more consequential move was the Nixon administration's historic 1972 grain deal with the Soviet Union. The largest of its kind, the $1.1 billion deal quadrupled wheat prices within months and initiated a severe though largely forgotten food crisis in poor countries.[29] While consumers in the North encountered gas lines and more expensive hamburgers, the oil-importing countries of the South found themselves priced out of global food markets as well as the fertilizers and other oil-based agricultural inputs they had adopted, with vigorous Western encouragement, during the

1960s Green Revolution. The NIEO's "Programme of Action" identified "fluctuating, temporary and excessively high-price levels" for agricultural inputs from the North as a central obstacle to development and called for new international bodies to stabilize prices and increase concessional food aid and technology transfer.[30]

Chapter 1 argues that US food policy leading up to and during the 1972–74 world food crisis was both a catalyst for OPEC's actions to raise oil prices in October 1973 and the first tool with which the United States—especially secretary of state Henry Kissinger—sought to break OPEC–Third World solidarity and rein in the NIEO. It also follows the planning and staging of the November 1974 World Food Conference in Rome—a signature Kissinger initiative that even his most intimate biographers have ignored.

At the World Food Conference, Kissinger hoped to take his Third World critics by surprise. In his carefully written (and rewritten) keynote, he announced the United States' commitment to a new global food bank, while blaming OPEC for driving up food costs due to high fertilizer prices. However, developing countries stuck to their structural critique of international economic relations and stood behind OPEC leaders Venezuela and Algeria, which promised their own new food and development programs to offset the costs to poor countries. Kissinger's proposals also suffered from internal opposition, as free-market reformers such as treasury secretary William Simon, Alan Greenspan, and secretary of agriculture Earl Butz charged Kissinger with acquiescing to the South's demands for global market intervention and sabotaging their own deregulatory crusade at home.

While the United States remained divided over its policy response to the NIEO, its closest allies in Europe were converging. In chapter 2 I argue that the NIEO both exposed deep divisions in the transatlantic alliance and ultimately prompted its renewal in the semi-institutional Group of 7. Kissinger, the architect of the new partnership, promoted economic managerialism among the North and economic concessions to the South as a way to break the "unholy alliance" between oil-importing developing nations and OPEC and to prevent both from striking separate deals with the European Community. Though never absolute, this move toward transatlantic unity in the emerging North-South dialogue stalled divergence in the North's economic policies, after more than a decade of troubling drift, while also weakening the resolve of the OPEC–No-PEC alliance and thus the South's negotiating power.

Chapter 3 examines the NIEO's impact on the early neoconservative movement. Although Gerald Ford's advisers saw the NIEO in terms of economic ideologies, a growing number of "new conservatives" believed the North-South divide represented a fateful struggle between US liberalism and its antiliberal Third World detractors. Their first victory came with Ford's appointment of self-described "Harry Truman Democrat" Daniel Patrick Moynihan as UN ambassador. His call for the United States to "go into opposition" against the postcolonial UN majority won him wide support at home but isolated the United States from its transatlantic partners. Moynihan's forced exit by Kissinger after just seven months on the job reflected the secretary of state's commitment to his own approach of conciliatory rhetoric and limited compromise. The chapter concludes with Kissinger's May 1976 charm offensive in Africa, which he had never previously visited in any official capacity. There, adopting the rhetoric of his hosts, Kissinger declared his support for "liberation on two scales," and in an opening speech at the UNCTAD meeting in Nairobi, he announced his government's commitment to negotiating a Common Fund for Commodities, a key plank of the NIEO platform.

These first three chapters make a novel, if counterintuitive, argument about Kissinger and the Third World. There has been more written about Kissinger in the last five decades than any other US diplomat ever. A full historiography would constitute a book in itself.[31] Many of these works highlight Kissinger's endorsement of governments and policies that permitted severe human rights violations in Latin America, Africa, and East Asia.[32] In focusing on Kissinger's economic diplomacy toward the South, this book in no way seeks to rehabilitate his legacy in those countries. But it does argue that in North-South economic negotiations, Kissinger's unwillingness to inject morality into foreign policy was an asset.

Though in private he dismissed the issue of human rights as sentimental nonsense, Kissinger was aware of its political salience in both North and South. Thus, Kissinger turned his reluctance to pursue Third World violators of human rights (especially liberal political rights or "negative freedoms") into an advantage, showing that nations with vastly differing political systems could settle global economic issues discretely from political ones. The World Food Conference was a perfect example. It took place fourteen months after the US-supported coup in Chile that ousted the democratically elected government of Salvador Allende, and throngs of (mostly Western) protesters surrounded Kissinger's motorcade each morning outside the stately palace where the delegates met.[33] Inside the conference, Third World delegates blasted the US position and the US government for its role in bringing about the crisis, but the only human rights concepts put forth were economic—that is, the right to food and the right to development.

The next three chapters focus on the Carter administration's approach to the NIEO, which was at once comprehensive and chaotic. Chapter 4 explains how Jimmy Carter went from being a little-known southern governor to US president through two important influences on his approach to foreign affairs: the Trilateral Commission, led by his future national security advisor Zbigniew Brzezinski, and the Overseas Development Council (ODC), an influential Washington-based think tank that also provided Carter with a number of new hires. The Trilateral Commission's idea of an interdependent world divided not between East and West but between North and South was the starting point for Carter's post-Vietnam foreign policy, while the ODC's promotion of a model of development based on meeting "basic human needs" became a major part of his administration's approach to human rights.

Chapter 5 takes a regional perspective to consider the NIEO's impact on the Carter administration's policy toward Latin America. Though remembered today for its censure of Southern Cone dictators, the administration intended its human rights policy to act as a positive incentive as well. State Department officials believed that including basic needs in its definition of human rights would encourage regional cooperation on development and moderate the North-South dialogue. However, key Latin American leaders became frustrated with Carter's evasive stance on structural North-South issues such as trade and debt. Many developing countries would pay a huge price for the lack of action on debt: the 1982 debt crisis, initiating what was known in Latin America as the "lost decade of development."

I then turn to the Carter administration's efforts to transform the North-South dialogue from within. By 1978, US officials conceded that political successes such as agreements on the Panama Canal and human rights had not lessened the South's support for the NIEO in North-South negotiations. In chapter 6 I show how, at secretary of state Cyrus Vance's urging, US policy for North-South negotiations came to focus on two "practical" development strategies: basic needs and appropriate technology transfer. The United States found some support for these policies at UNCTAD V and the UN Conference on Science and Technology for Development (UNCSTD), where the ODC's influential board chairman Father Theodore Hesburgh, president of the University of Notre Dame and Carter's personal friend, headed the US delegation. Against Hesburgh's advice, Carter and Vance refused to cede US control over any new development fund to Third World–dominated bodies. However, due to unexpected international and domestic pressure, the administration also failed to secure congressional funding for its own basic needs and appropriate technology counterinitiatives. This reduced the Carter administration's contributions to UNCTAD V and UNCSTD—the final two negotiating sessions of the North-South dialogue—to near zero.

In the Ford administration, neoconservatives and neoliberals had fought for influence over a realist Kissinger. In the Carter administration, liberal internationalists fought themselves. Both neoliberal and neoconservative ideological coherence precluded compromise with the NIEO. This was also true for Carter's world-order liberals, but with a twist. Kissinger had made a point of promising much more than he could deliver or suggesting ideas that he expected to fail. The Carter administration did the opposite—it promised only what it thought it could deliver, and this relative honesty was taken as parsimony, hostility, or indifference. In the end, world-order liberals' insistence on maintaining US primacy in international institutions outweighed their commitment to delivering more, and more effective, antipoverty aid.

In chapter 7 I explain how Ronald Reagan declined to continue any of Carter's reforms to US development policy or to convince Congress to meet Carter's other international commitments. This meant that the link between basic needs and human rights was severed, with important consequences for both. Human rights in US foreign policy reemerged in the 1980s as powerful weapons against Cold War adversaries accused of political abuses. At the same time, the Reagan administration restored US leadership in international financial institutions. Under the direction of A. W. Clausen, a former Bank of America CEO appointed by Reagan in 1981, the World Bank ended its involvement in global economic reform and turned instead to smaller-scale antipoverty projects. But it was at the IMF where neoliberalism's policy trifecta—privatization, liberalization, and fiscal discipline—became dogma as the Washington Consensus.[34] These efforts were first concentrated on the Latin American and African countries to which Western banks had loaned the petrodollars received from OPEC following the first oil crisis. The Atlantic alliance was strengthened around these and other changes occurring during the political and economic crises of the 1970s. What resulted, I conclude, was the reconstruction of an essentially Anglo-American market-based world system that had very little to do with the NIEO—the political, economic, and intellectual defeat of which enabled the new system's development and spread.

In the epilogue I place the NIEO in contemporary perspective by analyzing trends in global inequality and income since the 1980s. Drawing on the most recent data from scholars of US and global inequality, I show that although inequality between nations has in fact decreased under neoliberal globalization, the United States has returned to levels of economic inequality not seen since before the Great Depression. Contrary to prominent US foreign policy boosters and critics alike, I conclude that the greatest threat to the United States' global leadership and prosperity is not Americans' populism or isolationism but the gross maldistribution of income facilitated by political elites over the past four decades.

Chapter 1

Food Power and Free Markets

In the early 1970s, record high oil prices collided with an overheated US economy, a broken foreign aid program, rich-country protectionism, and the reorganization of US agricultural production to meet the needs of markets, not people.[1] While most Americans would remember 1972–74 as the end of cheap oil, for the worst off in poor countries, it meant the end of cheap food. The United Nations even created a new category—Most Seriously Affected (MSA)—for the thirty-three nations (mostly in Africa and the Middle East) where some half a billion people faced starvation.[2]

On May 1, 1974—International Labor Day—a diverse coalition of developing countries presented to the UN General Assembly a proposal for a New International Economic Order (NIEO).[3] Acting just months after Arab members of the Organization of Petroleum Exporting Countries (OPEC) had launched their embargo, during which time the price of oil quadrupled, the NIEO's Third World supporters hoped to negotiate a redistribution of money and power from the rich industrial North to the poor countries of the South. Their weapon was control over the price of major commodities—especially oil—that had made possible the United States' and Europe's spectacular prosperity after World War II. The NIEO's "Programme of Action" for food identified "fluctuating, temporary and excessively high-price levels" for agricultural inputs from the North as a central obstacle to development in the South, and it called for new international bodies to stabilize prices and increase conces-sional food aid and technology transfer.[4]

US food policy was both a catalyst for OPEC's decision to enact a spike in oil prices and the first tool with which the United States sought to break OPEC–Third World solidarity and rein in the NIEO. Secretary of state Henry Kissinger viewed food as the most powerful weapon against the Arab oil producers, all of which were large importers of US grain. The United States exercised enor-mous leverage over world food prices, as demonstrated in 1972, when a $1.1 billion deal with the Soviet Union tripled the price of wheat on international markets.[5] At the UN General Assembly in September 1974, Kissinger and presi-dent Gerald Ford charged OPEC with exacerbating the food crisis through its actions and insisted that high oil prices hurt the poorest countries the most.[6]

OPEC and even the MSA nations were unpersuaded by this logic. Instead, most developing countries believed that food prices were part of a larger sys-tem of unfair trade, one that overcharged them for rich countries' exports and underpaid for their own. The connection among the food crisis, the oil crisis, and the NIEO was not lost on contemporary observers. "What we have wit-nessed [in the last two years]," observed historian Geoffrey Barraclough in Au-gust 1975, "is the opening stage of a struggle for a new world order, a search for positions of strength in a global realignment, in which the weapons (backed, naturally, by the ultimate sanction of force) are food and fuel."[7]

Those weapons were on full display in November 1974 at the World Food Conference in Rome. Kissinger, who took the lead in organizing the confer-ence, sought to divide what he called the "unholy alliance" of OPEC and the rest of the Third World through limited compromise.[8] His plan was to use US food power to negotiate toward a global system of grain reserves for poor countries, so that a food shortage need never again turn into a crisis. Such an action, Kissinger believed, would convince poor and hungry countries that they had more to gain by cooperating with Washington to improve the existing global economic order than by trying to overthrow it with Algiers.

Kissinger's strategy faced many challenges, but the most immediate was internal. His willingness to endorse global market interventions was strongly opposed by the Nixon and Ford administrations' influential secretary of agri-culture, Earl Butz. An evangelist of free markets and self-reliance, Butz sought nothing less than "to remove the [US] government from the conduct of agri-culture, and the United States from the conduct of the world food economy."[9] He was backed by Ford's notably promarket and antistate (or "market funda-mentalist"[10]) economic team, especially treasury secretary William Simon and Alan Greenspan, head of the president's Council of Economic Advisers and a member of Ford's Economic Policy Board (EPB). Nor did Kissinger do himself any favors by running roughshod over the bureaucracies at the US Department of Agriculture (USDA) and the Treasury Department as he attempted to seize control of the administration's international economic policymaking to confront the NIEO. Ideological and personal disagreements between Kissinger and Ford's economic advisers over how to respond to the Third World's challenge would continue after the World Food Conference, reinforcing the OPEC–Third World alliance and further isolating the United States from its closest allies in western Europe.

US Economic Policy and the 1972–1974 World Food Crisis

The 1960s was a decade of promise in food production due to advances in agricultural technology in the North and agricultural modernization in the South. This Green Revolution meant that from 1960 to 1972, the global production of grains—the main food supply for most of the world—increased almost every year, saving millions from hunger but also dramatically reducing crop diversity and increasing dependence on fossil fuels.[11]

Rising incomes and populations in developing countries buffeted the global demand for grains. Not only did more people need to be fed; as poor people become richer, they tend to eat more dairy, poultry, and meat, which require large amounts of grain to raise.[12] Yet while incomes rose across the world, developing countries took a smaller part of the growing pie. Their share of world trade declined from 31 percent in 1950 to 21.4 percent in 1960 to just 17.2 percent in 1970, by which time the three largest economies—the United States, West Germany, and Japan—together accounted for more than a third.[13]

Overall growth in food supply and world trade masked these asymmetries, but they had serious consequences. Because the demand for food is highly inelastic, even small decreases in food supply can result in large price increases. This effect is exacerbated in poor countries, where most grain is produced for immediate consumption—feeding family and livestock—rather than sold.[14] Nor was the Green Revolution performing as well as its supporters had promised. "Agricultural output has grown so slowly [in developing countries]," the Council of Economic Advisers explained in 1967, "that food output per person in many countries is below pre–World War II levels." At the same time, "over half" of their annual growth in gross domestic product (GDP)—which, at 4.5 percent, was just shy of the UN's target for the Development Decade— "has been needed just to maintain their low level of living."[15]

US agricultural and trade policy presented another impediment to increasing food production in the Third World. Due to generous farm subsidies implemented during the Great Depression, by the mid-1960s the United States had become the world's leading exporter of grain. In response, the US government promoted cheap wheat exports and increased food aid through Public Law (PL) 480, also known as Food for Peace. What was not sold to developing countries, on highly advantageous terms, was stockpiled. Although this brought relatively stable, predictable, and low food prices for those countries, it gave neither farmers nor governments an incentive to invest in domestic production.

For a while, the United States' Cold War food policy paid considerable domestic dividends. Consistent US government purchases of farmers' surpluses boosted rural incomes during an unprecedented period of wage and employment growth in manufacturing centers and suburbs, and a powerful farm lobby in Washington grew to ensure that stockpiling was a bilateral commitment. But mounting federal deficits in the late 1960s led some politicians to question whether this commitment was worth the cost. President Richard Nixon complained that the United States was paying for the large majority of a scheme to stabilize world food prices, while the European Community (EC) discriminated against US food exports through its Common Agricultural Policy. The Nixon administration concluded that reducing stockpiles and holding back production would help US farmers by increasing world prices. From mid-1970 to mid-1972, the United States reduced its production of wheat by one-third, bringing down its share of global production from 15 percent to 10 percent.[16]

In June 1971 the Nixon administration moved to liberalize trade with the Soviet Union, eastern Europe, and China. The centerpiece of Nixon's overture was the promise of a massive sale of heavily subsidized grain to the Soviet Union. There was no actual grain shortage in the Soviet bloc. Facing an economic slowdown and short on hard currency, the Soviets planned to use the grain both as animal feed to maintain citizens' increased meat consumption (and thus loyalty) and as a commodity to sell on global markets for badly needed dollars. The deal also met several goals for the Nixon administration. It promoted détente, pleasing Kissinger; it was relatively cheap, pleasing the Treasury Department; it reduced US stockpiles, pleasing the USDA; and it raised prices, pleasing the farm bloc just in time for the 1972 elections. In what one journalist memorialized as the "Great American Grain Robbery," the Soviet Union alone absorbed about half of US carryover stocks in 1972 and more than one-quarter of total 1972 production.[17] In 1961 world food reserves—held mostly by the United States—could sustain world needs for 105 days; by 1974, those reserves could sustain needs for only thirty-three days.[18] The combination of lower production and the deliberate liquidation of stockpiles made the United States, and thus the world, ill prepared for any sudden shocks.[19]

The first shock came on August 15, 1971, when the Nixon administration ended the Bretton Woods gold exchange standard by allowing the dollar to float. Some countries still played ball, choosing to take more dollars rather than forcing the leader of the world's monetary system to devalue. But the writing was on the wall: countries such as West Germany and France refused to permit more and more inflation to support the lifestyles of US citizens or the quagmire in Vietnam, and traders in foreign exchange markets, believing the dollar to be overvalued, began to sell them rapidly. In May 1971 West Germany left the Bretton Woods system; in July, Switzerland and France asked for more than $140 million in gold. "I don't give a shit about the lira," Nixon insisted in June, and he asked his advisers to come up with a policy that would boost the domestic economy in time for the 1972 elections.[20] John Connally, his new non-economist treasury secretary, was entrusted with pulling together the views of Federal Reserve chairman Arthur Burns, undersecretary for international monetary affairs Paul Volcker, and Office of Management and Budget (OMB) director George Schulz. The administration's "New Economic Policy," announced August 15, consisted of the suspension of the dollar's convertibility into gold, a ninety-day wage and price freeze, a 10 percent cut in foreign aid, and a 10 percent import surcharge.[21]

The dollar's devaluation might have helped poor countries buy more US grain. In fact, Nixon intended to increase agricultural exports to balance US accounts, a strategy pursued more aggressively by Secretary Butz following the 1972 elections. However, the grain agreements with communist countries depleted the majority of the US surplus; at the same time, a series of bad weather events limited production in other important producers such as Australia, Argentina, India, and Peru.[22]

The devaluation also set off a series of events in international energy markets that had serious consequences for food prices. Throughout the 1950s, several Middle Eastern oil producers charged that Western governments were colluding with multinational oil companies (MOCs) to keep prices artificially low. Following the Anglo-Iranian Oil Company's refusal to cooperate on a new agreement with the Iranian government, prime minister Mohammed Mossadegh nationalized the country's oil industry. The Anglo-American coup that ousted Mossadegh from power in 1953 served as a powerful example of the limitations of the Third World's economic and political sovereignty in the postwar era.

Determined to increase their share of profits from the MOCs' exploitation of their reserves, the governments of Iran, Iraq, Kuwait, Saudi Arabia, and Ven-

ezuela met in Baghdad in 1960 to announce the formation of the Organization of the Petroleum Exporting Countries. Through most of the 1960s,
OPEC was essentially an informal bargaining group, confining its activities to
negotiating better profit-sharing agreements with MOCs. But because oil was
priced in dollars, the US devaluation caused a major drop in OPEC members'
real revenues—at the same time that prices were rising for just about everything else.

At first, OPEC pledged to price a barrel of oil against gold to maintain price
stability, to little effect. But on October 17, 1973, citing the US decision to resupply the Israeli military during the Arab-Israeli war, six Arab OPEC members
announced that they would stop oil exports to the United States and other supporters of Israel, including the Netherlands, Portugal, and South Africa.[23] At
the same time, OPEC leaders who did not join the boycott defended production cuts and high prices as long overdue. "Of course [the price of oil] is going
to rise," the shah of Iran told Italian journalist Oriana Fallaci in November.
"Certainly! And how!" The shah did not participate in the Arab countries' boycott, but he defended it with the clear economic logic of dependency theory:
"You've increased the price of wheat you sell us by 300 per cent, and the same
for sugar and cement. You've sent petrochemical prices skyrocketing. You buy
our crude oil and sell it back to us, refined as petrochemicals, at a hundred
times the price you've paid us. You make us pay more, scandalously more, for
everything, and it's only fair that, from now on, you should pay more for oil."[24]
Algeria's minister of oil agreed. The US decision to resupply Israel "at most
played the role of a catalyst, in taking a decision which was already well prepared and well justified on the economic level."[25] By the end of the embargo in
March 1974, the price of oil had quadrupled from about $3 per barrel to $12.

The 1971 devaluation had already increased the price of grain by as much
as 15 percent; after the 1972 wheat sale to the Soviet Union, grain prices quadrupled.[26] Better harvests and weather in early 1973 were promising, but the
oil shock dashed any hope of falling food prices. The growth of US agriculture was in large part the result of new fuel-intensive farming practices; the
same was true for the more modest gains in food production by developing
countries. The United States and EC responded by restricting food exports to
control domestic prices, but poor countries had no such defense against skyrocketing prices for the petroleum-based inputs required by modern agriculture. For decades, the Third World had lived off of cheap food imports from
the United States, Canada, and Europe, and the modernization packages promoted by both West and East prioritized industrialization over agricultural development. Now, poor countries would pay the price for their dependence on
the rich world's charity and misguided development schemes.

Western intellectuals pondered the morality of inaction but offered little guidance. Some even came down on the side of inaction in order to wean chronically dependent countries such as Bangladesh; others saw an application of medical-type triage—where rich countries decided which "patients" were worth trying to save—as the most humane option. "Cruel as it may sound," the president of the US National Academy of Sciences explained, "if the developed and affluent nations do not intend the colossal, all-out effort commensurate with this task, then it may be wiser to let nature take its course."[27] In other words, produce, pay, or perish.

Kissinger: Food, Oil, and Interdependence

Historians have argued that the oil crisis initiated a profound transformation in Kissinger's thinking, pushing him toward an awareness of global interdependence and the consequences of US economic policies for foreign policy objectives.[28] Kissinger himself certainly pushed this narrative. In a flattering January 1975 interview, *Business Week* concluded that "the outbreak of the October war in 1973, with the resultant oil embargo in the U.S.," had led Kissinger to undertake a "radical shift" in focus away from Southeast Asia and East-West relations and toward "international economics," where he had "taken over the lead role" in both the US government and abroad.[29]

This was both true and incomplete. Kissinger's reconsideration of international economics and national security came first from the world food crisis, though the significance of his response would soon be transformed by the energy question. On September 5, 1973, Kissinger sent out a National Security Council (NSC) memorandum outlining Nixon's growing concern about the food shortage's effects on allies. US agricultural policy had "long been a source of irritation in our relations with Europe," Kissinger summarized Nixon as saying, but "the recent emergency of protein and grain shortages has brought a new dimension . . . causing problems for many developing countries and for us in our relations with them."[30] Kissinger then asked the NSC to produce a study on the issue, and in response, it endorsed the idea of a "world food security system" involving an "international food stockpile agreement" to "ensure that in times of shortage, those with the least ability to pay would not be the first to suffer."[31]

Concern over the costs and consequences of US food policy was not new. In 1958, four years after its establishment, senator Hubert Humphrey wrote a scathing review of the PL 480 program and called for major reorganization and reform. Nor was the idea of a global food reserve new. Sir John Boyd Orr, the first director-general of the UN Food and Agriculture Organization (FAO), included such a reserve as part of his failed 1946 proposal for a World Food Board.[32] In 1959 George McGovern suggested the idea again in a letter to his Senate colleagues, and both Nixon and John F. Kennedy publicly supported a "multilateral surplus food distribution system" during the 1960 presidential campaign.[33]

Just weeks after his NSC memorandum, Kissinger would tell the UN General Assembly of his own support for such a system, which would be negotiated at a global conference on food the following year. Kissinger could not take sole credit for the idea; nor were his reasons entirely geostrategic. As D. John Shaw tells it, the idea for a global conference originated in discussions between Pakistani economist and FAO official Sartaj Aziz and former US Agency for International Development (USAID) official and president of the Overseas Development Council (ODC) James Grant, both of whom would play important intellectual and policy roles in North-South dialogue discussions in the 1970s and 1980s.[34] After their meeting, Grant persuaded Senator Humphrey, who frequently sought the ODC's advice on development policy, to take the idea to Kissinger, whose August 22 nomination for secretary of state still faced considerable opposition in the Senate. In exchange for Humphrey's support, the two decided that Kissinger would propose a global conference to address the world food crisis.[35]

On September 21, 1973, Kissinger's nomination passed the Senate; on September 23 he was sworn in. The next day, introducing himself as "the world's most junior Foreign Minister," Kissinger told the UN General Assembly of his proposal for a food conference to be held in November 1974 under FAO auspices (Aziz would act as undersecretary-general). "We will participate without preconditions, with a conciliatory attitude and a cooperative commitment," he insisted. "We ask only that others adopt the same approach." In tentative recognition of the Third World's larger complaints against the global economic system, Kissinger promised in the next sentence to "examine seriously" the Group of 77's Charter of Economic Rights and Duties of States (CERDS).[36]

In October 1973 OPEC initiated its blockade. By January 1974, the posted global price of oil had quadrupled, from $3 to $12 a barrel. Just a few months later, the Group of 77 (G-77) bloc of developing countries presented the NIEO at the UN's Sixth Special Session (and first on development). Heralded by Julius Nyerere of Tanzania as a "trade union for the poor nations," the NIEO called for a world order "based on equity [and] sovereign equality" and designed to "correct inequalities and redress existing injustices" through global redistribution and new international institutions responsive to Third World needs.[37]

OPEC members played key roles in developing and advancing the NIEO program. As chair of the Non-Aligned Movement, Algeria's Houari Boumediene was ideally positioned to lead the charge for economic decolonization. At home, Boumediene plastered Algiers with posters proclaiming OPEC "the shield of the Third World."[38] When he later refused to discuss oil prices with the rich countries unless they also agreed to address raw materials, it was the United States, not Algeria, that caved.

Venezuela was a second important link. President Carlos Andrés Pérez championed the NIEO from its inception, and the fact that he declined to participate in the Arab countries' boycott gave him more credibility in Western countries. On September 25, 1974, he took out a full-page ad in the *New York Times* defending OPEC against Ford's accusations at the UN and declaring his hope for an "equitable" grand bargain between North and South, brokered by OPEC. Like Boudmedienne, Pérez insisted that neither food nor energy could be separated from the larger problem of an existing international economic order designed to reinforce earlier patterns of inequality and dependence. "The World Food Conference [in November] will not be able to achieve its lofty objectives," Pérez warned, "if developing countries do not succeed in guaranteeing remunerative prices for the raw materials we produce, prices that are in the necessary and fitting balance with the prices of the manufactured goods we import."[39]

For US foreign policy, OPEC's advocacy for the NIEO upgraded the world food situation from a nuisance to a crisis. It also upgraded the US dominance in global food production from a burden to a powerful tool, at a time when traditional levers of US power were either ineffective or, as in the case of military intervention, potentially catastrophic. These two facts conditioned Kissinger's initial response to the NIEO and food's leading role in it. Just as Nixon did not "give a shit about the lira," Kissinger did not "give a damn about Bangladesh on humanitarian grounds. *I want it [food] for foreign policy.*" The United States had used food as a foreign policy tool for decades, but it had scarcely considered the long-term consequences for global food security. For Kissinger, committing to funding agricultural development in the Third World and taking the lead on an international reserve system would force OPEC to put its money where its mouth was. "This [food] is one of the few weapons we have to deal with oil prices," he insisted to newly installed president Gerald Ford in a September 1974 cabinet meeting on US participation at the World Food Conference. The United States could point out that OPEC's actions hit poor countries disproportionately, but food prices had begun their sharp rise in 1971, two years before the oil shock. At the same time, in 1973, 60 percent of PL 480 concessional aid went to just three strategic US allies: South Korea, South Vietnam, and Cambodia. "The President is scolding everyone at the United Nations for being miserly on energy, and the less we say we'll do on food, the less effect it has," Kissinger explained to Butz and Greenspan. "We are trying to tell the Third World they must be cooperative, and in turn we will try to cooperate."[40]

Butz: Food Power and the American Farmer

Kissinger's proposals for intergovernmental cooperation on food aligned him more with the liberal establishment than with other Ford cabinet members. "An internationally agreed system of food reserves is now in the self-interest of all nations," the ODC's Grant told Congress in 1973.[41] In June 1974 McGovern chaired hearings held by the Senate Select Committee on Nutrition on global food issues, at which he too called for an international system of food reserves. Five months later, senators McGovern, Humphrey, and Richard Clark joined Kissinger and Butz at the World Food Conference as members of an unofficial congressional delegation.[42]

Kissinger's biggest challenge before the conference was internal. Ford's economic advisers opposed Kissinger on both ideological (free market) and bureaucratic grounds. The Council of Economic Advisers conducted its analysis independently and was responsible to the president only. The treasury secretary was tasked with managing the country's overall financial stability, which in theory meant that they were responsible to all Americans but which in practice meant, in addition to the president, a few dozen powerful Wall Street investors and firms (nearly all holders of the office were alums). Not so for the secretary of agriculture, whose constituents in 1970 were spread across the country on some two-and-a-half million farms—down from three-and-a-half million ten years prior.[43] Earl Lauer Butz was the most consequential USDA head since Henry Wallace in the 1930s. In fact, his mission was to dismantle the system of price supports enacted during the New Deal to stabilize farm incomes. Under this arrangement, which continued into the postwar era, the government paid some farmers to keep land fallow and also bought farmers' excess grain. By buying and storing grain during times of surplus, releasing grain during droughts, and paying farmers to not plant too much, the US government could manage supply and guarantee that prices did not go too high, thereby hurting consumers, or too low, thereby hurting producers, while also ensuring that the land would be kept productive in the long term. Like Kissinger, Butz saw a major role for food in US foreign policy, and his disruptive approach to American agricultural production threatened Kissinger's entire North-South strategy.

Despite having a PhD in agricultural economics from Purdue University, where he eventually served as president, Butz was a controversial choice for secretary of agriculture. The first red flag for farmers was his service under (and outspoken praise for) Eisenhower's USDA head Ezra Taft Benson, "the most hated agriculture secretary ever" due to his strong antipathy toward New Deal reforms.[44] The second was his close ties to large US agribusiness conglomerates such as Ralston-Purina, where Butz's predecessor, Clifford M. Hardin, had already lined up a vice presidency at the time of his resignation as secretary. "He [Butz] is the worst possible choice I could imagine," the head of the National Farmers Organization stated, "one of those land-grant college educators who was supposed to assist all farmers in America, but who identified with giant agri-business corporations."[45] During his confirmation hearings, a coalition of liberal northern Democrats, conservative southern Democrats, and Farm Belt Republicans grilled Butz on his past statements predicting the end of the family farm and urging small farmers to "adapt or die" through "vertical integration."[46]

Not everyone in the Farm Belt opposed Butz's nomination. "The family farm has been in desperate straits for many years," the *Salt Lake City Tribune* explained in his defense. "Rising costs and declining farm prices have combined to clamp the small farmer in an increasingly untenable price squeeze."[47] Halfway through the hearings, the American Farm Bureau Federation, which claimed to represent two million "member families," became the first farm group to endorse Butz.[48] Still, his approval in the Senate by a vote of fifty-one to forty-four came only after Butz pledged, in writing, to take immediate action to increase farm incomes by raising corn prices. "You said you wanted an aggressive, articulate Secretary of Agriculture," he insisted at his swearing in. "You've got one. It may be that I'm more vigorous than you want."[49]

Butz moved fast. Less than twenty-four hours after taking office, he announced that the USDA would begin buying up corn in the open market "to firm up farm prices," thereby encouraging farmers to take advantage of a 1970 Farm Bill provision that removed many restrictions on planting quotas.[50] Butz was eager to defend higher domestic food prices, telling consumers they had never had it so good: Americans were eating more calories, and more red meat, and spending a smaller percentage of their incomes than ever before.[51]

Despite the religious fervor with which he condemned government spending and handouts—his negative comments on the widely popular food stamp program had dogged him during his confirmation hearings—in practice, Butz was no budget puritan. He earned the ire of treasury secretary George Shultz for siphoning a total of $700 million in "miscellaneous raids on the Treasury" for the corn buyback and other programs, but because "there is no one on the White House staff who knows much about agriculture," the *New York Times Magazine* reported, "he is relatively free of second-guessing."[52] Nixon wanted to win the Farm Belt in 1972, and with Butz's support—farm incomes for 1972 were a record $19.2 billion—he overwhelmingly did.[53]

Unlike his predecessors, Butz had no plans to sit on that surplus until a shortage struck. He instructed farmers to unleash their productive potential by planting corn and soybeans "fencerow to fencerow," assuring them that world markets would absorb what domestic markets could not. The 1971 Soviet wheat deal was the first move, accounting for one-third of the overall increase in agricultural exports in 1972; exports also increased substantially to eastern Europe, Latin America, Japan, and, for the first time in two decades, China.[54] In April 1973, at the height of the world food crisis, Butz announced to Nixon "[with] a great deal of pleasure . . . the virtual liquidation of farm products from the Commodity Credit Corporation," the linchpin of the New Deal system of managed farm prices. "This marks the first time in more than two decades that American agriculture can enjoy a market as free from the stifling effects of government stocks as it now can."[55]

This was only the beginning of the American farmer's new frontier. "This is a 'hinge point' in history," Butz told an audience in Chicago. "Agriculture is taking a dominant position in America's export trade." Indeed, US exports were down across the map *except* in agriculture, which Butz positioned as the cure for the US payments deficit. The result, he predicted, would be a virtuous circle comprising a hungry world, a cash-strapped US government, and US farmers with the "daring" and "imagination" to expand their farms and maybe get rich in the process: "Agriculture is already making a major contribution to America's trade balance. We have the potential to do even better. Overseas markets are growing. We can supply those markets, increase our exports, and strengthen our farm income."[56]

Butz was also quick to stress a second foreign policy benefit of his market reforms. "We are learning in this country, perhaps belatedly, how to use food as a positive factor in world diplomacy," he told a meeting of advertising executives in June 1974. This would not be like the "so-called 'Food for Peace' program" of the 1950s and 1960s, in which the US surplus was simply given away to improve the nation's image in the Third World. Instead, Butz cited the role of food exports in opening China, achieving détente with the Soviet Union, and reaching "peace and reconciliation" in Vietnam and the Middle East as proof that "food has become a major force for [international] negotiations." The United States' "food power" was indeed "a major weapon."[57]

The question in the middle of 1974 was how that weapon would be used toward OPEC and the Third World: was it a carrot, or was it a stick? There was a fine line between food power and food punishment. In late 1973 the White House rejected Butz's suggestion for a food embargo against OPEC members. As a State Department official remarked, food power was "power over people who are hungry—people we don't want to push around anyway."[58] Kissinger's proposal for a World Food Conference and promise to negotiate some sort of international reserve system indicated a more cooperative approach, but Butz was adamant that the United States avoid anything that might suggest a return to government intervention at home or a new system of intergovernmental management abroad.[59] Kissinger, State, and the NSC disagreed. From their perspective, private markets were inadequate for both the political and economic dimensions of the food issue.[60] Government-held stocks were a necessary part of any proposal—at least one that would be taken seriously by developing countries. Kissinger would not fall on his sword at the World Food Conference because of Butz's ideological opposition. "I am perfectly willing to take it to the President," he insisted.[61]

President Ford's chief economic advisers were no less skeptical of Kissinger's approach. One month before the World Food Conference convened in Rome, Kissinger shared a draft of his keynote address with Ford's EPB, consisting of treasury secretary William Simon, Ford's economic assistant William Seidman, Alan Greenspan, and OMB director Roy Ash. The opposition was unanimous. All backed Butz in objecting to Kissinger's insistence on including specific aid commitments, arguing that the United States should speak only broadly about its responsibility for ending the food crisis. This approach was exactly what Kissinger wanted to avoid. "Can we really say that 'all countries have responsibilities,' when we know that Bangladesh and the Sahel can't do anything, and that some others can do greater and still others lesser?" Such rhetoric would be roundly mocked by the Third World, negating the whole point of US leadership at the conference. "We should set forth a philosophy, try to convince people, not give an old-maidish lecture to others about what they should do," Kissinger insisted, and not for the last time. "We should be less schoolmasterish."[62]

Ford's economic advisers also objected to the implications of a globally coordinated system of food reserves. "All too frequently," the Treasury Department complained, high food prices were used "as a way of justifying, and among some developing countries excusing, the oil price increase." Did not Kissinger's plan for an international system of food reserves to regulate supply and price to some extent endorse this logic? The shah's analogy—if the price of wheat can triple in one year, why not the price of oil?—was misleading, given the effects of natural phenomena such as weather and poor crops on the global food supply. But Treasury's argument ignored several important decisions—the 1971 devaluation of the dollar, the 1972 grain sales to the Soviet Union, the

1973 decision to restrict food exports, and the lack of a meaningful response to famines in South Asia and Africa—implicating US policy in the food crisis.

Regardless of the economics, developing countries continued to see OPEC's actions as a legitimate response to decades of selfish and unfair treatment by the industrial countries. Algeria's and Venezuela's self-appointed leadership of the NIEO, announced barely a month after the Arab states ended their embargo against the United States, suggested the emergence of a new political economy for the energy and food crises defined primarily in North-South terms. Both the United States and OPEC had promised to aid oil-importing developing countries hurt by higher energy and food prices, but the World Food Conference was an opportunity for the United States to take the lead. As the State Department explained, "the US must demonstrate its willingness to use its food resources constructively if its position in trying to get OPEC countries to use oil responsibly is to have any credibility." Credibility on food would translate into credibility on oil, Kissinger reasoned. OPEC, not the United States, would be seen as the inflexible one, prolonging the Third World's food and energy deficits to line its own pockets.[63]

The 1974 World Food Conference

More than five thousand delegates and observers from 131 countries attended the World Food Conference, held in Rome's Palazzo dei Congressi on November 5–16, 1974.[64] Hundreds of journalists stalked the palace halls, which also contained representatives from 161 nongovernmental organizations (NGOs). More than two dozen influential social scientists and business leaders signed a declaration drafted before the conference by Barbara Ward (Lady Jackson), arguably the most important development expert of the decade.[65] The *New York Times* covered the conference extensively and published a series of explanatory articles on world hunger in the months before.[66]

Kissinger, whose keynote was expected to set the terms of the discussion, was not involved in conference preparation, which was carried out largely by the FAO. However, the State Department invited more than twenty members of Congress, including Senators Humphrey and McGovern, to accompany the US delegation.[67] Also present was the World Hunger Action Coalition, representing more than seventy civic and church groups; its US-based chairman would act as a liaison between the US delegation and the various NGOs.[68] All this suggested a new visibility for world hunger among Americans and a political base for more aid and global cooperation. "If a public relations opportunity like this won't get results," the conference's official newspaper wondered, "what will?"[69]

There were other reasons for optimism. According to the same paper, a "crude conjunction" of factors had propelled this crisis (as opposed to past ones) to the forefront of developed countries' agendas. Not only was this food crisis "the biggest ever"; its connection to the energy crisis and the NIEO had forced leaders in the United States and other rich countries to confront the national security implications of global inequality. The food crisis "has provoked in the massive industrial powers a kind of geopolitical change of life, for its logic is that a shared world must share resources, and the rich have the most to give," the author explained.[70]

Kissinger's keynote, the result of several months of interdepartmental wrangling and conflict, was a combination of high rhetoric, misleading accusations, and ambitious but vague proposals. As planned, he took aim at OPEC, naming "a political embargo and then abruptly raised prices for oil" as the reason for lower industrial and farm production in 1973–74 and for "accelerat[ing] a global inflation that was already at the margin of governments' ability to control." When producers' cartels restrict the supply of vital commodities to force political change, he explained, it is not the rich nations but "the poorest and weakest nations [that] suffer most." Citing the "special responsibility" of oil producers, he challenged OPEC members to use their dollar surpluses to fund long-term efforts for Third World agricultural development and to help at-risk countries meet current needs. After avoiding US responsibility for the current food crisis, Kissinger then assumed US leadership in preventing another. His five-point, twenty-five-year program included increasing food production in exporting countries, accelerating production in importing countries, improving the means of food distribution and financing, enhancing food quality, and ensuring security against food emergencies.[71]

There were important ironies in Kissinger's approach. For one, by blaming OPEC for all the global economy's problems, Kissinger effectively admitted that an organization of commodity producers from the South had single-handedly brought the global economy to its knees—and that the developed countries had been powerless to stop it. And while Kissinger held up the oil crisis as proof that producers' cartels hurt poor countries even more than rich ones, did not US monetary, trade, and agricultural policies produce the same effect for food—an even more vital resource? Most oil-importing developing countries said yes and continued to see OPEC as the necessary muscle behind the NIEO project. "These nations tend to speak of food as a matter of human rights," a US diplomat observed before the conference, "but they have applied practically no pressure on the oil producers to lower prices. Instead . . . they tend to applaud [OPEC's actions as a] redistribution of wealth."[72]

The good news was that Kissinger's proposals for reform were not much different from those of the FAO.[73] His vow that "within ten years no child [would] go to bed hungry" appeared in the final conference document and inspired the Universal Declaration on the Eradication of World Hunger, passed the following month by the UN General Assembly. Kissinger also endorsed the creation of a "reserve coordinating group to negotiate a detailed agreement on an international system of nationally-held grain reserves" of up to sixty million tons of food "above present levels." Though Kissinger commended FAO director-general Boerma's proposal for a reserve system, he made no mention of the fact that Boerma's plan involved the creation of a new UN body subject to the Security Council. At the same time, Kissinger nodded to the NIEO's call for global negotiations when he added, "This group's work should be carried out in close cooperation with other international efforts to improve the world trading system."[74]

OPEC members completely rejected Kissinger's line of reasoning. First, they denied that they were now wealthy nations with a "special responsibility" to fund development commensurate with the United States and other developed countries. "We are not rich," explained the deputy chief of the Saudi Arabian delegation. "Richness comes from structures, which we don't have. We import everything from needles and thread to automobiles at inflated prices."[75] Second, they dismissed the implication that they were to blame for the food crisis. "The food crisis has its roots in unfair policies of the developed countries, the enormous grain purchases of the Soviet Union, and the population explosion," said Iranian interior minister Jamshid Amouzegar. In any case, the delegates insisted, they were already giving between 6 and 8 percent of their GDP in aid, in contrast to the "old rich" countries in the North that gave well under 1 percent. "We have contributed more than our fair share [to ending the food crisis]," said a delegate from Kuwait's foreign ministry. "That is not talk but a fact. We were acting even before this conference was organized." Iran was "prepared to give—and give more," Amouzegar insisted, "provided we do not replace the traditional [Western] donors' contributions."[76]

Third, in response to Kissinger's challenge, eleven OPEC members proposed the establishment of a new multilateral institution to finance long-term Third World agricultural development. The proposal for an International Fund for Agricultural Development (IFAD), funded half by OPEC and half by the Organization for Economic Cooperation and Development (OECD), had thirty-four sponsors, including major European donors such as the Netherlands, as well as

Australia and New Zealand, both rich food exporters.[77] On November 14 the proposal passed in committee.[78] "I am absolutely certain [OPEC members] will contribute millions, no hundreds of millions of dollars [to the fund]," secretary-general Sayed Marei announced a few days later.[79]

Some saw hope in this effort. Jan Pronk, Dutch minister of development co-ordination in the 1970s and an active participant in several critical North-South forums, believed at the time that the "oil for food" concept was "brilliant." Pronk, one of the fund's cosponsors, insisted that it was not "an anti-Western resolution, because it was OPEC plus the Netherlands."[80] Given the much higher GDPs of OECD countries, the fifty-fifty split meant that OPEC was promising to give much more than its fair share to long-term agricultural development. However, it also meant that the rich countries could be outvoted by an OPEC–G-77 coalition, as the proposal divided voting power into thirds among the two donors (OECD and OPEC) and the recipients (other developing countries). Unprepared for this outcome, the US delegation publicly welcomed the IFAD while working behind the scenes to undermine it. In another committee, US officials proposed the "establishment of a less-rigid, more informal coordinating structure" for organizing development aid through bilateral channels and private investment, rather than government guarantees to a new fund shared with OPEC.[81]

Kissinger was confident that shaming the oil producers would drive a wedge between OPEC and the G-77, forcing them to choose between high oil prices and Third World solidarity. However, this strategy could work only if the United States backed up its rhetoric with commitments. On the one hand, the United States supported the creation of a World Food Council as a "high-level, limited-member UN organization" to oversee the enforcement of conference resolutions, including the creation of the IFAD. Kissinger's reserve system proposal also passed, as did a US resolution "urging major grain importers and exporters to begin urgent talks" through a "reserve coordination group." On the other hand, the US delegation worked to neuter any new institutions that might share US power or make specific resource commitments. Although the United States voted for the resolution, the World Food Council "would have no authority beyond moral suasion to force action on the part of governments or UN bodies," the US delegation reported. As for the IFAD, "the United States supported the proposal in hopes that it would be a vehicle for promoting development by the countries with surplus oil revenues, but the U.S. has no present intention of contributing to the Fund, and will continue directing its substantial multilateral contributions through existing institutions."[82]

Kissinger's lack of specificity on US commitments was glaring, and the reason why was obvious. "The Kissinger speech was vague and tentative because

Washington really [has] no policy on food," a Ford administration "food expert" told the *New York Times.* "My great concern is that he has come up with watered-down proposals emerging out of interdepartmental battles."[83]

Those interdepartmental battles were on display on November 6 when Butz, chair of the US delegation, took the stage for his address. (Kissinger was already en route to the Middle East to continue his shuttle diplomacy.) While Butz reiterated the US commitment to negotiating a reserve system, he laid down new market-based conditions absent in the Kissinger draft. "We do not favor food reserves of a magnitude that would perpetually depress prices, destroy farmer incentives, mask the deficiencies in national production efforts, or substitute government subsidies for commercial trade," Butz declared. Food aid and food reserves were "issues that arrive after food is produced, not before. The conference's "number one responsibility is to move the world toward a higher level of food production," he insisted, and the way to do that was not more government, but less. Butz held up his own free market reforms, such as removing production controls and limits on land use, as examples of how the United States was set to grow more food than ever next year. Developing country governments simply needed to allow their farmers to harness the same entrepreneurial spirit. "In my country, farmers respond to the incentive of profit. . . . In modern societies, these incentives are closely related to the ability to earn a fair return from one's investment—a decent reward for one's labor. I strongly suspect that this is true in other countries as well as my own."[84]

Butz's lecture on markets and self-reliance was exactly what Kissinger had warned against. "I want to avoid the Protestant missionary approach. I don't want to preach," he explained to Butz in an October White House meeting on US strategy. "What I want to do is convince the political leadership of these countries [the G-77] that we mean it when we call for cooperation."[85] More embarrassing, Butz's speech contradicted his own agency's analysis and public statements. In reports distributed at the conference, USDA officials blamed the root of the "current world food situation" on "government policies and basic human conditions (such as income distribution and poverty)."[86] Another report, prepared in December 1973 for the US Council for Agricultural Science and Technology and made public by Senator McGovern, determined that an international emergency food bank "would have little effect on United States farm prices and incomes. That little effect, however, would be positive."[87]

There was an even more glaring problem that both speeches shared: they said nothing new about what the United States was prepared to do about starvation *now.* Experts estimated that the thirty-three poor MSA countries needed to import sixteen to seventeen million tons of grain between the summers of 1974 and 1975; in Rome, those countries were short some seven million tons, at a cost of about $1.4 billion.[88] To put it simply: half a billion people across the Third World faced starvation if they did not receive food aid within the next eight months.[89]

Since June, US officials had been promising more aid, but the reality was much different. In fact, in the months before the conference, Bangladesh actually purchased more food from the United States than it received as aid. (The EC had also promised additional food aid, but none arrived before the conference.) Time was running out for the MSA countries: whether as aid or trade, food still needed to be moved from North American ports to cities in Africa and South Asia, which could take weeks if not months.[90]

A few days before the conference, Kissinger had raised expectations when he promised India, Pakistan, and Bangladesh extra food aid during visits to those countries. However, per Butz's advice and Ford's decision, both secretaries' speeches only restated Ford's promise at the September UN General Assembly to increase food assistance above present levels.

The food aid controversy had far-reaching effects on the conference. For one, delegates from MSA countries understandably focused their efforts on gaining a promise from rich countries on short-term aid and avoiding imminent starvation, rather than the long-term proposals being negotiated over their heads by the rich countries and OPEC. One official recalled a late-night session in the "hot, almost empty [plenary] hall," where the minister of agriculture of Rwanda described how the food situation in his country was "deteriorating from day to day. . . . Rwanda spoke, and nobody paid attention." Others acted more directly. On one occasion, delegates from Bangladesh arrived in Marei's office minutes before a press conference on the IFAD and "asked him to speak about how many people might die in Bangladesh in the next few weeks." After Butz's speech, Canada and Australia, the second and third largest wheat exporters, announced emergency aid increases; West Germany and Sweden followed suit, but the US position remained the same.[91]

Criticism from both foreign delegations and US congressional observers eventually proved too much, even for Butz. Halfway through the conference he signed and sent to Ford a letter drafted by the World Hunger Action Coalition "urgently requesting a minimum *volume* increase of 1 million tons of food aid for the 1975 fiscal year."[92] On the penultimate day of the conference, Ford announced that he could not approve the increase; further food aid, US officials explained, would be reviewed on a quarterly basis to avoid any sudden shocks to grain prices. To make matters worse, in the middle of the conference Butz flew to Egypt and Syria, where he announced new commercial grain sales to those countries.[93] The secretary made no secret of his displeasure at having his hand forced, "angrily criticizing" the politicians (led by McGovern and Humphrey) who had called for the increase. "Let me ask you a question," he barked at a *CBS Evening News* reporter questioning Ford's decision. "Does your wife have any—does your wife have any poor relation that you've got to help support. . . . Do you ever give them enough to satisfy them?"[94]

Kissinger's strategy for the World Food Conference—confronting OPEC while courting the G-77—was a failure. "The pressure was . . . on the members of OPEC right from the beginning," wrote one conference observer of Kissinger's strategy. "Put your money on the table . . . and we [the United States] will respond by doing something about immediate problems of world starvation by releasing more food aid."[95] Yet when OPEC did just that, the US delegation wilted. Interdepartmental battles prevented the food aid increase and isolated the United States from developing and developed countries alike. "We stuck out like a sore thumb," US delegation coordinator Edwin M. Martin lamented to Congress upon his return. "We have a long row to hoe in that respect."[96]

Instead, OPEC and G-77 leaders were emboldened and identified both food and energy even more strongly with the NIEO. The US delegation reported that, rather than expressing enthusiasm for Kissinger's reserve system or other proposals, the G-77 "called for radical adjustments in the current economic order and for reparations from developed to developing countries."[97] Venezuelan president Pérez denounced "the high prices the developed nations are charging us for the farming and industrial machines and other inputs that are essential to agriculture and the growth of our economies. . . . Unless the issue of international trade is faced squarely, it will not be possible to detect [the food crisis's] causes."[98] Algeria's Boumediene went further, listing the creation of a special fund for developing countries in the International Monetary Fund, reductions in developed country tariffs, renegotiation of international commodity agreements, greater regulation of multinational corporations, and the establishment of new international institutions as necessary to carry out the conference's program of action—in other words, the NIEO. The State Department telegram summarized, "DCs [Developed Countries] have great responsibility [for the crisis] and nonaligned will see that New [International] Economic Order prevails."[99]

In a fortuitous but nevertheless unsatisfying turn of events, widespread predictions of a weak 1974 harvest in major food producers proved false. Global grain prices plummeted in December and January, and in February 1975 the White House announced an increase of some two million tons over 1974 levels.[100] In theory, this meant that the conference's target of seven to eight million tons would be met, and for the next few years, the global price of wheat stabilized at around $3.50 a bushel—down almost half from its peak in February 1973, at the height of the oil crisis, but still almost double precrisis levels.[101] While images of starving children with distended bellies disappeared from televisions and newspapers, uncounted millions were still dependent on the West's charity for their next meal, and many were forever scarred by the wrenching long-term physical consequences of chronic malnutrition. One development expert told Congress a year later: "there has been no significant improvement in the precarious situation of the 460 million people whom the 1974 World Food Conference recognized to be malnourished or facing starvation."[102]

Also in February 1973, at the United States' request, the International Wheat Council (IWC) met to work out the implementation of Kissinger's reserve proposal. The White House was no closer to a unified strategy. The NSC reported in May 1975, around the time of the IWC's second meeting: "State and Agriculture, and to a lesser extent other agencies, have spent most of their time [since the conference] arguing about how the U.S. should implement [the reserve system proposal]." The difference was "fundamental, and the inflexible positions taken so far threaten to make a meaningful U.S. initiative possible." The disagreement was between State's "tight" system—according to the OMB, "essentially a price-fixing, international commodity agreement with nationally held buffer stocks and export controls in time of shortage"[103]—and Agriculture's "loose" system, "in which the agreement would be to consult on further action [in the event of a crisis] under pre-negotiated supply positions."[104] Butz won the battle, and at the IWC's third meeting in September, "representatives of the US agencies concerned" killed State's proposal.[105]

Kissinger's attempt to use US food power to shame OPEC was also unsuccessful. Not only did Kissinger endorse OPEC's proposal for an IFAD.[106] Throughout 1975 several OPEC countries announced numerous development funds and banks of their own with the stated goal of reinvesting oil profits to diversify Third World economies, mainly in the Middle East and Africa.[107] Although these efforts received neither adequate funding nor sustained focus, they shored up the South's solidarity through the energy and food crises. Kissinger underestimated not only OPEC's willingness to continue high oil prices at the expense of non–oil-importing developing countries but also the power of OPEC's example for other commodity producers. They were unwilling to ignore the role played by the developed countries, and the United States in particular, in their declining growth, export prices, and share of world trade during the North's age of affluence.

Throughout 1975–76 Kissinger expanded his conciliatory strategy in different forums. The United States' North-South policy evolved in the context of US-European-Japanese trilateral relations through the establishment of yearly summits. Once again, Kissinger took the lead in promoting these engagements, seeing them as a way to increase coordination among developed countries on a number of economic and security-related issues and to renew the West's sense of confidence and cohesion in the face of mounting energy, monetary, and fiscal challenges. Again, he fought with the EPB over how to present US economic policy—both North-South and North-North—in these meetings, but the results would begin to reveal more clearly the successes and failures of his NIEO containment strategy.

CHAPTER 2

North-North Dialogues
The NIEO and Transatlantic Relations

In 1972 Henry Kissinger was on a roll. That year he negotiated the Paris Peace Accords, initiating the formal end of the Vietnam War. With president Richard Nixon, he opened relations with China and concluded the first Strategic Arms Limitation Treaty, inaugurating a new era of détente with the Soviet Union. After Anwar Sadat expelled Soviet advisers from Egypt, Kissinger quickly established a back channel with Sadat's national security adviser to begin work on a new peace agreement with Israel and to consolidate the United States' role as the paramount superpower in the Middle East.[1]

Indeed, before 1973 Kissinger was everywhere but Europe, and his and Nixon's disregard was not without consequence. Europeans were ambivalent about the implications of détente: Willy Brandt pursued *Ostpolitik* with East Germany with the confidence provided by a tough US policy toward the Soviets, while the Conservative government in Britain feared being left out of US-Soviet negotiations and reciprocated by trying to keep the United States out of European conversations.[2] There was also fallout from Nixon's unilateral decision to float the dollar, which sent global currency markets into disarray and led European finance ministers and central banks to expand the money supply to avoid contraction. Then there were the effects of the US devaluation on global energy prices. In response to the cheapening of its dollar-priced oil, OPEC raised its rhetoric against the West and increased its excise tax against oil companies, which simply passed the cost on to US and European consumers.

Kissinger's belief in the importance of the Atlantic partnership was genuine, and after the globe-trotting of 1972, he set out to repair the rift. Neither 1973 nor 1974 would be his "Year of Europe," but by the end of President Ford's two-and-a-half-year term, the Atlantic alliance was stronger than it had been in more than a decade. The oil crisis and the New International Economic Order (NIEO) posed a real threat to US influence in western Europe, which depended on steady access to Third World commodities even more than the US did. But they also provided Kissinger with the opening he needed to repair transatlantic ties. Rather than destroying US-European relations, the Third World's challenge may have saved them, uniting developed countries around a political and economic consensus intended to sustain the postwar order. If this move toward unity did not always produce a common response to the fiscal, monetary, and energy crises of the mid-1970s, it did prevent any dramatic divergence in the developed countries' economic policies toward the Third World after more than a decade of troubling drifts.

After the NIEO's announcement, the United States insisted on separating energy—the most urgent of these crises, with its associated effects on fiscal and monetary capacity—from discussions about raw materials, but influential Third World leaders such as Algeria would not allow it. Fiscal and monetary policy convergence in the developed countries strengthened the West's hand when forced to discuss energy and raw materials together. It also increased confidence in the developed countries that these crises could be managed collectively and calmly through discussion among like-minded Northern elites, rather than resorting to protectionism and cutting separate deals with Southern energy and raw materials producers. This was Kissinger's main goal and a major boost for his strategy: Northern unity increased the likelihood of splitting the unholy alliance between OPEC and oil-importing developing countries while simultaneously decreasing the South's ability to conduct separate negotiations with Europeans.

Europe Comes Together, 1945–1972

On April 23, 1973—six months before OPEC's embargo and roughly a year before the NIEO was introduced—Kissinger announced the "Year of Europe." The US-European relationship had been "the cornerstone of all postwar foreign policy," he declared, but that era had come to an end. Europe's moves toward economic and political unity had created new tensions in transatlantic relations: Americans accused Europeans of free-riding on defense and taking economic self-interest too far, and Europeans accused Americans of being "out to divide Europe economically, or to desert Europe militarily, or to bypass Europe diplomatically." The "unforeseen" energy crisis raised the stakes of "atrophy . . . neglect, carelessness, or distrust" in the alliance. "New realities" required "new solutions." Kissinger promised that US officials would work out a revised Atlantic Charter, which Nixon would bring with him on his trip to Europe at the end of the year.[3]

Nixon never made that trip. His attention was diverted by calls for his resignation due to the Watergate cover-up, which did nothing to incentivize Europeans to increase their association with his faltering administration. As Kissinger put it during the 1973 Arab-Israeli war, Nixon was no longer seen as a "functional president."[4] Europeans also felt condescended to by Kissinger's sudden attention. French president Georges Pompidou remarked that for France, every year was the "Year of Europe"; as British prime minister Edward Heath noted in his memoirs, "For Kissinger to announce a year of Europe was like for me to stand on Trafalgar Square and announce that we were embarking on a year to save America!"[5] Regardless, the consequences of a united and independent Europe ran deeper than any single president or secretary of state. If anything, US efforts to create European unity following World War II had worked too well.

After 1945 the United States supported an economically and politically united Europe out of the conviction that prosperous and integrated European countries would have no incentive to turn to communism or return to war. The Marshall Plan had relatively few strings attached, but its $13.5 billion in aid to Europe was disbursed under a new US-backed mechanism—the Organization for European Economic Cooperation (OEEC), designed to develop intra-European trade and study the feasibility of a European customs union. In late 1949 the United States changed Marshall Plan requirements when it determined that credits were not being used sufficiently to achieve European economic integration. In 1950 the United States supported the creation of the European Payments Union under the OEEC's direction, designed to strengthen monetary cooperation among member states and to lessen Europe's dependence on US dollars.[6]

The United States also supported French proposals for the European Coal and Steel Community (ECSC). Launched in 1951, the ECSC was designed to prevent the possibility of war between Germany and France by integrating the production of coal and steel. Like the Marshall Plan, the ECSC would be open to any interested European nation, ensuring that no single nation would have a monopoly on the inputs of war. "This transformation will facilitate other action which has been impossible until this day," France's foreign minister Robert Schumann announced. "A new Europe will be born from this, a Europe which is solidly united and constructed around a strong framework."[7]

Once the framework was in place, expansion continued with consistent US support. In the 1957 Treaty of Rome, the ECSC's Common Market was expanded into the European Economic Community (EEC), governed by a set of new institutions including the European Commission, Assembly, and Court of Justice. In 1961 the OEEC was superseded by the Organization for Economic Cooperation and Development (OECD), which the United States and Canada joined, along with the OEEC's European founders.

Other developments in the 1960s also brought Europe closer together—and closer to the Third World. The roots of Europe's new economic relationship with the Third World began with the Treaty of Rome, before most decolonization took place (and before many Europeans accepted its inevitability). Over the objections of Germany and Belgium, Charles de Gaulle demanded that the treaty include new economic agreements with the French Community—the name of France's renewed imperial project—in exchange for his country's vote. Through the French Community's formal association with the EEC, France intended to strengthen its economic hold on its colonies, accord European legitimacy to the continuation of its empire, and transfer some of the costs of maintaining those relationships to other European countries. Without any consultation with its colonies, France's imperial preferences were extended to all EEC members, and the French Community was granted access on the same conditions to the EEC. Additionally, Europe would provide credits through the European Development Fund to French Community members.[8]

Decolonization further institutionalized EEC–Third World economic ties. It was not a wholly voluntary decision for European governments, some of which fought bitterly to hang on to their colonies well into the 1970s. But by the early 1960s, most European governments believed that formal independence was inevitable, and they set out to preserve political and economic arrangements with former colonies as the process unfolded.

Development aid was one important tool for securing the continued economic cooperation of former colonies and their integration into new postcolonial economic agreements with European states and the European Community (EC) at large. To that end, in the early 1960s the OECD set up the Development Assistance Committee to administer the European Development Fund in postcolonial territories. The EC soon became a major donor to the Third World and, like the United States and the Soviet Union, had its own interests to preserve.[9]

Preferential trade agreements were another tool, and such agreements between the EC and former colonies, mostly in Africa, multiplied throughout the 1960s. The first Yaoundé Convention in 1963 gave free access to EC markets for most exports, as well as additional European Development Fund credits, to the eighteen African states included in the Treaty of Rome (the Associated African and Malagasy States). The second Yaoundé Convention in 1969 proceeded along similar lines. The Treaty of Rome stated that "other countries of similar development" to the Associated African and Malagasy States could form similar agreements, so the Arusha and Lagos agreements attempted to expand preferences to African countries not covered under Yaoundé I and II. In 1971 the EC agreed to introduce the generalized system of preferences, lowering tariffs on exports from all developing countries.[10]

Developments in European political culture also encouraged a new EC policy toward the Third World. Historian Giuliano Garavini explains the shift in the European Left's priorities marked by the crises of 1968: "The liberation movements of the Third World, the protest movements of the young and the working classes, and the evolving neo-Marxist intellectual currents had opened Europe's doors to a partial rethinking of economic science, and to reconsider the damage caused to the nations of the Third World, to the Earth, and to all mankind by Western models of development."[11] Despite pushback from liberal and conservative parties and few real electoral victories, the general concerns raised by Europe's New Left were shared by more than just its supporters. The political orientation of the European governments that came to power in 1969–70 was a mixed bag: conservatives Edward Heath in Britain and Georges Pompidou in France; social democrats Willy Brandt in West Germany and Olof Palme in Sweden; and various Christian democrats in Italy, to name a few. Whether Europe was entering a "golden age of social democracy" or an age of "social-liberal coalition," all these governments responded to public opinion in similar ways.[12]

First, European governments heeded popular demands for a higher social wage and greater economic management. In OECD countries, the percentage of gross domestic product allocated for public spending increased just four points in the 1960s, to 31 percent; by 1980, it surpassed 45 percent. Second, Europeans recommitted to the project of unity. At the 1969 Hague Summit, Pompidou rejected his predecessor de Gaulle's hostility toward Britain's EC membership, paving the way for Britain's accession in 1973 under Heath (Ireland and Denmark also joined that year). The EC also strengthened the Common Agricultural Policy (CAP) with new tax provisions and tariffs and pledged a future economic and monetary union that would bring Europe closer than ever to Winston Churchill's "United States of Europe."[13] Last, the EC granted new trade concessions to the Third World through the Lomé Convention (discussed later), while also moving toward a common global position at the third

United Nations Conference on Trade and Development (UNCTAD) negotiations in Santiago, Chile.

Divergence at Santiago, 1972

The divide between European and US approaches to the Third World showed in preparations for UNCTAD III. Although differences within the EC remained—namely, over protectionist policies such as the CAP—many European countries devoted serious attention to improving relations with the coalition of developing countries known as the Group of 77 (G-77), some taking an openly critical position on international capitalism. The Italians' socialist commerce minister declared multinational corporations' "neo-capitalism" in the Third World "as atavistic as it is alarming," and Italy endorsed the G-77's push for a link between special drawing rights and development aid at the International Monetary Fund (IMF). The Dutch went even further, endorsing not only the special drawing rights–aid link but also the amendment of the EC's own protectionist agricultural policies and the renegotiation of existing commodity agreements. "Political parties, churches, and student movements today all have a passionate interest in cooperation between developed countries and developing countries," the Dutch minister for development cooperation explained in Santiago. "This is especially true in my country."[14]

France's calculations were more complicated. Finance minister Valery Giscard d'Estaing wanted to continue French leadership of Europe's policy toward the Third World, but he also wanted to defend the EC's favoritism toward African states as written into the Treaty of Rome. Before UNCTAD III, Giscard reiterated to African leaders their dependence on European aid, which may have led the Associated African and Malagasy States to focus their efforts at the conference on increased aid for the poorest developing countries (located mostly in Africa). Although Giscard endorsed new commodity agreements, he opposed any opening of European markets, reasoning to the mostly Latin American supporters of CAP liberalization that such measures would benefit primarily US agricultural exports.[15]

After studying the views of different agencies, the Nixon administration recommended "a forthcoming but low key approach" for UNCTAD III. This would "make the best of a difficult situation in which demands of the LDCs [less developed countries] are excessive." US officials were confident in the history of cooperation among developed countries, but they were also aware of Europe's desire to cut new deals with the Third World on commodities. Thus, the real divergence would be on support for individual commodity agreements, which the United States opposed. On these, "sharply divergent views . . . [with] the Europeans, and particularly the French," were likely.[16]

In fact, at UNCTAD the United States opposed the EC on a number of developed country (Group B) resolutions responding to G-77 proposals. It publicly dissociated itself from a Group B recommendation that the G-77 push for new concessions related to the General Agreement on Tariffs and Trade (GATT). It had one supporter in the EC, West Germany, which joined the United States in opposing French proposals for World Bank financing of buffer stocks and assistance in concluding commodity agreements. The United States also resisted Group B calls for improvements to the generalized system of preferences and new terms for debt relief and aid. Nevertheless, proceeding with negotiations required what one observer called "the continued unity of Group B around the lowest common denominator," that is, hard-liners outside of Europe, including Australia, New Zealand, and Canada, but led by the United States.[17]

Such differences should not have come as a great surprise. In fact, it should have been a surprise that they were not more severe. One month before Santiago, Peter Flanigan, Nixon's assistant for international economic affairs, had visited European capitals to gauge EC opinion on the upcoming negotiations. Flanigan was concerned with "the development of a spirit of economic isolationism or turning-inward on both sides of the Atlantic," and European reactions were not encouraging. Raymond Barre, the EC's commissioner for financial and monetary policy, justified the CAP's protectionism as an economic necessity and defended the expansion of reciprocal preferences with developing countries as "the inevitable consequence" of British entry into the European Free Trade Association. In other words, European economic integration, which the United States had done so much to promote, led naturally to efforts to protect European markets and develop preferential trade agreements with the Third World. Discussions with Giscard were "frank and not discouraging," even though France continued to defend the CAP and LDCs' preferences after Santiago. The British agreed that Europe needed to address the external tensions brought about by internal unity, but as a new EC member, Britain felt "a constraint . . . not to move out in front of the Six either too far or too fast." Talks with West German finance minister Karl Schiller were more encouraging, but "even he cautioned against expecting too much" in an "outward-looking" EC policy.[18]

The most damning talks were with the EC's new president, Dutch socialist Sicco Mansholt. Garavini argues that "predictions of an uninspired Community 'performance' at UNCTAD would have been realized if not for the nomination . . . precisely in connection with the beginning of discussions in Santiago, of Sicco Mansholt as President."[19] Although the actual effects of Group B's "lowest common denominator" performance are questionable, Mansholt was determined to use his role as EC president to reposition Europe's North-South policy as progressive, united, and distinct from that of the United States.

Mansholt was blunt, even abrasive, in his remarks to US officials. When Flanigan mentioned the continued importance of transatlantic economic cooperation, Mansholt "said that, in comparison with the 'minor' economic problems among developed countries, those between developed and developing economies were much more serious." Mansholt informed Flanigan "that he was not the least concerned with soyabeans ('to hell with your soyabeans')" and accused US officials of being unaware of the "real world," where "20 percent of the world was starving." He called the US performance at UNCTAD "disappointing" and warned Flanigan of "a serious confrontation between Europe and the U.S. . . . over trade and aid policies toward LDC's." Mansholt made assurances that "Europe will meet its obligations," Flanigan noted twice, "even if the U.S. will not."[20]

Mansholt was elaborating a more radical position for the EC than most member governments were prepared to pursue. Indeed, it is hard to imagine a British, German, or even French finance minister insisting to a US official at such a low point in transatlantic relations that "the problems Europe has with the U.S. are not important." But Mansholt *was* representative of a broad desire in European capitals to develop a more common and global North-South policy that implied a significant departure from US policy. The meeting ended with Mansholt accusing the United States of attempting to destroy Salvador Allende's socialist government in Chile by blocking loans from international financial institutions. This was especially significant because Allende, widely admired across the South for his nationalization of copper companies, had managed to secure his country's capital as the site for UNCTAD III. "He said that Allende was faced with a serious challenge from both the left and the right in Chile," Flanigan reported, "and that, if he went under, the country would give way to anarchy and, ultimately, become another Cuban-style dictatorship."[21]

The Year of Oil, 1973–1974

Kissinger did not share Mansholt's views on Chile or the South. "Nothing important can come from the South," he reportedly told Gabriel Valdés, Chile's foreign minister, in 1969. "The axis of history starts in Moscow, goes to Bonn, crosses over to Washington, and then goes to Tokyo. What happens in the South is of no importance." "Mr. Kissinger," Valdés responded, "you know nothing of the South." "And I don't care," Kissinger replied.[22]

As it turned out, Kissinger did care about the South, but for different reasons. Despite once describing Chile as "a dagger pointed straight to the heart of Antarctica," he told Congress that Allende's 1970 election was "a challenge to our national interest . . . Chile would soon be inciting anti-American policies, attacking hemispheric solidarity, making common cause with Cuba, and sooner or later establishing close relations with the Soviet Union."[23] Kissinger's association with the 1973 coup led by General Augusto Pinochet, resulting in the popular socialist leader's death, would only exacerbate distrust in the South toward his initiatives for LDCs following the oil crisis and the NIEO. It also contributed to an underappreciated reaction in Europe comparing US behavior in Chile with the Soviet Union's repression of the Prague Spring in 1968. Both cases "brought home the lesson, particularly relevant to the European situation, that the two superpowers interpreted their self-interest in such a way as to preclude any meeting point between democracy and socialist parties within their respective spheres of influence."[24]

Kissinger would not perceive the South's importance beyond its place in US-Soviet relations until the aftermath of the oil crisis and the announcement of the NIEO. Instead, with China opened, détente under way, and the Vietnam War drawing down, in the beginning of 1973 Kissinger turned to building partnerships with the European governments he and President Nixon had neglected. This proved more difficult than both had imagined, not least due to the evolving domestic scandals consuming the president's attention. As Kissinger recalled with understatement, "Nixon's relations with Europe's leaders lacked any particular intimacy . . . [and] he had few opportunities to put into practice his deep commitment to Atlantic relationships."[25] Most damning in Nixon's eyes was the apparently related resurgence of socialism and European unity, of which he complained to Kissinger bitterly.[26]

Kissinger was more determined to make a change in transatlantic relations. Since the early 1960s he had expressed support for a "federal idea" for world governance. This was not the global federalism of Wendell Willkie or Norman Cousins but a more restricted vision based on semi-formal partnership among the Western democracies within his "axis of history." In 1961 Kissinger explained his concept of an "Atlantic Confederacy" involving an "Executive Committee" of transatlantic leaders who "would forge a common position for negotiations with the Soviet Union . . . formulate overtures for peace and stability in Europe, and . . . pool their resources to increase the military pressures on Moscow to avoid conflict." He condemned the United States' rigid opposition to de Gaulle's proposed directorate of US, British, and French leaders: "No attempt was made to explore de Gaulle's reaction to the possibility of a wider forum." Key to such a proposal was the inclusion of West Germany. "European history demonstrates," Kissinger remarked, "that stability in Europe is unattainable except through the cooperation of Britain, France, and Germany."[27]

Stability in postwar Europe was indeed attained and maintained through British, French, and German cooperation, but an unintended consequence was the increased exclusion of the United States from key decisions. US-European policy discussions proceeded in the 1960s on an ad hoc basis, leading in the early 1970s to European suspicion of détente, accusations of selfishness in trade and monetary policy, and an underappreciated but real divergence in political and economic relations with the South. On this last point Kissinger was especially blind. His overwhelming focus throughout his academic and government career had been East-West security. On international economics, Kissinger said little. On the South—which, as Europeans and LDCs understood the term, implied a division based on economic relationships—at best, he said nothing; at worst, he was stridently dismissive.

Though it did not push Kissinger to renegotiate economic ties with the Third World at large—this would come after the NIEO—the 1973–74 oil crisis demonstrated the limitations of his focus on Cold War security. However, lack of appreciation for the political economics of oil extended across the Atlantic. Blind to the fact that oil had actually become cheaper in the 1950s and 1960s (when adjusted for inflation), few Western leaders realized the extent to which their unprecedented prosperity and growth—their golden age—depended on OPEC's cooperation in keeping prices low. Western Europe had become particularly vulnerable: In 1950 coal and coke (managed by the ECSC) accounted for 83 percent of western Europe's energy consumption, and oil accounted for just 8.3 percent. By 1970, coal and coke's share had declined to 29 percent, while oil's share had increased to 60 percent of total consumption.[28]

The United States was less vulnerable—in 1973 it produced two-thirds of its own oil consumption—but it was by no means immune.[29] US oil producers were entirely unprepared for production cuts in the Middle East and lacked the means to increase domestic production to match the gap. The most visible manifestation was long lines at gas stations across the nation, but the effects reverberated throughout the economy. "No economic event in a long generation, excluding only wartime upheavals, has so seriously disrupted our economy as the manipulation of oil prices and supplies over the past year," Federal Reserve chairman Arthur Burns told Congress in 1974. The world was in the midst of a global commodity boom; in 1972–73 wholesale prices of industrial commodities surged 10 percent. At the same time, US industrial plants were operating at full capacity, and many major industrial materials were already in short supply. "Inflationary expectations were therefore becoming more deeply ingrained at the very time when inflation was curtailing the purchasing power of worker incomes and creating some weakness for big-ticket items in consumer markets," Burns explained. "Thus, the oil embargo, together with the huge increase in oil prices that began in the fall of 1973, contributed to the twin economic problems plaguing us in 1974—namely, high rates of inflation and weakness in production."[30]

Although all developed economies were hit hard—growth in the OECD countries dropped from 5 to 6 percent in 1972–73 to just 0.5 percent in 1974 and 0.3 percent in 1975—the oil crisis did not initially produce a common response.[31] The major European countries and Japan distanced themselves from US policy throughout the Arab-Israeli war. Only Portugal and the Netherlands allowed US planes resupplying Israel to stop and refuel at their bases. Arab OPEC members responded by including those two countries in their oil blockade. "The Europeans, especially the French, are playing a lousy game," Nixon lamented. "The British are in trouble, so it's easy . . . to kick the United States around."[32]

The most immediate concern for Europe was economic, but the British and French also resented their deliberate exclusion by Kissinger from any Middle East peace process. In the months after the embargo, the European Community issued a declaration calling for an immediate cease-fire and a return to 1967 borders. Their "general strategy," Nixon administration officials explained, was to get the United States to "carry the burden" toward a settlement while endeavoring (particularly the French and British) to "obtain a seat at any international conference" and to launch bilateral dialogues with oil producers through "more or less quiet efforts" to resume production for their countries.[33] The efforts may have been quiet, but the results spoke loudly: by the end of 1973, Britain, France, Germany, and Japan had each signed or promised separate deals with Saudi Arabia, Iran, Iraq, Kuwait, Abu Dhabi, and Algeria.[34]

The US response was twofold and at first glance contradictory. In November 1973 the Nixon administration announced Project Independence. It intended to achieve energy security through increased production in the Western Hemisphere, diversification of fuel sources, and energy-saving measures at home. The EC had announced similar measures for conservation, but, combined with bilateral arrangements, the two programs suggested a new fragmentation of oil politics, with the United States and Europe pursuing separate and perhaps opposing strategies. For the New York Times, Nixon's insistence that, by 1980, "Americans will not have to rely on any source of oil but their own" sounded like "the economic nationalism of the nineteen-thirties, with its disastrous influence toward international tension and war."[35]

This analysis missed the combined effect of Project Independence and the second, largely unannounced part of US strategy: multilateral cooperation with Europe. According to the State Department, the energy crisis had "silver linings" for US power. The Saudi and Kuwaiti embargo (or "inconvenience") showed that the United States was the strongest economic power (unlike Europe, "it cannot be shut down"); forced public attention on the need for long-term economic supplies; increased pressure on the Israelis; and, most important, provided "an opportunity to revitalize our alliances by moving toward cooperation across the energy front."[36]

Kissinger quickly began meeting with European officials to warn them of the consequences of bilateral arrangements. They "will be difficult to organize," he told German officials, "and if we fail to achieve agreement on a cooperative effort, we will have to go our own way and make our own bilaterals." Because of US control over production in the Western Hemisphere, which would be expanded under Project Independence, the United States was "in a far stronger position to do this." The Germans agreed, noting that if the United States responded with its own bilateral deals, "it would destroy NATO." Kissinger believed that despite OPEC's impact on the OECD, the United States remained the strongest country, while Europe's move toward bilateralism only showed its leaders' desperation. A joint response by developed countries, led by the United States, could bring transatlantic cooperation to new levels, all under firm US leadership. Britain and Japan had signaled their willingness for a multilateral effort, but the Germans still wondered about the French. "I am almost certain that they will come along," Kissinger insisted, "because they will realize they will have no alternative."[37]

In February 1974, just four months after OPEC's embargo began, the United States, Canada, and twelve other industrialized countries, including Japan, met in Washington to discuss a common response to the energy crisis. Both the United States and Europe recognized the discord preceding these meetings. A few days earlier, Lord Cromer, Britain's ambassador to the United States, had lamented to Nixon how "unfortunate" it was "that the Year of Europe initiative came at the time of the EC's first joining together." However, that coming together also revealed fundamental disagreements within the EC. "When we joined," Cromer continued, "France had the Common Agricultural Policy set up and they wanted nothing changed. We haven't had the leverage on the French which we have needed, but with rising commodity prices, French influence may decline."[38]

Kissinger still worried about the Europeans moving ahead on bilateral talks with oil producers, a strategy spearheaded by France. He and treasury secretary William Simon agreed that the EC's announcement of negotiations two days before the meetings in Washington was "dangerous" and "scary"; the implication was that the Europeans would back the Arab states in any future joint energy negotiations, forcing the burden of compromise onto the United States. According to Kissinger, the EC was being "led by France and others too weak to resist." But Kissinger believed that European unity was not strong enough to overcome individual states' self-interest, best represented by the finance ministers. "The foreign ministers are idiots," he remarked, but in monetary discussions, "there is no feeling of confrontation." Nixon thus instructed Simon to "talk turkey" with the "technical types"—that is, the finance ministers—because "they don't have to posture like foreign ministers."[39]

At the Washington Energy Conference, the foreign ministers all agreed on the "unprecedented" nature of the crisis and pledged "a substantial increase in international cooperation in all fields," implying a willingness to open negotiations on other North-South issues.[40] Kissinger stressed the implications of Europe's bilateral strategy while also promoting his idea for an International Energy Agency (IEA), which he had announced the month before. Much like the global food reserve system Kissinger would propose later that year at the World Food Conference, the IEA would govern an international system of oil reserves to be released in times of crisis. Although the attendees admitted that LDCs faced problems caused by high oil prices, the IEA was directed primarily toward developed countries. In a sense, the IEA would act as an extension of Nixon's Project Independence across the West.

The conference was an important step forward for Kissinger's strategy, which sought to deal with Europeans individually rather than as a community. He also benefited from existing EC tensions. In the words of one European commentator, "What happened in Washington did not provoke a crisis in the Community. Rather, it demonstrated the state of crisis that had already existed in the Community."[41] The EC's political structure left it at a serious disadvantage in negotiations with the United States, which had come to the conference with a unified strategy it could adopt as needed. The EC, however, had never formed an energy strategy beyond the ECSC, which meant little after Europe's energy needs transitioned so dramatically from coal to oil. The EC could not suddenly develop a strategy in the middle of negotiations with Washington. There was a leadership vacuum in the EC, and as both US and European officials recognized, that vacuum was being filled by France, to the delight of no one but the French. Throughout the conference, France objected to US proposals and even declined to sign the final communiqué. Instead, foreign minister Michel Jobert delivered a dissent rejecting Kissinger's IEA and any idea of a developed country consumers' organization.[42]

"The French are determined to unify all [EC members] against the United States," Kissinger said after the conference. "I am convinced we must break the EC."[43] In its response to the energy crisis, however, the EC was breaking itself. The French considered the IEA too confrontational and told Britain that Europe must develop its own energy strategy before adopting joint measures with the United States. But given OPEC's decision in January to raise prices again—and Washington's relative economic strength through it all—the others did not want to wait. France's "notably graceless" objections only pushed other European delegations, led by Britain and Germany, closer toward the United States. For Sir Edward Tomkins, Britain's ambassador to France, the conference brought "to a point of uncomfortable focus the central problem of our convergences and divergences with the French over the position of Europe vis-à-vis the United States and over the balance of our European and Atlantic connections."[44] With the exception of France, the remaining eight European delegations at the conference agreed that cooperation and coordination with the United States, not bilateral deals with OPEC, would be Europe's strategy for dealing with the energy crisis.

The North Comes Together, 1974–1975

European governments' attempts to renegotiate and expand trade relations with the Third World were an important component of their move toward political, economic, and institutional unity. But the energy crisis challenged this and other assumptions about the future of Europe. The European project thrived during a time of economic growth and easy access to raw materials in the 1960s, but the abrupt end of cheap oil revealed the inherent weakness of the EC's political structure when individual states experienced severe economic distress. The EC's president could serve as an effective continentwide ambassador when there was general agreement on technical issues and when the benefits were clear, such as extending preferences to LDCs before the energy crisis. But the crisis revealed the EC's ultimate inability to produce a common, forward-looking energy strategy without the support, or at least the acquiescence, of the United States. It also showed that despite the EC's growth and unity, major stakeholders such as Britain and West Germany would not toss aside their respective economic and political ties to the United States—especially when détente suggested a greater sharing of the defense burden at a time when their governments had neither the will nor the means to do so.

Dramatic and rapid international change following the Washington Energy Conference would once again transform transatlantic relations. The developed countries' overwhelming focus in 1973 was high energy prices and their consequences—low growth and inflation. This was not the case across the South. While officials in Washington, London, and Paris feared the end of ever-rising prosperity, high food prices brought on by a combination of drought, depleted US wheat reserves, the dollar's devaluation, and high oil prices were forcing millions in the Third World to go without food. Leaders across the South saw the energy and food crises as interlinked, and many blamed the international economic architecture, designed and managed by the United States, as the main culprit. Despite the recognition that high oil prices were contributing to the food crisis as well as to the general contraction in worldwide economic growth, there was a sense throughout the Third World that only a crisis in the developed countries, rather than the polite politics of UNCTAD, would lead to real changes in global trade, finance, and development.

The promise of that opportunity for change was embodied in the Group of 77's "Declaration on the Establishment of the New International Economic Order," announced on May 1, 1974, at the UN's Sixth Special Session on Raw Materials and Development. Algeria's president Houari Boumediene, a leader of both OPEC and the Non-Aligned Movement, gave the keynote address outlining the demands for increased aid, technology transfers, commodity cartels, and other proposals long familiar to UNCTAD participants. Boumediene received a standing ovation lasting three to four minutes from the General Assembly, where his foreign minister, Abdelaziz Bouteflika, held the presidency. Pakistani economist Sartaj Aziz recalled the feeling in the South after the Algerian leader's dramatic speech:

> So that evening, there was a dinner at the Pakistani minister's house. [Ghanian official and future UNCTAD secretary-general] Ken Dadzie was there, [UN ambassador] Donald Mills of Jamaica was there, and some other delegates. We were all talking about Boumediene's speech and feeling very good about it. Somebody said, "You know, Boumediene is not alone. *The Third World has come of age.* Look at Nyerere of Tanzania, look at Michael Manley in Jamaica, look at Anwar Sadat in Egypt, look at King Faisal in Saudi Arabia, look at Bhutto in Pakistan, and Bandaranaike in Sri Lanka." There were about eight to ten leaders who had become world-class statesmen in the Third World.

There was also a belief that the time had come when developed countries, stable and united in their politics and economics, could no longer act with imperial certainty and arrogance in their dealings with developing countries. "On the other side, in the developed world," Aziz continued, "there was a strange vacuum developing. Nixon had just been Watergated. Pompidou of France was dying. Wilson was not a very strong leader in Great Britain."[45]

These assessments did not anticipate changes in leadership in the developed countries that would fill this vacuum. In March, Edward Heath's Conservative government in Britain was replaced by a Labour government under former prime minister Harold Wilson. According to Kissinger, Wilson "wasted no time in restoring the special relationship" with the United States.[46] Foreign secretary James Callaghan, who would replace Wilson as prime minister two years later, immediately instructed the Foreign Office to improve Anglo-American relations.[47] "The same ever-so-polite needling familiar from the Heath period which had been designed to underscore the new priority of Europe in British policy" was gone, Callaghan informed Kissinger. He said, "'Henry and I are going to work together. If there are any disagreements, bring them to me, and Henry and I will solve them.'"[48]

After Pompidou's death in April and Brandt's resignation in May, two pro-Atlantic finance ministers, Valery Giscard d'Estaing and Helmut Schmidt, assumed power in France and West Germany, respectively. Both had long histories of cooperation with Washington as members of the so-called Library Group, whose members first met in the White House library in early 1973. The Library Group consisted of the finance ministers (or equivalent) of the United States, Britain, France, Germany, and Japan; it was an informal forum that allowed the participants to hold high-level discussions without political considerations, which the Europeans attributed to Nixon's abrupt dismantling of the Bretton Woods system in 1971.

Kissinger especially admired Giscard. Unlike Pompidou's foreign minister Jobert, who was an "idiot," Giscard, like Kissinger, was "an extraordinarily perceptive student of global trends" whose analytical ability and centrism led him to see "the challenges faced by the West in ways that paralleled our own."[49] Kissinger's priorities also aligned with those of Schmidt, whose support for Kissinger's proposals at the Washington Energy Conference had led Jobert to accuse him of betraying European unity. Schmidt diminished any worries about détente's consequences for West Germany, assuring Ford and Kissinger that Germany had "no doubts" about the US commitment to its security. Instead, "convinced that only collective action by the industrial democracies could avert a collapse of the postwar social order," he prioritized international economic issues, especially efforts to unite the United States and Europe in mounting a common response to the energy crisis.[50] Like Giscard, with whom he had developed a close friendship during Library Group meetings, Schmidt believed that European unity could in fact enhance the alliance. As he described his government's foreign policy just after taking office, "We subscribe to political unification in Europe in partnership with the United States."[51]

These changes in Northern governments were profound. By reaffirming the primacy of transatlantic cooperation, leaders in West Germany and especially France were removing central obstacles to Kissinger's model for global governance. Britain could commit to the European Economic Community without fear of prejudicing its relations with the United States; France implied that it would no longer use its dominance within the EC as political leverage over either the United States or its European partners; and West Germany, whose diplomatic power had suffered under the de Gaulle and Pompidou governments, could assert itself as a political force commensurate with its economic strength and security importance. Ford and Kissinger moved quickly to take advantage of these changes, holding separate meetings with the leaders of Japan, Austria, Canada, Germany, and France throughout December 1974 to discuss cooperation on energy and monetary policies.

The results came quickly. The most important breakthrough was with Giscard, whom Ford spoke with at a well-publicized summit on the French island of Martinique. The key achievement was an agreement between the two to strengthen consumer solidarity before a major North-South event scheduled for March 1975. Originally Giscard's initiative, the Conference on International Economic Cooperation (CIEC), or the Paris dialogue, was launched to separate discussions on oil from those on raw materials after the LDCs' insistence on their linkage in the UN's Seventh Special Session. Kissinger explained that without coordination before the conference, the developed countries "would be beaten to death" by OPEC and the LDCs. The new arrangement with France was a "solution broader than energy."[52] As Giscard told Ford, "We can't make an agreement [on energy] without the support—not just the consent—of the United States."[53] "The civil war in the Atlantic community, where each has to choose between the U.S. and France, should be moderated if France carries out its obligations," Kissinger concluded after the Martinique meeting. "We have made a big step toward the cohesion of the industrial countries."[54]

North-North Dialogue at Rambouillet, November 1975

In late 1975 two major meetings—one involving only the North and the other (the CIEC) involving both the North and the South—tested but in the end strengthened rich-country cohesion. The first was the November summit held in Rambouillet, France, with the leaders of the United States, Britain, West

Germany, France, Italy, and Japan (the G-6). The idea originated in Library Group discussions in 1973, when Schmidt suggested to US treasury secretary Shultz that "Atlantic Finance Ministers . . . periodically meet very privately to consult on the whole range of interrelated commercial, financial, energy, etc. problems."[55] Schmidt and Giscard expanded the idea to informal discussions between the two of them when CIEC preparatory talks broke down in April 1975 over Algeria's insistence that all raw materials be included in the discussions. At the Conference on Security and Cooperation in Europe that summer, Giscard, Schmidt, and Ford agreed to begin preparations for a summit, managed closely by their "personal representatives" to avoid any bureaucratic obstacles.[56]

The summit's broad purpose was to restore the West's psychological confidence in the face of interrelated fiscal, monetary, energy, and raw materials problems. To achieve this, the summit leaders would discuss—or affirm—a predetermined agenda including trade, monetary policy, energy, North-South relations, and East-West relations. One major goal for the Europeans was to obtain a US commitment to fiscal stimulus, which would boost growth and confidence in weaker European countries and, over time, reduce inflation across the OECD. "If an economic conference should take place this year, we shouldn't expect too many results," Schmidt told Ford and Kissinger. But "if we could create the impression we intend to work together and coordinate our policies, that will be enough."[57]

Ford and Kissinger both embraced the summit. It fit with Ford's preference for personal diplomacy between heads of state, as well as his desire to distance himself from Nixon's legacy of suspicion and neglect in Europe. For Kissinger, the summit would assist his strategy since the Washington Energy Conference, which was to deal with international economic issues—especially North-South issues—on a political basis between US and European leaders. The summit could send a message to developing countries in advance of the resumption of CIEC talks in December, one month after Rambouillet. Kissinger explained: "We should try to break what the Chancellor [Schmidt] correctly called the unholy alliance between the LDCs and OPEC. This can happen, and we can achieve our results, if they know that their disruptive actions could stop discussions on commodities or that they will pay a price in terms of cooperation, or military exports. In this way we can combat our dependence with a coherent strategy."[58] This was the stick; the carrot was a willingness to cut new deals with oil producers prepared to abandon the NIEO. "We agree on the need for cooperation with producers," Kissinger insisted. "With cooperation we can separate the moderates from the radicals within OPEC, the LDCs from the OPEC countries, and prevent a lot of other 'PECs.'"[59]

Once again, Ford's promarket economic advisers resisted. Treasury secretary William Simon accused Giscard of using the summit to return the international monetary system to fixed exchange rates.[60] He and others also doubted the emphasis on fiscal stimulus; instead, Simon, William Seidman, and Alan Greenspan all agreed that "we should emphasize what we are trying to do structurally to revitalize the private sector, through deregulation, etc."[61] To them, the summit risked institutionalizing Keynesian solutions to problems that actually had their roots in Keynesian policies. "Interference by governments in the operation of an open world market system is counterproductive," explained Flanigan, the president's pro–Wall Street adviser. "This is the basic philosophy of our approach to international economic problems."[62]

Ford's economic team directed its greatest hostility at Kissinger's North-South strategy. Since the oil crisis and the NIEO, Kissinger had announced, with minimal consultation outside of the State Department, numerous initiatives designed to win the support of moderate LDCs and weaken their support for OPEC. Building on his proposal at the 1974 World Food Conference for an international system of food reserves, Kissinger presented his initiatives in an important speech at the UN's Seventh Special Session in September 1975, where he insisted on the United States' willingness to enter discussions with LDCs on raw materials and development in good faith.

There and elsewhere, Kissinger made it clear that the United States would not accept the NIEO, stressing improvement of the existing system instead. To Simon and others, however, Kissinger's public admission that developing countries had legitimate concerns, if illegitimate demands, called into question the entire free-enterprise project at home and abroad. "The principles of free markets and free enterprise are, after all, what we stand for and what we believe in," Simon and Seidman's Economic Policy Board wrote in response to Kissinger's proposals. "If we fail to speak out in their defense, no one else will be able to do so."[63]

In advance of Rambouillet, Simon and Seidman pressed their case to Ford. If the United States promised "'new solutions or new arrangements'" with the South at Rambouillet, "the world will perceive this as a willingness on our part to compromise our basic system." Instead of calling for increased aid and new commodity agreements, as Kissinger had done at the UN, the pair argued that the United States should emphasize the merits of free markets. For Ford's neoliberal advisers, failing to issue strong statements of support at Rambouillet for global market-based solutions would signal a lack of commitment to domestic market-based reforms. Kissinger's approach, they told Ford, would jeopardize "the principles you have been building at home and our economy and military strengths will increasingly count for less in the world."[64]

Kissinger held that the United States would gain nothing by countering the NIEO with a vision of the market that was unpopular even in developed countries. Put simply, the United States would not win an ideological fight with the LDCs, OPEC, or its partners in Europe, who were more dependent on foreign oil and commodities and more politically receptive to some of the NIEO's statist measures. "If we insist on theoretical positions," Kissinger explained to Ford, "Schmidt will separate from us on raw materials. . . . He will not follow us on a confrontation course with the LDC's. If he won't, neither will France, Great Britain, or Japan."[65]

Indeed, elements in Europe had already separated on that issue. Schmidt, Giscard, and Wilson's shared emphasis on restoring the transatlantic alliance and cooperating on energy did not prevent them from endorsing ongoing EC efforts to cut separate deals with LDCs on raw materials. The Lomé Convention, signed in February 1975 by the EC and seventy-one African, Caribbean, and Pacific (ACP) countries, provided nonreciprocal preferences for most ACP exports to Europe, in addition to $3 billion in development aid. Hailed across Europe as a success and well received by several participating LDCs, the convention was a direct response to the NIEO, its preamble pledging "a new model for relations between developed and developing states, compatible with the aspirations of the international community towards a more just and more balanced economic order." EC officials saw Lomé as an achievement of both European unity and Europe's new relationship with its former colonies. Claude Cheysson, a member of the European Commission that negotiated the 1975 agreement, concluded: "All this work has produced an agreement which, I say with some pride, is unique in the world and in history. Never before has there been any attempt to do anything of this kind. It is the first time in history that an entire continent has undertaken a collective commitment."[66]

Despite the EC's measures and the neoliberals' opposition, Kissinger's State Department was confident that his pre-Rambouillet raw materials strategy was beginning to show results. Officials concluded that since Kissinger's overtures at the UN, the OPEC-LDC alliance was weakening, with "moderates" opting for "pragmatic cooperation with the West—where their economic interests necessarily lie." As many had predicted, OPEC price increases were beginning to put LDCs' finances under severe strain, especially in fast-growing moderate countries with strong political and economic ties to the United States, such as Brazil, Mexico, Egypt, and South Korea. Expecting that the "more radical non-aligned" LDCs and OPEC would counter at the CIEC with new aid proposals and a new "political and ideological base for LDC unity," State recommended that, to consolidate gains and discourage additional EC-LDC negotiations, the United States should assume a position of leadership at Rambouillet. The strategy combined firmness on some points and flexibility on others. President Ford should commit to negotiating commodities on a case-by-case basis but reject the South's plans for indexation and a Common Fund buffer program, encourage new financing measures through the IMF and private markets for debt relief but oppose debt moratoriums and forgiveness, and stress the centrality of recovery in the industrial countries to LDC growth.[67]

The United States largely pursued this strategy at Rambouillet, and for the most part, so did Europe. At the Third Session on Energy, Raw Materials, and Development, Ford and his counterparts all agreed on the need to break the "unholy alliance" between OPEC and the LDCs, but strategies on how to do this at the CIEC varied. Above all, the Europeans were concerned about the consequences of confrontation. To them, even the appearance of confrontation would reverse any progress they had made in moderating the South's demands since the UN's Seventh Special Session. Delegates praised Kissinger's UN proposal for a Development Security Fund in the IMF to stabilize LDC export earnings, which was similar to the EC's UN proposals. But since then, Europeans were no less vulnerable to additional price shocks from the South. Inflation had already been rising throughout 1972–73; the oil crisis induced contraction not only through higher costs for energy and related goods but also through diminished expectations of the business community, which held back investment for fear of higher prices for oil and, after the NIEO, other raw materials.[68] "This disruption cannot continue," Schmidt insisted. "Germany has no raw materials except intelligence, technology, and of course coal." Kissinger stressed that it would be "suicidal" to enter the CIEC without cohesion among the oil importers and insisted that "cooperation among us is not confrontational vis-à-vis OPEC." But this would not be enough. "Attacks can strengthen the solidarity of the LDCs," Giscard responded. "We must show the developing countries that we are aware of their problems."[69]

Here the industrial countries converged on one central point. Early on, Wilson had suggested a "Marshall Plan type initiative" that would ward off protectionist measures in both North and South, but this was unlikely. As Wilson himself admitted, "We will be able to offer the developing countries little [in aid]" because of the North's own economic problems, "and certainly far less than the minimum they feel is their right. And even in holding the line we set ourselves a most difficult task." Thus, the cheapest—and most politically and economically effective—response was new commodity arrangements designed in cooperation with the developed countries. Such agreements would seek to stabilize LDCs' export earnings rather than prices, which the LDCs' demand for cartels and indexation promised. "The prospects for individual commodity agreements [as opposed to cartelization and indexation] are not too discouraging," Wilson noted. "But we have to face the fact that the OPEC syndrome is catching on. There are already phosphate-pecs, bauxite-pecs, banana-pecs, and others."[70]

Wilson stressed as an example his initiatives for commodity stabilization at the Commonwealth Heads of Government Conference in Kingston, Jamaica, six months prior to Rambouillet. The Commonwealth group represented a quarter of the UN's population, Wilson pointed out, and this and other centers of decision making and engagement could prove essential in moderating the South's demands. Kissinger's proposal showed the "common ground" already present in the North on a basic approach to commodities. "At the Seventh Special Session [of the UN], the UK's proposals at Kingston, the united approach by the EC and the wide ranging US proposals [by Kissinger] led to the final resolution of the session," Wilson said. "We must demonstrate in the future the same unity that we then achieved or the Group of 77 will divide us."[71]

Schmidt adopted a slightly different approach. While insisting that the developed countries should "educate the developing countries to understand, think, and operate in market economy terms," he also envisioned "something analogous to the Lomé agreement" expanded worldwide. Such a system would stabilize export earnings by providing payments to LDCs in bad times; in times of surplus, the LDCs would pay the money back. It was not a giveaway—it would be managed through the IMF, which would charge interest on late payments. But the industrial countries could use funds otherwise directed toward development aid to subsidize some of the interest. By combining controls, support, and intervention with financial discipline, "this would be more than the Lomé model. It could be done with all industrialized countries on one side and all the developing countries on the other. It would take into account total raw materials exports. And this could be in the upcoming dialogue."[72]

Giscard agreed with Schmidt and Wilson on the difficulty of increasing aid, again citing tight budgets in developed countries and the risk of worldwide inflation. Instead, Giscard suggested, "we can set up reasonable and effective arrangements in commodities." He too endorsed a worldwide system to ensure LDC export stabilization. "Such a system would contribute to the stability of the world economy," Giscard emphasized. "We should show awareness [at the CIEC] of the importance of continuous improvement in the lot of the LDC's."[73]

North-North Dialogue at Puerto Rico, June 1976

After a deep dip in 1975, the US economy was coming back. Unemployment was still high—around 7.9 percent in January 1976, down slightly from the previous year—but the number of employed was increasing without a corresponding jump in inflation. "It is my feeling that the meeting in Rambouillet was very important," President Ford told EC commissioner Francis-Xavier Ortoli two months after the summit. "It had psychological as well as substantive benefits." Ortoli agreed that "the cooperative approach has helped. We have avoided counter-productive measures. So things are not so bad. We are pleased with the results of Rambouillet."[74]

Ford and Ortoli's optimism was premature, at least with regard to the health of Northern economies. Throughout 1976 inflation increased across Europe as the governments of Britain, Italy, and other weak industrial economies borrowed to meet their budgets, threatening the return to protectionism that many had feared. As Daniel Sargent explains, Greenspan and Simon, who had been less than enthusiastic about using political summitry for economic policy, now favored it, but not for the same reason as Kissinger. Greenspan and Simon wanted to use the second G-7 summit, scheduled for June 1976 in Puerto Rico, to impose market discipline on the "sick" countries. Simon advised Ford to offer financial assistance to Italy with strict budgetary conditionalities, while Greenspan warned against "a new wave of inflation" brought on by post-Rambouillet stimulus in western Europe.[75] Greenspan rejected the Keynesian consensus still dominant in Europe and in most of the United States, explaining that "stable growth presupposes a shift of resources into investment and away from public and private consumption." He also anticipated the IMF's "structural adjustment" packages—essentially, the face of the IMF for poor countries and antiglobalization activists from the Reagan administration to the present. Rather than bilateral aid, the difficult "domestic corrective measures" for European deficit countries should be administered through "a general mechanism in the context of the IMF, which will be able to provide financial assistance to developed countries in special need, preconditioned on special corrective programs to insure a return of sound economic equilibrium."[76] This was similar to what Schmidt had proposed at Rambouillet for LDCs.

The State Department "expressed skepticism" against "punitive" measures but still favored another summit. Ford and Giscard met and agreed that "responsible" and not "punitive" measures were needed.[77] Kissinger, no ideologue but no free-spender either, agreed that the Puerto Rico summit could be used to ensure more responsible spending among allies. But the word *responsible* is instructive here. One of the key questions of interdependence theorists was whether democracy prevented industrial countries from making the tough decisions necessary for economic adjustment. This had many implications. A 1975 report by the Trilateral Commission titled "The Crisis of Democracy" accused the citizens of Western democracies in the 1960s of a fundamental contradiction in their demand for government "to increase its functions, and to decrease its authority."[78] In a background paper on the major industrial countries for the Puerto Rico summit, the Economic Policy Board made the same diagnosis: "Governments [in the 1960s] committed themselves to ameliorate social inequities at home and abroad and to achieve an ever rising standard of living. However socially commendable, these commitments proved to be too ambitious in economic terms—both in what they actually attempted to achieve and in the expectations they raised among the public. Thus, the major task for the next several years is both economic and political—*not only to regain acceptable levels of output but also to set realistic goals that are accepted by the public at large."*[79] Kissinger had reached a similar conclusion, though typically, his comments were more about politics than economics: "If the British are smart, it could be in their interest to be pressured into agreement on conditions, so that they can say that the only reason they imposed stringent conditions on the British economy is because of those American SOBs."[80]

Thus, Ford and Schmidt (the latter as head of Europe's only surplus country) went to the Puerto Rico summit in June 1976 looking to discipline the debtors. They faced opposition to their primary goal of fighting inflation over reducing unemployment, especially from Britain's embattled prime minister James Callaghan. Shortly after Puerto Rico, however, Callaghan was repeating the same reasoning to his own supporters. He told the 1976 Labour Party conference that the "option [to increase spending] no longer exists. And in so far as it ever did exist, it only worked on each occasion . . . by injecting a bigger dose of inflation into the economy, followed by a higher level of unemployment as the next step." Asking for assistance from the United States, West Germany, and the IMF, he found only the IMF willing to help—and not without the strict conditions Simon and Greenspan favored.

The Rambouillet and Puerto Rico summits showed that an understanding of postwar Keynesian economics in the industrial countries both persisted and was rejected during the global economic crisis of the 1970s. At Rambouillet, President Ford and his counterparts agreed on a sort of global Keynesianism for the world economy. While keeping an eye on inflation, the theory went, the healthier developed countries should continue spending because their purchasing power would stimulate both weaker OECD neighbors and the developing world through increased demand for their exports—later called locomotive theory by officials in the Carter administration. Locomotive theory was also a way for developed countries to avoid the kind of global structural changes called for by the South, without abandoning the key features of the global Keynesian approach. However, some in the North, especially the

Scandinavian countries and the Netherlands, all of which were left out of the G-6 and G-7 summits, pushed for more radical North-South measures within the European Commission. In addition to endorsing indexation and debt relief, they favored direct transfers to LDCs for global stimulus—a different global application of domestic Keynesian principles that was increasingly out of touch with understandings of economics and out of favor among the governments of the major industrial countries. These differences would cause some problems in the Northern coalition at the CIEC, where, unlike in previous talks, the EC would have common representation.[81]

Kissinger's State Department still endorsed locomotive theory and rejected large fiscal transfers to the South, as well as calls from its Treasury Department colleagues to punish profligate European governments. The consensus remained that government was the solution, in that it should be better managed—even held to task by its creditors—but not shrunk or attacked on principle, especially during a severe economic crisis. For Kissinger, the state's economic power was above all a political lever, essential for domestic stability and international bargaining. But for neoliberals in the Ford administration, government *was* the problem. Big budgets were the result of big government, not just the politicians who managed them. The solution was to remove politics from economics by transferring the enforcement of discipline from individual countries to the IMF—which, of course, reflected the policy and ideological preferences of Washington (and, specifically, the US Treasury).

For Kissinger, the summits' main success was unrelated to the neoliberals' ideological concerns. Rambouillet's "greatest contribution" was that it provided the "kind of political *directoire* of the industrial democracies" that he had advocated since de Gaulle proposed the idea in the 1960s.[82] The Rambouillet directorate excluded the most progressive European countries such as Sweden and the Netherlands, which advocated greater concessions on commodities and debt relief at EC discussions. Rather, at the directorate's center were Britain, Germany, and France, now in closer economic cooperation with the United States since the Marshall Plan. Even in their area of greatest divergence—energy and raw materials—they were close to united. By the time of the CIEC, the major developed countries had agreed to (1) prioritize breaking the OPEC-LDC alliance, (2) stress the impact of the oil cartel's actions for LDCs' prospects, and (3) block the LDCs' calls for debt relief and indexation and limit commodity reform to export, not price, stabilization.

This convergence validated Kissinger's efforts since 1973 to renew the transatlantic alliance around a shared purpose. That shared purpose came from, quite unexpectedly for all involved, the imperative to counter the Third World's challenge to Western countries' economic stability, in the face of what appeared to be a massive structural crisis. But what had once threatened divergence among the world's most powerful economies now suggested convergence around the maintenance of an entire global order that none sought to abandon.

Due to a combination of Kissinger and Ford's persistence; propitious changes of leadership in Britain, Germany, and France; and the increased threat of oil and raw material shortages in the West, transatlantic leaders in the mid-1970s started to realize the truth of the interdependence over which they obsessed in public speeches. Interdependence could be managed only within a stable international order. The EC had tried to create its own alternative order in the early 1970s by isolating the United States through exclusive raw materials agreements with LDCs and then exclusive energy agreements with the OPEC countries after the oil crisis began. But the United States' relative strength through the crisis communicated the consequences of this strategy, as it could make its own deals that undercut the Europeans. Equally important was the fact that Europe still leaned on the United States for subsidized security. If the United States reduced its commitments, the Europeans' budgets would gain a burden that no nation could carry in good economic times or in bad.

This did not mean that US-European divergence on energy and raw materials was no longer a risk. Nor did it mean that the Third World's challenge was over. After the first meeting of the CIEC in December 1975, national security adviser Brent Scowcroft warned Ford that "[US] dependence on these countries [LDCs] for markets and raw materials is increasing. And their political and economic influence is growing." And he still worried about "the Europeans and the Japanese," both of whom were "far more dependent on the Third World than is the US." The United States should use the CIEC to "pursue a variety of policy options, both bilateral," with Third World producers, "and multilateral," with producers and European consumers, "to better secure its economic (trade, investment, and raw materials) and political interests."[83]

Outside of the CIEC, the United States pursued its North-South policy options at the fourth UNCTAD meeting in Nairobi, Kenya. The State Department placed great importance on UNCTAD IV, for several reasons. Policy toward UNCTAD, which would focus on commodities and debt relief, could not be separated from the CIEC; it would arise in all future discussions with developed and developing country leaders, and any success would require substantial effort from the executive branch. UNCTAD "has special meaning for the developing world," State reported to Kissinger, "having prepared the intellectual foundations of much of the New International Economic Order." It was especially important that the United States take UNCTAD seriously now; in the past, it had not. Further, despite the developed countries' convergence on commodities and debt relief and on the link between special drawing rights at the

IMF and foreign aid, the United States was "almost isolated" from Europe. "If we can squelch divisive proposals among DCs [developed countries]," State concluded, "UNCTAD IV gives us the chance to further harmonize DC policies toward the Third World."[84]

Kissinger sought to demonstrate his government's commitment by giving the keynote address at UNCTAD IV, making him the first cabinet-level US official to participate in a meeting of UNCTAD. The address was the centerpiece of a multicountry goodwill tour of Africa in the final months of his tenure. It was Kissinger's first official trip to Africa as secretary of state, and this was evident in his conversations with African leaders. The Ford administration's attention to the continent had been limited to involvement in a proxy war in Angola with the Soviet Union and implicit support for white minority rule in South Africa and Rhodesia. The trip was complicated by the actions of UN ambassador Daniel Patrick Moynihan, who had contradicted Kissinger's North-South overtures at the UN with dramatic denunciations of Third World—and especially African—leaders. Moynihan used the Third World's human rights record to counter its calls for economic redistribution; he also publicly and privately called out Kissinger, his boss, for failing to stand up for human rights in East-West relations. These developments coincided with a human rights movement that both of Ford's opponents in the 1976 presidential elections, Republican Ronald Reagan and Democrat Jimmy Carter, used for their own ends. All these trends would come together in Kissinger's final major initiative for both North-South policy in the Ford administration and his own career in government.

CHAPTER 3

Neoconservatives and the NIEO at the United Nations

Prompted by allegations from investigative journalists and the findings of US senator Sam Ervin, chair of the Senate Watergate Committee, in January 1975 Congress established a new intelligence committee tasked with investigating and publicizing illegal activities by the CIA abroad and at home. It found that "all six administrations from Franklin Roosevelt's through Richard Nixon's—four Democrats and two Republicans—had secretly abused their powers," wrote Frederick A. O. Schwarz Jr., the committee's general counsel. "This was probably the committee's single most important finding."[1] Regardless, the bipartisan committee had a decidedly Democratic stamp, and while no president would have granted it everything it requested, the task (and consequences) of disclosure and denial fell to president Gerald Ford.

This reaction against executive power and secrecy was a consequence of the United States' Third World policy under Nixon and Ford, but it was not the only one. In the early 1970s Americans of both parties came to resent what they saw as ruling-class passivity toward the nation's declining global power and the Third World's rise. In speech after speech at the United Nations, Third World representatives called the postwar economic order unequal and immoral, and OPEC leaders such as Algeria and Venezuela singled out the United States for its selfishness. *Newsweek* told Americans that the global conflict between the "haves" and the "have-nots" was "The World's New Cold War," encouraging their sense of siege.[2] The liberal internationalist establishment agreed. "The main axis of conflict at most international conferences today," Zbigniew Brzezinski, director of the hyperelite Trilateral Commission, explained in 1975, "is not between the Western world and the Communist world but between the advanced countries and the developing countries."[3]

Kissinger's eagerness to pacify the South through concessions on trade and aid led to conflict with Ford's neoliberal economic advisers, who considered the G-77's proposals to regulate international commodity prices directly counter to their own mission to end price controls at home. But while William Simon and Alan Greenspan focused on the economic principles at stake, another set of actors, largely from outside government, saw an even greater threat emanating from the South. The North-South conflict was not simply a battle between rich and poor nations, Irving Kristol, one leading voice, explained in the *Wall Street Journal*; it was "much more a question of one's attitude towards liberal political and economic systems, and toward liberal civilization in general."[4]

In 1973 sociologist Michael Harrington used the term *neoconservative* to describe Kristol and other former liberals who opposed the Democratic Party's embrace of interest-group politics and ambitious social engineering through welfare programs.[5] For neoconservatives, this was embodied in the "New Politics" of 1972 Democratic presidential nominee George McGovern, which was part of an attempt to forge a new base of support from younger feminists, environmentalists, black activists, and others who had come of age politically in the 1960s. According to neoconservatives, Democrats had drunk the New Left Kool-Aid. As one writer put it in *Commentary*, the New Politics movement elevated "TV militants" like Jesse Jackson over NAACP moderates, pandered to the counterculture, and generally accepted the New Left's charge that "the average American had been brainwashed by the Establishment and was tainted by racism."[6] For neoconservatives, these politics were being played out internationally at the United Nations, where State Department diplomats allowed the Third World's attacks on US liberalism to go unchallenged. In the 1980s and beyond neoconservatives took pride in their dismissal of the UN's relevance and authority, but in the 1970s they wanted to stay and fight for an institution they believed was worth saving. Their first major victory came in 1975, when Kissinger appointed Daniel Patrick Moynihan, a former ambassador to India and Kennedy and Johnson administration official, as his ambassador to the UN.

Most histories of neoconservatism overwhelmingly focus on neoconservatives' attitudes toward détente and human rights in the Soviet Union, but Moynihan's UN tenure was a watershed moment for the movement. Although their prescriptions differed, both Moynihan and Kissinger believed that what developing countries said at the UN—and how they organized to say it—mattered.

While Kissinger was able to rebuff the neoliberals' calls for free-market bro-mides, he was less able to control Moynihan's bold, often chauvinistic assertions of the political, economic, and moral superiority of US liberalism. Moynihan's combative neoconservatism threatened Kissinger's attempts to articulate an ap-proach to the Third World that was more in line with western Europe's, and their private and public disputes led to Moynihan's resignation in February 1976 after just seven months on the job. It also made Moynihan more popular than ever at home. Americans found his assessment of the UN compelling: he de-scribed it as a club of tin-pot dictators and racist fanatics denouncing the United States in one breath and demanding money in the next. Months later, voters elected him to the US Senate, where he represented New York State until his retirement in 2001.

Two months after Moynihan's departure, Kissinger tried to reverse the fall-out through a major visit to thirteen countries in Africa—his first and last of-ficial visit to the continent. During the trip Kissinger praised African socialists such as Tanzania's Julius Nyerere, renounced US support for minority rule in southern Africa, and connected support for majority rule to economic devel-opment and the North-South dialogue. He also became the first high-ranking US official to address the United Nations Conference on Trade and Develop-ment (UNCTAD), where he presented another significant policy reversal: en-dorsement of the G-77's call for a Common Fund to support global commodity prices. Kissinger's trip was intended not only as an affirmation of the US gov-ernment's good-faith participation in the North-South dialogue but also as a rejection of Moynihan's legacy at the UN, marking the end of a brief but key phase in neoconservatism's ascendancy in US foreign relations.

Moynihan in Opposition

Like all political labels, the term *neoconservative* has a varied and contested his-tory. As one author put it, "From the 1960s to the 2000s, neoconservatism trans-formed itself so thoroughly as to become unrecognizable."[7] Since at least 1979 there has been no shortage of histories, most of them written by partisan attack-ers or defenders of either neoconservatism's founders or its post-2001 iteration.[8] More helpfully, other scholars have identified different neoconservative move-ments, thereby distinguishing the philosophies of Cold War liberals in the 1970s, such as *Commentary* editor Norman Podhoretz and sociologists Daniel Bell and Nathan Glazer, from the more rigid antistatism of the George W. Bush administration.[9]

Daniel Patrick Moynihan was one of those Cold War liberals and a central figure in the history of neoconservatism. Born in 1927 in Tulsa, Oklahoma, Moynihan moved to New York City as a child, where he shined shoes before graduating high school and finding work as a longshoreman. Unlike future friends Podhoretz and Kristol, Moynihan was never a member of the New York Intellectuals, a fabled group of anti-Stalinist leftist writers and literary critics who debated aesthetics and Trotskyism with equal fervor. Instead, after a year at City College, Moynihan enlisted in the navy, during which time he graduated from Tufts University.

Despite subsequently earning an MA and PhD in international relations from Tufts' Fletcher School, Moynihan was not initially interested in foreign affairs; indeed, in a great irony, the future ambassador failed the State Department's Foreign Service exam. Instead, following the completion of his dissertation in 1961, Moynihan joined the Kennedy administration—the embodiment of the tough "vital center" liberalism to which he subscribed—as an assistant secretary of labor.

During this time Moynihan gained national attention for a controversial report he authored on black poverty. Because he asserted a causal link between black family instability and black poverty, many accused Moynihan of blaming the victim (and worse). It did not help that the report became public knowledge in August 1965, the same month as the Watts riots in Los Angeles. Civil rights leader Whitney Young Jr. called Moynihan's thesis a "gross distortion," while Harvard psychologist William Ryan accused him of harboring a "new ideology" in which blacks were "savages."[10] "I am now known as a racist across the land," Moynihan despaired to NAACP director Roy Wilkins.[11]

The controversy over the "Moynihan Report" was a turning point in Moynihan's relationship to the Democratic Party. "The reaction of the liberal Left to the issue of the Negro family was decisive," he wrote in a reply to his critics. "They would have none of it. No one was going to talk about their poor people that way." By this time, Moynihan "was a neoconservative in all but name."[12] Like Podhoretz and Glazer, Moynihan believed that he had not abandoned liberalism; rather, in its rejection of consensus politics, resistance to internal criticism, and unwillingness to confront its radical elements, liberalism had abandoned him. Following his resignation from the Johnson administration in 1965, Moynihan, a board member of the Americans for Democratic Action, called for a "formal alliance between liberals and conservatives" to combat the "nihilist terrorism" and "erosion of authority" in US cities and universities. In 1966, Moynihan joined the faculty of Harvard's Graduate School of Education, where he taught and directed a Joint Center for Urban Studies with the Massachusetts Institute of Technology. Preferring the term "liberal dissenter," Moynihan mocked the "mob of college professors, millionaires, flower children, and Radcliffe girls" that he blamed for Johnson's decision not to run for president in 1968.[13]

Through it all, Moynihan's stock on the right began to rise. While Podhoretz declared "full-scale war" on the New Left from the pages of *Commentary*—marking its crowning as the neoconservatives' principal organ[14]—Moynihan joined the Nixon administration in 1970 as a special counselor to the president on race relations and urban affairs. When the press picked up on another memo that was widely interpreted as urging Nixon to neglect the black community, Moynihan saw history repeating itself as farce. As if he needed another excuse to abandon his sympathies for the American Left, in response to the "benign neglect" memo, members of Students for a Democratic Society reportedly threatened to trash his house in Cambridge, Massachusetts—the same day antiwar protesters hung a Vietcong flag from Peace Corps headquarters in Washington.[15]

In January 1971 Moynihan returned to Harvard but remained in the Nixon administration part time as a special observer to the United Nations. He was shocked by the Third World–ist consensus of UN committee agendas and reports; the Economic, Cultural, and Social Council's 1970 "Report on the World Social Situation," for instance, was a "totalitarian tract" that he compared to a "hastily written undergraduate thesis." Most troubling for Moynihan was the State Department's lack of a reaction. "It is incomprehensible to me," he told UN ambassador George H. W. Bush, "that a State Department that would take the nation into a hopeless and disastrous war in Asia in defense of abstract principles about democracy is not able—or in some perverse way—not willing—to summon the intellectual competence to defend democracy in a United Nations debate."[16]

In late 1972, for the second time in two years, Nixon offered Moynihan the job of UN ambassador. Believing that the "[UN] corpse had already begun to decompose," he turned it down in favor of becoming ambassador to India, Nixon's other offer. Moynihan's main achievement was the renegotiation of a large food loan India owed to the United States, but his experience abroad left him convinced of a fundamental crisis in US–Third World relations. In letters to Podhoretz and Glazer—now coeditor (with Kristol) of the neoconservative journal *The Public Interest*—he denounced Nixon and Kissinger's hesitancy to resupply Israel during the 1973 war, the Europeans' refusal to support the United States when it did send arms, and especially the anti-Israeli sentiments of the "leftist, 'anti-colonial'" government of Indira Gandhi. "I came here thinking that liberty was losing in the world," Moynihan concluded. "I leave thinking that liberty may well be lost."[17]

If the Moynihan Report and "benign neglect" episodes confirmed his views of the domestic "totalitarian Left," Moynihan's experiences as a diplomat convinced him that an analogue of that same virus had infected the making of US foreign policy. He was not alone among neoconservatives. In 1972 New Politics advocates in the Democratic Party united around liberal antiwar candidate McGovern, who edged out neoconservative favorites Henry Jackson and Hubert Humphrey for the presidential nomination. In response, Jackson supporters formed the Coalition for a Democratic Majority (CDM), urging the party to return to a more aggressive policy toward the Soviet Union and, importantly, the promotion of democracy and human rights.[18] Neoconservatives feared the loss of Truman- and Kennedyesque containment within the Democratic Party, but the Republican Party was no more welcoming, as the Nixon administration embraced détente and balance-of-power politics and opposed many of the social programs neoconservatives still favored. Thus, while McGovern campaigned on the slogan "Come Home, America," the CDM issued its last plea to liberals: "Come Home, Democrats."[19]

More important for Moynihan was that the foreign policy establishment had seemingly lost the will to defend the United States—not so much with weapons but with words. In a 1974 *Commentary* essay titled "Was Woodrow Wilson Right?" he determined that US elites were in the middle of a "crisis of faith . . . demoralized, even victimized" by a combination of the radical Left at home and the "poisonously anti-American" political elites in "most of the rest of the world."[20] The problem was not just that US elites had lost hope; it was also that few, if any, of them actually understood what they were up against. From Moynihan's perspective, it was not hard to find a parallel between US liberals' refusal to acknowledge the uncomfortable truths he raised about black poverty in 1965 and the unwillingness of US foreign policy elites to stand up and defend liberalism against its antiliberal and antidemocratic Third World detractors. In a not-so-subtle jab at his State Department colleagues, Moynihan told the *New York Times* while serving as a UN delegate, "I will not split the difference between a totalitarian society and an open one, or suggest that there's good to be said on both sides."[21]

After his resignation as ambassador to India in late 1974, Moynihan, at Podhoretz's urging, collected these ideas for a lengthy essay in *Commentary*'s March 1975 issue. He began working on it as soon as he returned to Harvard in early January; a month later, Podhoretz, a gifted publicity hound, called a press conference to announce the article's release. Within days, Moynihan, who had already graced the cover of *Time* in 1966, was back in the national spotlight for a major television interview.[22]

In "The United States in Opposition," Moynihan gave both a historical over-view of the Third World's ideology and a prescription for how to combat it. His explanation of "what happened in the early 1970s" was highly idiosyncratic and clearly reflected his recent time in India and his profoundly Anglocentric view of history (and perhaps the aftertaste of two lonely, bitter years as a Fulbright scholar at the London School of Economics). Moynihan located that ideology's origins in the "general corpus of British socialist opinion" from 1890 to 1950, which harbored both "a suspicion of, almost a bias against economic develop-ment" and an "aristocratical disdain" of the US model of capitalist develop-ment. In short, he argued that colonial elites, educated in the Marxist-inflected Fabianism popular at the LSE, took this ideology back to their countries, where they asserted a right to not only political independence from their colonizers but also economic reparations from the developed capitalist world writ large. "Before very long," Moynihan explained, "the arithmetical majority and the ideological coherence of those new nations brought them to dominance in the United Nations and, indeed, in any world forum characterized by universal membership."

More important than his explanation of the Third World's ideology was his diagnosis of current US policy. Part of the problem was that Americans did not even recognize that the Third World held a distinctive, coherent ideol-ogy. The Third World countries' first act as a bloc, he explained, was the po-litical move to establish the Non-Aligned Movement, but in 1964 they became an economic bloc too, with the establishment of the G-77 caucus in the United Nations. By this point, "it was clear enough that the Third World . . . was not going communist," but neither was it going liberal. Rather than discouraging this slide toward statism and anti-Americanism, Moynihan charged, the United States, through "blind acquiescence and even agreement . . . kept endorsing principles for whose logical outcome it was wholly unprepared and with which it could never actually go along." In a thinly disguised jab at Kissinger, Moyni-han cited the 1974 World Food Conference (a Kissinger initiative) and responses to the New International Economic Order and Charter of Economic Rights and Duties of States as the latest examples of the State Department's failure of will.

There was only one choice for beleaguered US policymakers: "*The United States goes into opposition. This is our circumstance. We are a minority. We are* outvoted. This is neither an unprecedented nor an intolerable situation. The question is what do we make of it." He concluded by listing three areas in which the United States must defend itself against attack—international lib-eralism, the world economy, and political and civil liberties—and called for the

US to stand up for liberalism's political and economic achievements in both the UN General Assembly and special organizations. "It is past time we ceased to apologize for an imperfect democracy," Moynihan asserted, and not for the last time. "Find its equal. It is time we grew out of our initial—not a little condescending—supersensitivity about the feelings of new nations. It is time we commenced to treat them as equals, a respect to which they are entitled."[23]

The article caused the sensation it sought and quickly made its way to Kissinger, who allegedly read it straight through an afternoon appointment. When he proposed to Ford that Moynihan "head a group about behaving more aggressively at the UN," the president suggested instead that Moynihan lead the US delegation. Kissinger recalled in his memoirs that he had recommended Moynihan for the position, but Ford remembered it differently: "Henry was not in favor of sending Moynihan to the UN and warned that he might use it as a political stepping stone."[24] Regardless, Ford was in favor, and in a meeting with the new ambassador and the president, Kissinger agreed, noting, "That Commentary article is one of the most important articles in a long time. That is why it is essential to have him at the UN."[25] In addition to a preponderance of neoliberal economic officials, the Ford administration now had a powerful representative of another trend in the fractured and transitional politics of the time: neoconservatism.

Both Kissinger and Ford still had doubts about Moynihan. Ford asked whether he "would carry out orders," to which Kissinger replied, "You—and the press—would know when he disagreed." One consideration was Moynihan's views on the Middle East, of which Kissinger was already aware. "One major problem you will have is on Israel," he warned the new ambassador. "They are desperately looking for a spokesman and they will work on you. . . . I don't want Israel to get the idea that our UN mission is an extension of theirs. . . . We have to show Israel that they don't run us." Moynihan agreed: "The American Jews have got to be Americans." Kissinger was wary but nevertheless believed that Moynihan could be managed. "He will give us fits," he told Ford, "but he will do well."[26]

Kissinger's ambivalence about Moynihan's appointment was understandable. Although his status as a hard-nosed foreign policy realist has been challenged, Kissinger was certainly not a Wilsonian like Moynihan.[27] More important, Moynihan's call for the United States to go into opposition at the UN ran counter to the more conciliatory approach Kissinger had been moving toward since the World Food Conference. The secretary of state already had the Treasury Department and Council of Economic Advisers accusing him of selling out US economic values and interests to placate Third World statists and socialists. Why would he risk turning an even more outspoken critic into such a public liability when his own rhetoric had moved firmly in the opposite direction?

Podhoretz argued that Moynihan had been brought on "to shore up the right flank without having to pay too much for it," since Kissinger believed the UN was essentially "harmless." This is unpersuasive. Kissinger paid unprecedented attention to the United Nations in 1975–76, even traveling to Nairobi to address the fourth meeting of UNCTAD, making him the only cabinet-level US official to do so up to that point (Cyrus Vance addressed UNCTAD four years later, but this act has not been repeated since). Nor was Kissinger persuaded by Moynihan's account of the Third World's ideology, which, in an early meeting, they both agreed was "exaggerated" and "overblown."[28]

Instead, Moynihan had been brought on precisely *because* Kissinger believed that the Third World's ideological offensive at the United Nations was important. "Until the Sixth Special Session," the State Department explained in May 1974, "most LDCs seemed to go along with NAGC [Non-Aligned Country Group] political positions and economic rhetoric, but to look to [the] Group of 77 for real progress on specific economic aims." However, the NIEO demonstrated a "new-found LDC capacity" to ignore political and economic heterogeneity and unite around the confrontational tactics of "militant" Third World leaders in OPEC and the Non-Aligned Movement. Even though their resolutions were not binding or enforceable, the effect of this leadership at the UN both muted "more pragmatic LDC approaches to economic and political issues" and "isolated increasingly [the United States] as [the] apparent protector of [the] status quo on . . . self-determination, racial equality, and distribution of global resources."[29]

Kissinger did not have to endorse Moynihan's prescription—"the United States goes into opposition"—to appreciate his diagnosis that, as the composition of the UN changed, so did its politics and significance. When OPEC leaders used arguments developed primarily in UN agencies to justify restrictions on oil production, they were drawing on organizations and bodies of knowledge that the United States had, through its silence, effectively endorsed back when the oil weapon was seen as an empty threat. Its deployment in 1973 demonstrated both developed countries' dependence on Third World resources and, in western Europe's subsequent scramble for new energy deals with Iran, Iraq, Saudi Arabia, and others, the limits of developed country solidarity. "We are now living in a never-never land, I am certain," Kissinger despaired in early 1974, where "tiny, poor and weak nations can hold up for ransom some of the industrialized world."[30]

"The Commentary article makes two points," Moynihan explained to Kissinger and Ford upon his appointment: "We are still acting in the same posture we had in the past when we had a majority—so we still seek a consensus. The only consensus now is screw the United States. The reputation of the US keeps eroding and that reputation is important to us." "We even cooperate in resolutions directed through codewords against us," Kissinger agreed. "How we are going to behave," in both the General Assembly and specialized agencies like UNCTAD, "is important. . . . *We need a strategy.*"[31]

The Seventh Special Session, September 1975

At the time of Moynihan's appointment in April 1975, the National Security Council (NSC) was in the midst of a major North-South strategy review. Kissinger's leadership at the World Food Conference in November 1974 was a start, but any gains were undercut by public disputes between secretary of agriculture Earl Butz and US congressional delegates over food aid levels. Regardless, the NIEO leadership showed no indication of dropping its confrontational strategy in future negotiations and refused to be swayed by Kissinger's argument that a showdown over oil and other commodities would hurt poor countries the most.

One month after the World Food Conference, the General Assembly met and overwhelmingly approved the Charter of Economic Rights and Duties of States (CERDS). The brainchild of Mexican president Luis Echeverría, CERDS attempted to provide some legal context for the NIEO by outlining new "resolutions and codes of conduct in relations between the North and South."[32] To Kissinger's dismay, US ambassador John Scali had "brow-beaten enough Europeans" to vote *against* the charter, rather than trying to convince a majority of developed countries to merely abstain (as Kissinger had instructed).[33] Instead, the United States inadvertently organized a lonely and ambivalent opposition around itself, angering not only the Third World but also its allies, five of which reluctantly joined the small "no" chorus. Unaware that it was even fighting a battle, the United States lost twice. It was no wonder that Moynihan singled out these poor diplomatic performances in his *Commentary* article.

Expectations were justifiably low for the Conference on International Economic Cooperation (CIEC), the producer-consumer meeting to be held in Paris in April. It was an attempt by French president Valery Giscard d'Estaing to bring together a Group of 19 developing countries and a Group of 8 developed countries to work out some grand bargain on energy outside of global NIEO negotiations in the UN. The first preparatory meetings in February were over before they began. Algeria insisted on discussing raw materials alongside energy at the conference; the United States claimed it had agreed to attend the "prepcon" only on the condition that raw materials would be excluded altogether. "The French chairman has been a disgrace," Kissinger told Ford. The conference "will break up if we don't cave." "Damn right," Ford replied. "You can tell [our diplomats] to come home."[34]

The CIEC's failure caused a reckoning inside the NSC. "Based on the experience of the prepcon," Robert Hormats wrote to Kissinger, "it is clear that for both political and economic reasons the US must more seriously address issues of raw materials and development." To avoid the United States being blamed for its failure, the CIEC would have to be resumed, which meant caving in to Algeria. Refusal to do so would have important consequences beyond the Third World; without hope of a conference, Hormats worried, Europeans would pull their support for Kissinger's International Energy Agency, already on life support due to continued French ambivalence. "Domestic constituencies [in Europe] sensitive to implied confrontation with producers" would attack the IEA and the United States, he explained, "as having sabotaged the consumer/producer dialogue and forced other consumers to go along with the treachery."[35]

Hormats recommended two paths forward. First, Kissinger would continue to strengthen North-North cooperation. At the Conference on Security and Cooperation in Europe in July, Ford, Giscard, and German chancellor Helmut Schmidt revived the idea of a formal summit of industrial country leaders to discuss a predetermined agenda including trade, energy, finance, North-South, and East-West issues. "If an economic conference should take place this year, we shouldn't expect too many results," Schmidt told Ford and Kissinger. But "if we could create the impression we intend to work together and coordinate our policies, that will be enough."[36]

Second, Hormats said it was "imperative" that the United States develop a new position on commodities before September, when the General Assembly would meet for its Seventh Special Session on Raw Materials and Development. The purpose of the Seventh Special Session was to consider progress made toward realizing the NIEO since its announcement at the previous special session in May 1974, and expectations were low on both sides. By bringing to the session a "major initiative on commodities," the United States could take the lead and set the tone early on. "In so doing," Hormats stated, "we would try to strengthen the position of the moderates on commodities and, subsequently, to encourage a more reasonable position by the OPEC moderates and developing countries in the [CIEC]."[37]

According to Kissinger, announcing US willingness to negotiate new commodity agreements would isolate Third World radicals and weaken the argument for comprehensive global negotiations. By proposing multiple negotiations on commodities instead of one grand package or commission, the United States could "break off the [Third World] moderates into various associations or groups and get them to join us in order to minimize the chances of confrontation."[38] This strategy would also strengthen the cohesion of the other developed countries, which could now approve of the new US position without losing points in the South. As Kissinger explained to Moynihan: "Our basic strategy must be to hold the industrialized powers behind us and to split the Third World. We can only do that if we start with a lofty tone and a forthcoming stance. That alone will permit us to hold the industrialized countries together. Bloc formation in the Third World can be inhibited only if we focus attention on practical measures in which they have a tangible stake." By offering "forward-looking" proposals on commodities at the Seventh Special Session, the United States would have something to offer not just to developing countries but also to the European Community, which was split among a conservative Germany, a moderate Britain and Italy, a liberal France and the Netherlands, and a socialist Scandinavia. "I don't want to take an ideological stance and simply argue the virtues of the market economy," Kissinger emphasized to Moynihan. "We must speak early in the session and put forward specific and progressive ideas—something for our friends to hold on to."[39]

At the beginning of the special session on September 1, Moynihan read Kissinger's dramatic two-and-a-half-hour speech to the General Assembly. Rejecting the "charity and dependency . . . methods of development assistance of the 1950's and 60s," Kissinger called instead for new protections for commodity producers, preferential treatment for developing countries' exports, new finance mechanisms in the International Monetary Fund (IMF) for the "least developed countries," and increases in public and private financing for Third World industrialization. Specifically, he rejected the previous US position (supported by the Treasury Department) of opposing new commodity agreements, agreeing to discuss them on a "case-by-case basis"; proposed the creation of a new facility within the IMF to stabilize developing countries' export earnings (as an alternative to price indexation); and promised to resume the CIEC with both energy and raw materials as discussion topics. After fifteen days of close negotiations between assistant secretary of state for economic affairs Thomas Enders—Kissinger's economics guru—and Manuel Pérez-Guerrero—the influential former UNCTAD secretary-general and Venezuela's finance minister— delegates unanimously approved a sixteen-page resolution that, Time noted, "contained more than two dozen references to the proposals made by the U.S. at the start of the session." In a notable victory for the United States, in exchange for possible price-stabilizing agreements for specific commodities—namely, copper and tin—the developing countries dropped their insistence on including indexation in the resolution.[40]

The new US approach to the North-South divide was welcomed across Europe and the Third World. Britain's ambassador to the UN Ivor Richard declared Kissinger's address "the most significant American speech on economic policy since the Marshall Plan," a comparison also made by the Swedish media. In France the left-wing *Quotidien de Paris* saw a "profound revision" of US foreign economic policy, and *Le Monde* noted that even hard-liners like Algeria were saying that "the Americans for the first time are using a language understandable to the countries on the road to development."[41] The *Nairobi Standard* reported that "the world's developing and industrialized nations are now on the brink of a workable compromise," and Mexico City's *Novedades* interpreted the US position as an endorsement of CERDS. An outlier was Venezuela, which took issue with Kissinger's characterization of oil price increases as "arbitrary and monopolistic."[42] Only the Soviet Union appeared uninterested in the US overtures, continuing its policy of self-recusal on the NIEO. The overwhelming consensus in both North and South was that the Seventh Special Session marked a turning point—the beginning of a North-South *dialogue*. "We have spoken with each other rather than to each other," insisted Jan Pronk, Dutch minister of development and the Seventh Special Session's ad hoc committee chairman.[43]

The results of the Seventh Special Session met all of Kissinger's objectives. First, his speech had brought the US position on commodities much closer to the Europeans', whose negotiating solidarity was needed before resuming the CIEC in December. Second, it seemed that the engaged and forthcoming US stance had the intended effect on the Third World bloc. "The majority in the third-world group didn't want an ideological showdown or political victories," one Third World delegate told the *New York Times*. "That's why the extremists were defeated and we started talking business with the Americans." Also significant was a sense that, in the end, the United States had more to offer developing countries than OPEC did. Even Abdelaziz Bouteflika, the outspoken Algerian foreign minister and General Assembly president, acknowledged as much, telling the General Assembly that the Third World "knows that it must count on the understanding and agreement of the major powers for the satisfaction of its most obvious rights."[44]

Kissinger did not believe the United States could "win" the debate at the special session, but it could influence the final results to be much more favorable to US interests. "I would like a reasonable outcome in which we are not totally isolated," he told Moynihan in the session's hectic final days.[45] Instead of enabling radicals and isolating allies through defensiveness and hostility—as the United States had done with the NIEO and CERDS—Enders and Moynihan worked behind the scenes to ensure a final resolution that reflected compromise from both sides. They were helped by Kissinger's proposals, which he correctly expected would change the terms of the debate from a grand bargain into several discrete negotiations. As an added bonus, the inclusion of twelve Kissinger proposals in the final resolution showed a significant degree of US leadership.[46]

Not all the credit for the special session went to Kissinger. *Newsweek* attributed the unexpected "note of civility" at the UN to Moynihan, adding that the "highbrow Horatio Alger . . . has won almost nothing but praise for his patience and diplomatic skill."[47] "The diplomatic outcome certainly vindicates Ambassador Moynihan's basic approach," the editorial staff of the *Wall Street Journal* proclaimed. "Rather than play the European game and swallow as much, and a bit more, of the Third World's demands as the U.S. could tolerate, the U.S. set out to be responsible opposition."[48]

A Fighting Irishman at the UN

Discussions at the Seventh Special Session stuck to economics, and so did Moynihan, following Kissinger's instructions to ensure a "reasonable outcome." That Moynihan did so was surprising. In August the nonaligned nations had met in Lima, Peru, to agree on a collective agenda for the session. Their opening statement celebrating their vanguard role in the "struggle against imperialism, colonialism, neocolonialism, [and] racism" was boilerplate, and most US diplomats would not have glanced twice. Moynihan, however, was particularly troubled by one more ism on that list: Zionism. Not only was this "hardly the substance of economics," he scoffed. This "talk about declaring Zionism to be a form of racism . . . reeked of the concentration camp and gas chamber. No person sensitive to the idea of liberty would want in any way to be associated with such language."[49]

Nor was he made hopeful by a panel discussion with Zbigniew Brzezinski. President of the two-year-old Trilateral Commission and soon to be Jimmy Carter's chief foreign policy adviser, Brzezinski embodied the world-order liberalism that neoconservatives detested. Brzezinski and other liberal internationalists, largely from the Trilateral Commission, would dominate Carter's foreign policy team, with the self-appointed mission of "making the world safe for interdependence."[50] "The dominant struggle in the world [is] between the West and the Third World," Moynihan paraphrased Brzezinski, "with the Soviets the primary beneficiaries."[51] The policy details were spelled out in a dozen Trilateral Commission reports, but the basic assumption was clear: the United States would have to acknowledge the Third World's rising influence in an interdependent world and deal with its economic demands on that basis.

For a brief moment, however, the UN seemed a less divided place. The special session's promising conclusion on the morning of September 17 also marked the end of the Third World's control of the presidency of the General Assembly—scheduled to begin its thirtieth session that very afternoon. Bouteflika was out; in his place was Gaston Thorn, the centrist prime minister of Luxembourg and future European Commission president. "French without resentment, and German without guilt, he was the best we could have hoped for," Moynihan recalled. "The auspices had rarely been better."[52]

From Algeria to Zaire, delegates opened the General Assembly with praise for the "truly historic" and "universal and cooperative process" for global economic dialogue established at the Seventh Special Session.[53] Back from his Middle East negotiations, Kissinger reaffirmed to his fellow foreign ministers the new "spirit of conciliation" in North-South relations. Borrowing the rhetoric of his critics, Kissinger declared that there was "no longer any dispute" that human rights were a legitimate concern and standard for all governments' behavior. But he also insisted that it was possible to "fashion unity while cherishing diversity," leaving the definition of human rights—and what action the United States would take regarding violations—undefined and thus uncontroversial. Conciliation, not confrontation, was the clear message: "Let us fashion together a new world order. Let its arrangements be just. Let the new nations help shape it and feel it is theirs. Let the old nations use their strengths and skills for the benefit of all mankind. Let us all work together to enrich the spirit and to ennoble mankind."[54]

Of course, Kissinger sought no such "new world order"; his goal was to hold on to the old one, by whatever modifications necessary. In policy terms, this meant swallowing US pride and accepting Algeria's demand that CIEC discussions include both energy and raw materials; making concessions on commodity policy, from new individual agreements and buffer stocks to eventual endorsement of a Common Fund, an International Fund for Agricultural Development with US contributions and OPEC influence; and billions for an IMF special fund for developing countries' balance-of-payments problems. At the heart of it all was the transatlantic alliance, strained by external crises—high prices for energy and raw materials—and struggling under internal crises—low growth and inflation. "If we insist on theoretical positions [in the North-South dialogue]," Kissinger explained to Ford, "Schmidt will separate from us on raw materials. . . . He will not follow us on a confrontation course with the LDC's. If he won't, neither will France, Great Britain, or Japan."[55] North-North economic disharmony also threatened critical East-West policy objectives such as NATO unity and détente—one of several "hard" security issues stressed by interdependence advocates (and future Carter officials) Brzezinski and Richard Cooper.[56] If avoiding these outcomes required aping the Third World's talk about a "new world order"—and ignoring its rhetoric about Western racism, Zionism, and imperialism—then so be it.

While Kissinger declared his intent to "fashion unity while cherishing diversity," Moynihan took diversity to a different conclusion. In August he broke with thirty years' practice among US ambassadors and used his vote on the Security Council to veto the UN application of a new nation—the (communist) Democratic Republic of Vietnam. According to Moynihan, the State Department's opposition to his vote was "unanimous": "To do so would outrage the General Assembly, jeopardize everything that was at stake in the Special Session, and bring on the expulsion of Israel," a senior official reportedly told him. Ford approved Moynihan's actions, and State worked hard to minimize the expected damage by defanging his final speech. Regardless, in Moynihan's estimate, his "reasonable opposition" strategy had been vindicated: "There was *no* reaction to our veto. . . . If anything, the United Nations seemed to have been reminded of American power."[57]

The Vietnam incident was the "opening shot" in Moynihan's war at Turtle Bay. "We would make the connection between the unwillingness to tolerate democracy at the U.N.," he explained, "and the refusal [by Third World countries] to allow it at home."[58] That is, if the UN would admit North Vietnam, a communist state that did not allow free opposition, then, by that logic, it must also admit capitalist nonmembers such as South Korea and South Vietnam. For Moynihan, the Third World's rejection of those terms was a perfect example of the "tyranny of the majority" at the General Assembly, where (he alleged) postcolonial and poor nations weaponized democracy against liberalism.[59]

Moynihan did not coin the catchy "tyranny of the majority" phrase. In fact, neoconservatives used it in the 1960s to describe the antiliberal tendencies of mass politics in the United States, especially the idea of "participatory democracy" advocated by the radical student Left.[60] In this context, the tyranny of the majority is another example of how neoconservatives' vision of domestic politics shaped their—and the nation's—understanding of foreign policy. Every Sunday, Moynihan drove this message home to the viewers of political talk shows. As he explained on *Meet the Press*: "We are not about to be lectured by police states on the processes of electoral democracy.[61]

If Idi Amin's Uganda was not a police state, it was only a matter of semantics. So when the unpredictable dictator addressed the General Assembly on

August 1, Moynihan was listening. Amin began with praise for the Seventh Special Session, including a "special tribute to the United States authorities . . . who approved a change in the American attitude and policy towards the third world." He transitioned into harsh but typical denunciations of US imperialism and declarations of support for the Soviet Union and China, but he saved his greatest wrath for the state of Israel and its "Zionist" supporters in the United States—who, through their ownership of "virtually all the banking institutions, the major manufacturing and processing industries and the major means of communication," Amin claimed, had "colonized" the US government. There was only one solution: Americans must "rid their society of the Zionists," and the world community must ensure the "extinction of Israel as a state."[62]

The State Department was no friend of Amin. After he sent a telegram to UN secretary-general Kurt Waldheim applauding the massacre of Israeli athletes at the 1972 Olympic games in Munich, State canceled a $10 million loan and called his words "deeply shocking" and "totally incomprehensible." But for Moynihan, the State Department missed the point. Amin's comments might have been dismissed as the ramblings of an unhinged racist—if not for the fact that, less than two months prior, the Organization of African Unity (OAU), which Amin chaired, had passed its own resolution likening "the racist regime in occupied Palestine" to the "racist regimes in Zimbabwe and South Africa," citing their "common imperialist origins." Amin may have put it most crudely, Moynihan concluded, but his was clearly not a minority opinion—and only Israel seemed to realize the implications of the global community's implicit endorsement.[63]

In *Commentary*, Moynihan had insisted that the United States must take what is said and done at the UN seriously. Kissinger agreed with this assessment but was less concerned about the actual language used by Third World states than about how these expressions of collective opposition encouraged similar bloc behavior on other multilateral and global issues—namely, energy and commodities. Amin was powerful in Uganda but, his chairmanship of the OAU notwithstanding a marginal force in Third World politics; as a whole, Third World states were much more unified around and capable of taking action on the NIEO than they were on Israel. But for neoconservatives, such attacks could not be separated: they were part of the same ideological assault on the sacred principles of Western, and particularly US, liberal democracy. As chairman of the OAU, Amin "spoke for forty-six African nations," Moynihan charged, "but in truth in that moment he spoke for the authoritarian majority in the General Assembly itself."[64]

When the State Department's initial reaction was silence, Moynihan decided that "it was time to create a crisis."[65] He skipped a scheduled dinner for

Amin that night and traveled to San Francisco, where he addressed an AFL-CIO audience gathered by George Meany—just the type of right-wing liberals the neoconservatives believed the Democrats were abandoning. Few could—and only the delegate from Dahomey later did—argue with his characterization of Amin as a "racist murderer." What angered Moynihan's African colleagues in Turtle Bay was his claim that Amin's leadership of the OAU was "no accident." This was factually incorrect—the chair rotates among member states—and several African diplomats had in fact openly criticized Amin's speech. Some of the continent's leading newspapers even rivaled Moynihan in their rhetoric. For instance, Nigeria's *Daily Star* called the speech "the most racist act ever seen at the United Nations," and Kenya's *Daily Nation* made it "perfectly clear" that when Amin "speaks about the expulsion of Israel he does not represent African opinion."[66]

Back home, the reaction to Moynihan's comments was overwhelmingly positive. "With a mood of cynicism widespread in America, it doesn't hurt to be reminded that there is a difference between democracy and totalitarianism," the *Wall Street Journal* wrote in response.[67] A remarkable 70 percent of Americans approved of Moynihan's approach, one poll concluded, while only 16 percent believed the ambassador should "be more diplomatic and tactful."[68] Significantly, the poll found that Moynihan had even more support among Democrats (71 percent) than Republicans (66 percent). Moynihan also received public statements of support from Clarence Mitchell Jr., the NAACP's head lobbyist who had backed him during the controversy over his report on black poverty, and Bayard Rustin, another influential black civil rights activist who had already become a major actor in the neoconservative movement.[69]

Moynihan believed that he was speaking truth to power not only at the UN but also in Foggy Bottom, telling the *New York Times* that the State Department "machine" was "emasculating" his speeches.[70] While President Ford bent to this groundswell of public support and told reporters that Moynihan "said what needed to be said," Kissinger did the opposite. *Newsweek* reported that the secretary "blew his stack" before quickly putting out a statement distancing the State Department from Moynihan's remarks. Not only had Moynihan insulted the OAU; he had also singled out Indira Gandhi's authoritarian leanings in India, about which Kissinger had instructed US diplomats to keep quiet.[71] "The President didn't know what he was supporting," Kissinger grumbled.[72]

The Amin fiasco was a prelude to one of the most controversial votes in UN history: General Assembly Resolution 3379, which declared Zionism a "form of racism and racial discrimination" and a "threat to world peace." The resolution had been in the works at least since August, when the nonaligned countries simultaneously denounced the resistance of the "large consumption economies" to the NIEO and celebrated their own resistance to the North's "imperialism, colonialism, neocolonialism, racism, Zionism, apartheid, and any other form of foreign domination."[73]

Without Moynihan's public relations campaign before and after the vote, the resolution might have been passed and forgotten about, and indeed, this is what Kissinger had hoped for. The State Department tried to prevent Ford from giving a statement (prepared by Moynihan) about the upcoming vote, arguing that it would neither influence the vote nor produce any serious foreign policy benefits.[74] Moynihan also went to Congress to drum up support for a strongly worded resolution, and again, Kissinger intervened to soften the language. But Moynihan made it clear he had no intention of backing down— he only agreed that, on November 10, the day the General Assembly voted, he would not speak until after the final vote had been taken. All Kissinger could do was tell Moynihan to tone it down. "We have been overdoing the defense of Zionism as a philosophy and a system," he insisted that afternoon through an intermediary. "Ask [Moynihan] to cut it back. We are conducting foreign policy. This is not a synagogue."[75]

The General Assembly passed Resolution 3379 with seventy-two in favor, thirty-five against, and thirty-two abstentions. The overwhelming majority of support and sponsors came from North Africa, the Middle East, and the Eastern Bloc. Most parts of Latin America and sub-Saharan Africa joined the United States, Canada, western Europe, and Australia—the "large consumption economies"—in voting nay.

Contrary to Moynihan's insistence, the reasons for many countries' votes went beyond anti-Semitism or antiliberalism. "Brazil, seeking Arab oil and investments, refused to go along [with the United States]," *Newsweek* reported, while "some Black African nations did not want to dilute the [resolution's] attack on South Africa."[76] Kissinger's staff also saw this brighter side, noting that, "among sub-Saharan Black African states without a significant Islamic population and not under a politically 'radical' influence, 26 either opposed equating Zionism with racism or abstained, while only 2 in that category did link it." More important for African countries were persistent promises, made at the beginning of the oil crisis, that "they would receive far more aid than they actually have from the Arabs, in return for breaking relations with Israel and voting sympathetically on Arab causes."[77] Still, some delegations—including "several experienced American diplomatists"—cited Moynihan's repeated attacks on the General Assembly and the Third World as the reason for their support or abstention. As one African delegate put it, "All I can tell you is that our vote was mainly against Moynihan."[78]

The American public felt the opposite way. After his speech denouncing the "infamous act" that had just taken place—a phrase coined by Norman Podhoretz, who, along with Suzanne Weaver, had helped write Moynihan's speech the night before—one poll found that more than 70 percent of Americans supported both his actions and his style.[79] "The cheers have been coming from both conservatives, who have historically distrusted the U.N., and liberals, whose commitment to the organization is not as automatic as it used to be," *Time* explained in a flattering profile of the "fighting Irishman."[80] On November 12 tens of thousands of people gathered for a rally in New York City to protest the vote, which more than a dozen prominent diplomats, religious officials, and leaders from the labor, civil rights, and women's movements called an "outrage," a "curse," and an "abomination." Carrying signs that read "U.N. Nothing" and "Brazil, You Stink! And You Too Mexico!" the demonstrators broke out into "applause," the *New York Times* reported, "every time a speaker mentioned Daniel P. Moynihan."[81]

Moynihan's defiance of Kissinger's policies did not stop with the Third World. Neoconservative intellectuals were also pleased by his public criticisms of détente, which they had been describing as appeasement since 1972. The first jab came in June, when Moynihan appeared at another Meany-organized AFL-CIO dinner, this time honoring Soviet dissident Alexander Solzhenitsyn. Fearing that the president's attendance would offend the Soviets just weeks before the Helsinki negotiations, Kissinger had persuaded Ford to decline Meany's invitation. The only other cabinet official to appear was defense secretary James Schlesinger, whom Kissinger openly despised.[82] And while Kissinger privately (and to his Soviet counterparts) dismissed the concessions to human rights contained in Helsinki's Basket Three (One and Two covered borders and trade, respectively), just days after the Zionism vote Moynihan introduced a UN resolution calling for the immediate release of all political prisoners worldwide. "I am being told if he does not put it forward everyone will know I vetoed it," Kissinger complained. "As far as I know I am being blackmailed to proceed with that resolution."[83] When Kissinger denied him access to State Department resources, Moynihan formed an alliance with the human rights group Freedom House, a longtime supporter of Eastern Bloc dissidents, to draft a "universal standard for human rights" for the UN's use.[84] The proposal went nowhere, but that was beside the point. The "lesson," Moynihan said of the controversy over his OAU comments, "is that if you want an audience, start a fight."[85]

This was too much for Kissinger. Moynihan was a "laughing stock," he told Brent Scowcroft, his successor as national security adviser, and a "disaster in Europe."[86] With the developed countries still reeling from the previous year's oil shock and fearing, as British prime minister Harold Wilson put it at the first G-7 meeting in November, more "phosphate-pecs, bauxite-pecs, banana-pecs, and others," Moynihan could not have chosen a worse time to start a war of words with Third World commodity producers.[87] In December Wilson's UN ambassador Ivor Richard compared Moynihan "variously to a trigger-happy Wyatt Earp, a vengeful Savonarola and a demented King Lear 'raging amidst the storm on the blasted heath.'"[88] Reasoning that Richard would never make such statements without Wilson's approval and that Wilson would never give the okay without first running it by Kissinger, Moynihan sniped back. On January 23 he sent a memo to all US embassies that included a list of incidents showing that, due to his actions, "governments are beginning to think that anti-American postures at the UN are not without cost." Moynihan contrasted these successes with "a large faction" of the State Department that "has an interest in our performance being judged to have failed."[89] The memo was then leaked to the press, almost certainly by Moynihan's office.

Ford and Kissinger gave measured public statements of support for Moynihan, but these were nothing more than polite formalisms ahead of his impending departure. Both the president and the secretary of state "deplore Moynihan in private," wrote James Reston, Kissinger's preferred source for leaks at the *New York Times*. "Having put him in the job, they can neither tame nor repudiate him."[90] On February 2, after just over seven months in the position, Ambassador Moynihan resigned.

"Moynihan has enraged Third World delegates, discomfited his Western European colleagues, and brought cheer to the hearts of Americans," *Time* summarized his last months as the US representative to the UN.[91] Whether liberal Democrats had abandoned him in the 1960s or the other way around, Moynihan's attacks on antiliberalism and anti-Americanism at the UN brought him wide esteem from other right-wing liberals alienated by the Democratic Party's apparent embrace of egalitarianism, multiculturalism, and noninterventionism. As Kissinger had suspected, Moynihan wasted little time in securing political support for a run for office from party power brokers—namely, "liberal Democrats and black leaders so that [he] could address their misgivings about his opinions of socialism and racial issues." In early June 1976, just four months after stepping down, Moynihan declared his candidacy for the Democratic nomination for US senator from New York. After narrowly defeating liberal incumbent Bella Abzug for the nomination, he easily triumphed in the general election over his conservative Republican rival James Buckley—thus making Moynihan "the first neoconservative intellectual to be elected to public office."[92]

Apartheid and the North-South Dialogue: "Liberation on Two Scales"

The deterioration of North-South relations at the UN under Moynihan's tenure coincided with two important developments suggesting a strengthening of the US position. In 1973 Kissinger had set about rebuilding the postwar transatlantic partnership between the United States and western Europe, which, at the time, was mired in fallout from Nixon's New Economic Policy and détente. The oil shock later that year and the announcement of the NIEO in the spring of 1974 gave greater urgency to these efforts. After a series of discrete but stalled attempts at macroeconomic cooperation, in November 1975 the United States, Britain, France, Italy, West Germany, and Japan met in Rambouillet, France, to agree on a coordinated response to the interrelated fiscal, monetary, and energy crises.

The second event was the reopening of the Conference on International Economic Cooperation in December. In fact, a major purpose of the Rambouillet summit had been to strengthen developed country solidarity before the CIEC as a counter to the developing countries' own unity—especially after Moynihan's performance at the UN, which, except for the Seventh Special Session, had weakened the former and strengthened the latter. Only after establishing a common stance on energy and commodities—that is, forming a developed country bloc—Kissinger explained at Rambouillet, could the United States and western Europe negotiate with any sort of credible leverage.[93] "We agree on the need for cooperation with producers," Kissinger insisted. "With cooperation we can separate the moderates from the radicals within OPEC, the LDCs from the OPEC countries, and prevent a lot of other 'PECs.'"[94]

Still, two massive obstacles remained for Kissinger's goal of winning Third World moderates; both were regionally specific but had global implications. The first was the Panama Canal. Negotiations over the canal's status (started and stalled in the Johnson administration and renewed by President Nixon in 1973) played a role in Kissinger's bid to win the cooperation of influential Latin American leaders such as Venezuela's Carlos Andrés Pérez and Mexico's Luis Echeverría on trade, energy, and commodities. "If these [canal] negotiations fail," Kissinger told Ford, "we will be beaten to death in every international forum and there will be riots all over Latin America."[95]

The second obstacle was apartheid. In the Truman and Eisenhower administrations, South Africa was a reliable supporter of the United States' global Cold War agenda. Washington reciprocated by abstaining on antiapartheid resolutions in the UN, sharing scientific and military technology, and promoting investment by US multinationals.[96] Liberals in the Kennedy and Johnson administrations changed some policies, voicing support in principle for African self-determination and endorsing a worldwide arms embargo, but they still refused to back additional economic sanctions that might harm US businesses. However, the international isolation of Ian Smith's government in Rhodesia in the late 1960s and a growing global movement against apartheid—as well as the achievements of the US civil rights movement—made the United States' lack of a firm policy an increasing liability, which the Soviet Union was quick to exploit in its own relationships with postcolonial African governments. The longer South Africa existed as a pariah state, the worse the United States looked for identifying strategically with the white government's leadership. "The time has come for the U.S. and the European countries with interests in South Africa to begin a dialogue with the South African leaders," Bouteflika instructed Kissinger in December 1974, just days after the vote on the Charter of Economic Rights and Duties of States. "You cannot pursue any longer a policy which is in disharmony with the rest of the world."[97]

The situations in South Africa and Rhodesia were complicated by events elsewhere on the continent. In Angola the departing Portuguese—undergoing their own "Carnation Revolution" following the removal of right-wing dictator Antonio Salazar in 1974—left opposing nationalist factions to fight their way to power. Each side soon received arms: the pro-US National Liberation Front of Angola (FNLA) from the CIA, and the pro-Soviet People's Movement for the Liberation of Angola (MPLA) from Cuba. It was a classic Cold War proxy battle and, for that reason, an apparent defiance of détente.[98]

The State Department's Africa bureau doubted the benefits of intervention, but Kissinger pressed forward. When Congress got wind of the secret program in late 1975 and banned any additional military aid to the FNLA, the United States lost its only bit of leverage. Kissinger was caught in a bind. Most African governments opposed US intervention, but they also opposed Soviet influence in Angola; for that reason, several governments, including Nigeria, Ghana, and Tanzania, gave aid to the MPLA.[99] At the same time, the US embassy in Ethiopia reported that many African governments believed the United States and South Africa were in "de facto collusion, if only because both support opponents of [the] MPLA regime."[100] The stakes were therefore high. "A communist victory in Angola would quicken events in southern Africa, encourage radicalism and discourage moderates," Kissinger explained to Ford. "When you added to that the Cuban troops and the congressional action preventing us from giving further support in Angola, we left our OAU supporters high and dry and all trends toward radicalization in Africa were speeded up."[101]

Hovering over Angola and apartheid in early 1976 was the North-South dialogue, and US strategists' inability to address each problem discretely was a clear demonstration of the new realities of global interdependence. Although Latin America took a larger share of overall US exports, African commodities— especially coffee, cocoa, cobalt, chrome, iron ore, and diamonds—were essential to US industrial production and household consumption. "Thirty to sixty percent of our consumption" of those commodities comes from Africa, Kissinger reported to Ford; the figures were even higher for Europe's reliance on African commodities.[102] As major producers of raw materials, African states played a particularly important role in international commodity negotiations, especially because, unlike the Organization of American States, the OAU debated and developed common positions independently of US input or influence. "There are only two states with which we have any major military assistance role, that is, Kenya and Zaire," Kissinger told congressional leaders. "For the rest of Africa what is needed is a sense of direction and a sense of confidence in the United States."[103] That sense of direction was expected to come from three new policies: clear support for a transition to majority rule in South Africa and Rhodesia, withdrawal of US arms in Angola, and a new commitment to the continent's economic development. In exchange, Kissinger expected African leaders to resist Soviet and Cuban interference in Angola, South Africa, and elsewhere, as well as to back down from confrontational tactics in North-South negotiations.[104]

For these reasons, Kissinger planned a multicountry trip to Africa that would conclude with a major North-South policy speech delivered at the fourth meeting of the UN Conference on Trade and Development in late April. While the CIEC's membership was restricted to a Group of 19 from the South and a Group of 8 from the North, UNCTAD, which had met every four years since its founding in 1964, was a permanent and open UN-affiliated forum where the heterogeneous developing countries of the G-77 could organize largely on their own terms. "UNCTAD as an organization has special meaning for the developing world," the State Department explained, "having prepared the intellectual foundations of much of the New International Economic Order and frequently being the LDCs' preferred vehicle for carrying out policies ranging from commodities to technology."[105] In fact, after the United States agreed to resume CIEC talks at the Seventh Special Session, several developing countries sponsored a General Assembly resolution "designed to create a link between the CIEC and the UN . . . where they have equal representation, an equal chance to be heard, opportunities to coordinate their positions, extensive secretariat support, and the majority vote."[106] For these reasons, it was important to ensure that UNCTAD IV concluded with as little acrimony as possible. The "alternative," the State Department warned, would be "a complete breakdown in [the] North-South dialogue which would [include the] CIEC."[107]

Kissinger's presence would mark the first time a cabinet-level US official attended a meeting of UNCTAD; it was also his first official visit to Africa.[108] Thus, the trip was the subject of a great deal of flurried interdepartmental and intergovernmental coordination. In March and April Kissinger held a series of meetings with the NSC, Treasury Department, congressional leaders, and thirty-eight African ambassadors to solicit input on a strategy. "There are two burning issues in Africa," Liberia's ambassador to the United States told Kissinger: "first of all independence and majority rule and second, economic development." The Somali ambassador also emphasized "liberation on two scales" as the "two major ideas" animating the continent. Kissinger's own motives and sympathies varied; he told Ford of his "basic sympathy with the white Rhodesians," but he also recognized that "black Africa is absolutely united on this issue."[109] However, his framing of the trip to African ambassadors was a clear repudiation of the Moynihan-neoconservative approach toward the South in general and Africa in particular:

The relationship between the developed and developing nations (which is one of the crucial problems of our period) must find its reflection— and its solution—in Africa. . . . This cannot be done in an atmosphere of confrontation on either side. We are not going there in an attitude of confrontation, nor are we going there to tell Africans how to organize their internal affairs. We are going there . . . to see whether we can respond to the economic needs of Africa and the political aspirations for majority rule of the African peoples.

Whereas just months earlier Moynihan had identified African unity as a shameful enabler of anti-Semitism and authoritarianism, Kissinger now praised its central role in human rights and economic development. "We think that the future of Africa can best be achieved by Africans," he repeated, "and for this we believe that African unity is essential."[110]

Kissinger emphasized this morally inflected vision of US foreign policy in his visits to African capitals. "President Ford has sent me to this continent to witness firsthand the aspirations of the peoples of Africa for national dignity, racial justice, and economic advance," he told an audience in Liberia. "America's own moral values summon us to this policy."[111] That policy, he explained in Zambia, now included "the unequivocal commitment of the United States to human rights, as expressed in the principles of the U.N. Charter and the Universal Declaration of Human Rights," and US "support [for] self-determination, majority rule, equal rights, and human dignity for all the people of southern Africa—in the name of moral principle, international law, and world peace."[112] Privately, Kissinger called human rights "sentimental nonsense," but the speech reportedly brought Zambian president Kenneth Kaunda to tears. After decades of US support for white rule, Kaunda remarked, "We could not believe this was a Secretary of State from Washington, D.C."[113]

Kissinger also insisted that the United States was ready to respond to the Third World's multidimensional vision of rights, in which political independence and economic development went hand in hand. As he had at the Seventh Special Session, he made sure that his own language—if not his actual intentions—matched those of his African counterparts. "I have come here to make clear that the United States associates itself with the two great aspirations of the independent nations of Africa," Kissinger stated upon his arrival in Nairobi, "the aspiration to human dignity and racial equality and the aspiration to economic progress."[114] Thus, the United States would work with African governments, he insisted in Lusaka, "to help them achieve the economic progress which will give meaning to their political independence and dignity to their struggle for equality." Kissinger then promised a series of new measures for African development in particular and Third World development in general, which he would reveal at the UNCTAD meeting in Nairobi. "This is the first time that an American Secretary of State . . . [has] come on such a mission," he emphasized, "reflecting the importance we attach to the economic development of southern Africa."[115]

UNCTAD IV, April–May 1976

The idea of liberation on two scales was front and center when the delegates convened at the Kenyatta Centre—at the time, Kenya's tallest building—in late April 1976 for UNCTAD IV. More than five hundred journalists were in attendance, as was UN secretary-general Kurt Waldheim. The significance of the conference's location and timing—in close temporal proximity to the CIEC and the first UNCTAD meeting after the NIEO's announcement—was something Western delegates were compelled to acknowledge. "The achievement of political independence does not represent the end of the struggle," Waldheim told the delegates at the beginning of the conference. "We are now engaged upon the achievement of economic decolonization, and upon the creation of a new international economic order."[116]

After the developed countries tried to reduce divergence on North-South matters at the Rambouillet summit, the G-77 met in the Philippines in Febru-

ary 1976 to strengthen its own common front before UNCTAD. Two contentious issues emerged from the Manila declaration. First, the G-77 proposed an
"integrated programme for commodities" that aimed to manage commodity
price fluctuations through the use of a "Common Fund"—essentially, a bank
that would support prices by buying and selling a wide range of commodities
centrally held in buffer stocks. This was not a new proposal from developing
countries—they had been calling for a "comprehensive strategy," including a
"central fund to finance a number of international buffer stocks," since UNC-
TAD II in 1968—but it was the first time such a fund would be seriously discussed post oil crisis and post NIEO.[117]

Second, members of the G-77 agreed that their growing debt burdens were
not simply the result of high oil prices, as the United States and others insisted.
Rather, they viewed their debt problems as "springing from the system of international economic relations in which they were such unequal and disadvantaged
partners." The developing countries therefore called for an international debt
conference to be held under UNCTAD's aegis so that debt could be dealt with
comprehensively and with equal participation from debtors. Specifically, they
urged writing off the debts of the poorest "Most Seriously Affected" (MSA)
countries and waiving service payments on debts from other MSA countries
until the UN lifted the designation.[118]

The developed countries—Group B in UNCTAD parlance—were by no
means united on the issue of the Common Fund. The Netherlands and Norway endorsed the G-77's approach, which West Germany staunchly opposed.
France supported the creation of individual commodity agreements but suggested that "after a while the creation of a Central Fund [sic] may reveal itself
as convenient."[119] All recognized, however, the consequences of a flat-out rejection of the Common Fund and Integrated Programme. At CIEC discussions
in Paris, the nineteen developing countries warned that the conference would
be jeopardized without "substantial results" at UNCTAD; similarly, UNCTAD
secretary-general Gamani Corea called negotiations in Nairobi "the first—and
perhaps last—test to measure the validity of the entire concept of cooperation between producers and consumers in terms of commodities."[120]

Kissinger's new policy on commodities was twofold. He accepted the G-77's
argument that a "piecemeal approach" to commodities was inadequate and
agreed that some "integrated commodities program was necessary." But rather
than rejecting the Common Fund—which, importantly, he never mentioned
by name—Kissinger proposed his own "comprehensive approach," the central element of which was an International Resources Bank (IRB) for commodity financing. The IRB approached commodity prices from a different angle:
instead of financing the creation of buffer stocks, as the Common Fund

proposed, the IRB would "mobilize capital for sound resource development projects" by issuing "commodity bonds" for private and public investors. Those bonds would be supported by a $1 billion capitalization from OPEC and the developed countries and guarantees from the World Bank, with which the IRB would be associated. Kissinger did not rule out buffer stocks altogether but suggested that if they were necessary, they could fall under the IRB's aegis.[121] Kissinger did not expect to end developing countries' support for the Common Fund, but he hoped the IRB would at least demonstrate that the United States took their concerns seriously. The idea, as the *New York Times* put it, was to "[give] an inch to avoid going the mile."[122]

Although the Group B countries showed some flexibility on commodities, they were close to united in their opposition to the G-77's proposals on debt. OPEC continued to deny responsibility for the sharp rise in the Third World's debt, but the numbers were hard to ignore: by 1976, just two years after the oil crisis, developing countries' public debts had grown from $9 billion to $35 billion.[123] It was also true that the volume of that debt was relatively concentrated: just ten oil-importing, or "No-PEC," nations accounted for more than 64 percent of developing countries' public and publicly guaranteed debts.[124] Of course, for every debtor there was a lender, and overwhelmingly those lenders were New York, London, and Paris banks looking for higher returns than were available in developed countries' markets on the petrodollars they had accumulated from OPEC during and after the 1973 shock.[125] Again, Kissinger gave an inch, endorsing the creation of an "appropriate forum" to "examine problems of acute financing and debt service difficulties" but rejecting the idea of writing off existing debts or committing to any proposed guidelines.[126]

Secretary-General Corea regretted UNCTAD's focus on the Common Fund, which, he recalled, "dominated the Conference in a manner that was quite without precedent." His own hope was to gain "an acceptance, even if qualified, on the principle of a Fund" so that progress could also be made on other suddenly more urgent matters—namely, debt. The fund came to overshadow debt and other commodity issues for several reasons, including an "air of militancy and a disposition to bring matters to a head" among developing countries and the fact that few developed countries had come to the conference with a definite position on the fund.[127] The official Group B line eventually fell back to endorsing commodity price stabilization on a case-by-case basis, to which the G-77 reacted angrily. "Even a man on a galloping horse," ambassador Herbert Walker of Jamaica charged, "would see that there was no Common Fund there!"[128]

Deadlock over the Common Fund required extension of the conference for two days, during which time a deal was finally hammered out between a select group of G-77 and Group B leaders.[129] In exchange for Group B formally endorsing the Integrated Programme for Commodities and agreeing to begin serious discussions in UNCTAD toward establishing a Common Fund, the G-77 agreed to refer Kissinger's counterproposal, the IRB, to the "permanent machinery of UNCTAD for further study."[130] Both decisions were reflected in formal resolutions at the end of the conference.

Corea saw a silver lining in UNCTAD IV's results. Although what the developed countries would make of their promise to negotiate a Common Fund remained unanswerable, "for the first time, a comprehensive and interrelated framework" for dealing with commodity price fluctuations had been established. This was meaningful for two reasons. The resolution's adoption was indeed a "reflection of the climate of the times, the new atmosphere created by the goal of a New International Economic Order, the change in international economic relations following the rise of oil prices, the sense of leverage among the developing countries, and the desire of the developed countries for cooperation in North-South relations."[131] In other words, Third World advocacy and solidarity since the oil crisis had not been for nothing. But the Integrated Programme resolution—and the binding negotiations it promised—also marked a culmination of UNCTAD's efforts since its founding to be more than just an idea generator and a debate forum.[132] "Resolution 93(IV) amply fulfilled this goal," Corea maintained, making it a "matter for deep satisfaction."[133]

The same could not be said for debt, about which Corea was "quite frankly . . . disappointed."[134] Although forced to commit to something resembling a Common Fund, Group B countries appreciated the consequent lack of focus on debt. "The resolution of the confrontation over the common fund combined with Conference schedule pressure, resulted in an agreement on LDC debt problems which was far less forthcoming than we had anticipated," lead US negotiator Charles Robinson wrote to Kissinger. The G-77 did secure Group B acceptance of a special meeting on debt within UNCTAD, which, during the Carter administration, led to the cancellation of some of the poorest countries' debts. But this committed the United States to nothing beyond the old case-by-case policy it had going in. "I believe this to be a most favorable result," Robinson stated, "particularly given the determination of the LDCs to achieve a more meaningful concession."[135]

Nor, for that matter, did US officials see themselves as all that committed to the Common Fund. From Robinson's perspective, the US delegation had promised only to attend more meetings. The United States had no more committed to establishing a Common Fund on the G-77's terms, Robinson explained, than the G-77 had agreed to dropping the fund and adopting the IRB—the resolution for which several G-77 countries had, to the Americans' chagrin, voted against in the final count. Although the United States would attend Common Fund meetings, every effort would be made to "bring increasing pressure on the G-77 with the objective of gaining support for the IRB," including in the preparatory meetings.[136] Nor was the IRB the Common Fund competitor it had been presented as. "The IRB was called a 'bank' only to give it more sex appeal with the LDCs," Robinson explained a few months later, "and we agree that we should avoid [the] establishment of a new international bureaucracy."[137] With all this in mind, then, the chief US delegate could declare the conference a "reasonable success." The United States had set out to prevent the "complete collapse" of the conference and, with it, the CIEC. In other words, it had tried to buy time—and in this, it succeeded.[138]

In June 1980—exactly four years after the United States and other Group B countries accepted the G-77's Integrated Programme for Commodities and committed themselves to its realization—the participating developed and developing countries signed the final agreement to establish the Common Fund. There were, of course, limitations, the most obvious of which was the fund's limited capital base—down to $400 million from the hoped-for $6 billion—which diminished its ability to stabilize prices through stockpiling. But Gamani Corea, who had shepherded the "long and arduous" negotiations in UNCTAD, still saw a bright side. Considering developed countries' hard and, after Nairobi, soft opposition to creating the Common Fund; divisions over the fund's objectives, importance, and financing within the G-77 itself; the communist bloc's nonattitude toward the fund and similar commodity initiatives; and, no less crucially, OPEC's failure to deliver on its promise of massive diplomatic and economic support, the fund's very existence was indeed an achievement.[139]

The Common Fund was expected to begin operations no more than two years later, but a more urgent issue quickly and dramatically transformed the priorities of North and South alike. In August 1982, eleven months after twenty-two world leaders met in Cancún to try to revive what had become a stale and stalled North-South dialogue, Mexico's finance minister announced that his country was no longer able to service its debt.[140] Sensing a continent-wide crisis, commercial banks in New York, London, and Paris abruptly halted their lending to Latin America and demanded payment on existing short-term loans. The result was a dramatic loss of income, wages, and gross national product across the South and in Latin America and Africa in particular, the effects of which would make the 1980s "a lost decade of development for most of the developing world."[141]

"Regrettably, in the light of the crisis of later years," Corea reflected, "UNC-TAD [IV]'s lone and prophetic warnings on the emerging debt situation were ignored by all sides—by developed and developing countries alike."[142] This assessment is incomplete. In fact, as soon as the Nairobi negotiations concluded in May 1976, debt competed with indexation as the top issue for the nineteen developing countries at the reopening of the CIEC. "[Manuel] Pérez-Guerrero [former UNCTAD secretary-general and CIEC cochair] and other G-19 delegates said that the G-19 now views G-8 acceptance of its demands on these two issues as important tests of our 'political will' in CIEC," the State Department explained in July, "and that without a satisfactory solution the commissions cannot begin their substantive work in September."[143] The discussions continued into December, but with no meaningful progress, and in a General Assembly resolution that month, developing countries registered their "profound concern at the adverse effect which the failure of the conference will have on international economic co-operation."[144]

There was one more reason why the G-19 wanted to postpone discussions: the 1976 US presidential election.[145] The North-South dialogue was not a major issue in either the primaries or the general election, but US policy toward the Third World certainly was. On the conservative right, Ronald Reagan blasted incumbent Gerald Ford over his administration's—really, Kissinger's State Department's—efforts to renegotiate the Panama Canal treaties. "We built it, we paid for it, it's ours, and we're going to keep it!" Reagan exclaimed during the Florida Republican primary. In 1975 neoconservatives, still committed to retaining their influence in the Democratic Party, once again rallied around Henry "Scoop" Jackson as their candidate. Ben Wattenberg and Elliott Abrams, members of the Coalition for a Democratic Majority, ran Jackson's campaign, while the rest of the CDM "did all it could to support him without crossing the legal line of open endorsement." After Jackson's defeat by little-known Georgia governor Jimmy Carter, the CDM focused on rewriting the Democratic Party's convention platform. "Moynihan, who had just joined the CDM," Justin Vaisse writes, "worked with Wattenberg . . . to achieve a moderate platform that would not yield on foreign policy issues to pro–Third World leftists. . . . The platform contained no hint of American guilt or apology and no mention of moral equivalence."[146]

Neoconservatives claimed they saw Carter as a blank slate in 1976 and were surprised at his foreign policy positions after the nomination.[147] In fact, in the general election he endorsed several of the neoconservatives' key themes, such as suspicion of détente and support for the human rights of Eastern Bloc dissidents. Carter also adopted the neoconservatives' moralistic language, but his usage suggested an interpretation drawn from the party's new social egalitarianism and world-order liberalism rather than the views of the right-wing Democrats who had written the convention platform. Like Moynihan before him, Carter attacked the Ford administration's actions during the 1974 World Food Conference. But while Moynihan accused the administration of doing too much to placate the Third World, Carter said it had done too little. Instead of being the "arms merchant of the world," Carter insisted during the televised foreign policy debate with Ford in October, the United States' "strength derive[s] from doing what's right—caring for the poor, providing food, becoming the breadbasket of the world."[148]

The neoconservatives should not have been too surprised. Carter's vision in 1976–77 was exactly the one promoted by the prophets of world-order liberalism at the Trilateral Commission, who had been advising him on foreign policy since he began attending commission meetings in 1974. They were joined in the campaign—and after Carter was elected, in the administration—by a number of economists, academics, and former foreign policy officials from the Overseas Development Council, the first US think tank devoted entirely to the study and advocacy of international development. These groups' largely shared view of an interdependent world being shaped chiefly by engagement between the trilateral countries of the North—the United States, western Europe, and Japan—and the developing South dominated the interpretation and implementation of Carter's main foreign policy initiatives, especially toward the Third World.

The overall approach to North-South policy—a renewed emphasis on trilateral cooperation with western Europe and Japan, concessions on trade and increased foreign aid to developing countries, and the resolution of symbolic global issues such as apartheid and the Panama Canal—was not substantially different from Kissinger's after the Seventh Special Session. But the decision to give serious consideration to human rights in the making of US foreign policy—to define the political, economic, and strategic roles and limits of human rights—produced major distinctions that would open up new possibilities in the North-South dialogue while closing off older ones. Humanitarian goals such as access to food, shelter, health care, and other basic human needs were elevated, while action on global structural issues such as the Common Fund and debt repayment were not. Those decisions would have profound consequences for the course of international development, finance, and trade in the 1980s, during which UNCTAD's "lone and prophetic warnings" about a looming crisis would come to fruition.

CHAPTER 4

Interdependence, Development, and Jimmy Carter

When governor Jimmy Carter announced his candidacy for the Democratic nomination for president at the end of 1974, even the leading newspaper in his home state of Georgia could not resist poking fun at his chances: its headline read, "Jimmy Who Is Running for What!?"[1] Six months later, Carter's name recognition registered at 2 percent nationally.[2] Nevertheless, absent any clear front-runner, the one-term governor and born-again Christian played up his outsider status to defeat well-known Democrats, including California governor Jerry Brown and senators Frank Church and Henry Jackson, for the nomination.

Carter continued to play the role of Washington outsider in the general election, running as a reformer against unelected insider Gerald Ford. He persistently associated Ford with the network of corruption surrounding Richard Nixon, and Ford's pardon of his predecessor shortly after taking office provided Carter with a powerful symbol. Throughout 1976 Carter directed his attacks at the Nixon-Kissinger-Ford style of foreign policy, which, he explained, meant neglecting allies in western Europe and Japan, selling out human rights in the Soviet Union for détente, and failing to engage the developing countries in a cooperative and mutually productive dialogue. More potent were the moral charges. The Nixon-Kissinger-Ford moniker deliberately placed the secretary of state in the middle: "The President is not really in charge," Carter's talking points for an October debate read. "Our policies are

Kissinger's ideas and his goals, which are often derived in secret." This "covert, manipulative, and deceptive" foreign policy ran "against the basic principles of this country, because Kissinger is obsessed with power blocs, with spheres of influence."[3] Rather than secretly aiding "friendly dictators," Carter promised "a government that is as honest and decent and fair and competent and truthful and idealistic as are the American people."[4]

Carter indeed began his campaign as an outsider in all senses. Unlike his competition, he grew up on a farm in a small segregated town, he did not attend an Ivy League college or law school, and he had spent relatively little time in Washington. Most of all, he lacked fluency in the politics, history, and vocabulary of foreign policy that his more experienced rivals had acquired through decades of experience in the Capitol. The Ford campaign and many in the press frequently cited Carter's inexperience in national and foreign affairs and called his emphasis on morality in foreign policy naïve, even dangerous.

Carter's ambitious and righteous rhetoric surely contrasted with Kissinger's carefulness and the occasional dark humor he fed to the press, but under the surface was a set of policies informed by some of the best and brightest of the liberal internationalist establishment. Two influential foreign policy networks, the Trilateral Commission and the Overseas Development Council, provided Carter with a coherent, if abridged, education in foreign affairs during the campaign (as well as dozens of highly educated and experienced staff for his administration).

Both groups had been formed in reaction to aspects of Nixon's foreign policy, which they thought inadequate to deal with the increasing challenges of economic and political interdependence. Both were also transformed by the twin events of 1973–74: the first oil crisis and the campaign for a New International Economic Order (NIEO). In their view, these events globalized the challenges of interdependence and demanded new and comprehensive global solutions for the poverty that was destabilizing and radicalizing the South. During the Carter administration, their policies were supposed to transform both the North-South dialogue and the United States' relationship with the Third World. But their gains were uneven, as Carter officials proved unable to translate progress on human rights, the Panama Canal, and foreign aid into moderation on the NIEO and other global economic issues.

Carter and Interdependence: The Trilateral Commission

The most central concept to Carter's foreign policy before and during his presidency was interdependence. In its initial and most basic meaning, *interde-*

pendence referred to the interaction between traditional security objectives (especially in Europe) and foreign economic policy. The term gained currency within the study of international relations in 1968 with the publication of a book by Richard N. Cooper, who later became one of Carter's main foreign policy advisers. Cooper was concerned about the growing divide in transatlantic relations during the 1960s, as the Johnson administration shifted attention and resources toward Southeast Asia and away from western Europe. He identified economic disagreements between the industrial countries—between the United States and Japan on textiles, the United States and the European Community on agriculture, and France and Germany on monetary policy—as the greatest threat to the Western alliance, an essential pillar of world stability that successive US administrations had taken for granted during two decades of economic growth and political consensus.[5]

By the early 1970s, most of the foreign policy establishment accepted interdependence as a useful conceptual device, although its precise meaning varied. In 1969 President Nixon suggested to the United Nations that interdependence meant a greater sharing of the defense burden—a jab at the free-riding Europeans who refused to back the US war in Vietnam.[6] By 1973, Nixon's thinking was closer to Cooper's. In September Nixon voiced concern "about the foreign policy repercussions" of US agricultural policy, particularly in Europe but also in the developing countries.[7] Transatlantic relations had been neglected by Nixon-Kissinger initiatives in pursuit of détente with the Soviet Union, normalization with China, and peace with North Vietnam, and in early 1973 Kissinger set out to renew that partnership. In his "Year of Europe" speech, Kissinger kept his references to interdependence mostly within the Atlantic framework, suggesting that a "new Atlantic Charter" would renew the alliance and promise global stability. But the growing energy crisis in late 1973 and the NIEO declaration in May 1974 pushed Kissinger to acknowledge a "new age of interdependence" in which, he told the UN General Assembly in September, "inflation and the threat of global decline hang over the economies of rich and poor alike."[8] By the time Carter launched his campaign for the Democratic nomination, it was not just the United States and Europe that were interdependent. Both developed and developing countries now spoke of interdependence between rich and poor, North and South, in a newly profound way.

Before Nixon and Kissinger pivoted back to the West, a network of transatlantic elites from business, academia, and government organized around the idea of reasserting US-European-Japanese cooperation in global affairs. The Trilateral Commission was launched in 1972 as an initiative of David Rockefeller, CEO of Chase Manhattan Bank and chairman of the influential Council on Foreign Relations. Like other establishment internationalists, Rockefeller was a staunch Atlanticist concerned about the effects of Nixon's foreign eco-nomic policy on the trilateral alliance of the United States, western Europe, and Japan. David's brother Nelson, a former governor of New York, was a longtime patron of Kissinger, whom he valued as a brilliant scholar with fresh views on maintaining transatlantic relations. However, David Rockefeller was disturbed by Nixon's willingness to dismantle the Bretton Woods system, im-pose economic controls, and introduce tariffs without consulting other trilat-eral leaders. Kissinger's well-known aversion to international economics—his overwhelming focus in academia and government had been on security—and preoccupation with Southeast Asia and China did not suggest a sudden change in priorities. Thus, two years before government finance leaders from the United States, Britain, Germany, France, and Japan began informal Library Group discussions at the White House—the precursor to the formal G-7 sum-mits involving trilateral heads of state—Rockefeller institutionalized his own forum, bringing together trilateral elites to confront the growing interdepen-dence of their countries' economic and foreign policies.

To help with the project, Rockefeller selected young Columbia University professor and noted Sovietologist Zbigniew Brzezinski. Like Kissinger, Brzez-inski was a brilliant immigrant from Europe who believed that his adopted country had a special role to play in ensuring global stability. Both had also been deeply affected as young men by the rise of the Nazi Party: Kissinger as a middle-class Jew in a small town in Bavaria, and Brzezinski as the son of a prominent Polish diplomat posted in Berlin. After receiving his undergradu-ate degree at McGill University in Montreal, Brzezinski moved to Harvard for his PhD and then to Columbia in 1961, where he led its new Institute for Com-munist Affairs. At this time Brzezinski joined the Council on Foreign Rela-tions, where he and Kissinger became friendly rivals.[9]

In 1970 Brzezinski entered the interdependence debate with the publica-tion of *Between Two Ages: America's Role in the Technetronic Era*. Its focus on new transnational forces changing the parameters of states' economic and politi-cal autonomy fit with the conclusions of other scholars writing on interde-pendence, such as Cooper, Charles Kindleberger, and Raymond Vernon; however, it also contained a great deal of futurist speculation bordering on eugenics that Brzezinski soon dropped. The book was out of print by 1976. What caught Rockefeller's attention was a section on the development of a "planetary consciousness" among transnational elites. Because of the United States' strength, Brzezinski argued, rivals (friendly or otherwise) would unite in blocs to challenge it from a position of collective strength. Europe was al-ready doing this, but current US foreign policy threatened the orientation of the elites behind the project, who might continue the kind of regionalism and economic nationalism that can lead to a world of closed economies, technologies, and societies. Still, Brzezinski expected that with US leadership, a new class of "transnational elites . . . highly internationalist or globalist in spirit and outlook" would form a genuine and self-conscious "community of the developed nations" to manage collectively the challenges of global economic and technological transformation.[10]

The Trilateral Commission began operations in 1972 with the explicit intention of fostering that community. "The more Atlanticist part of the American foreign policy community" behind the commission, *Foreign Affairs* noted, believed that "the relative balance of economic strengths had so changed [under Nixon] that the United States could no longer play the role of [sole] economic leader."[11] Such pro-Atlanticists included future Carter campaign advisers and administration officials Richard Cooper, Fred Bergsten, Henry Owen, Gerard Smith, Richard Gardner, Cyrus Vance, Harold Brown, and, of course, Brzezinski, the Trilateral Commission's first executive director; many other future Carter officials, such as Robert Bowie and Samuel Huntington, contributed to commission reports.

At the commission's founding, managing interdependence was an overwhelmingly Northern problem and responsibility. "Persons from other nations," members agreed in July 1972, would be "brought into the work of the Commission [only] at appropriate times." In these early meetings, some talked about new Marshall Plans and Monnet Plans for the trilateral countries and even "a new 'conception' of the international order as fresh as that once posited by Keynes."[12] The reference to Keynes and Bretton Woods was apt: as in 1944, few of the representatives considered what that order would mean for the developing countries, and none spoke of the developing countries' participation in shaping this new conception.

This changed in 1973. Just as it had done with Kissinger, the oil shock and NIEO (and the subsequent alliance of the developing countries and OPEC) transformed the priorities of the Trilateral Commission. "There are critical turning points in history when the lives and fortunes of large numbers of human beings hang upon the decisions by a small handful of national leaders," Richard Gardner wrote in July 1974 in the commission's third report. "The oil embargo—the fourfold increase in fertilizer prices—the higher costs and severe shortages of food and fertilizer—the unprecedented concurrence of acute inflation and recession across the industrialized world—these events have gravely strained the fabric of international economic relations. In particular, they have detonated an explosion in North-South economic relations that has been building up for years. . . . In short, they have raised the most troubling questions about the world's ability to manage its interdependence through peaceful international cooperation."[13] Over the next two years, eight of the first twelve reports by the commission's task forces dealt with North-South issues, including energy, commodities, trade, finance, international institutions, and maritime law. Despite some fresh ideas, the task forces' rhetoric largely matched Kissinger's. They recognized the need for a "general restructuring of North-South relations," including a mutual recognition of interdependence, "cooperation instead of confrontation," and "burden-sharing between the Trilateral world and the OPEC countries." Their concern for development may have been less cynical than Kissinger's, but their solutions required no serious redistribution of power in the world economy. The first North-South report focused on the most immediate effects of the oil crisis in the developing world—namely, "some thirty low-income countries of the 'Fourth World' who have been particularly hard hit by skyrocketing costs of oil, food, fertilizer and industrial goods." In particular, the commission recommended "an extraordinary act of cooperation" between the trilateral countries and OPEC, with both contributing $1.5 billion to a special action fund to meet the emergency needs of the resource-poor Fourth World in 1974–75.[14]

The commission's multipurpose, multilateral development fund did not happen. Instead, at the World Food Conference in November 1974, Kissinger called OPEC's bluff with regard to its concern for oil-importing developing countries. Together they negotiated a significantly more limited and less capitalized fund, the International Fund for Agricultural Development. The IFAD would not come into existence until 1977, by which time the worst effects of the crisis had passed (in part due to the UN's Emergency Fund, approved by the General Assembly during the Sixth Special Session announcing the NIEO). Thus, in a follow-up report the commission directed attention to "the problem of North-South development beyond the emergency period"—that is, 1976–80, the next president's term. The "much more formidable" problem was how to increase official development aid by $6 billion a year, per the recommendations of World Bank governor Robert McNamara. This issue was more formidable indeed: as the report pointed out, from 1963 to 1973, OECD citizens' real incomes grew by 60 percent, while the real value of OECD aid declined by 7 percent. Aid from the trilateral countries was getting smaller during times of plenty; there was even less appetite for more aid in times of scarcity and uncertainty. As Kissinger had argued to Ford's economic advisers who opposed his initiatives at the World Food Conference, the report concluded that only increases in real aid levels would give the trilateral countries "any credibility in aid discussions with OPEC members."[15] But even if $3 billion could be raised in the North, OPEC was not likely to match it. The World Bank estimated that for 1980, the combined gross national products (GNPs) of OPEC countries (excluding Nigeria and Indonesia) was just 6 percent of the combined GNPs of the trilateral countries. Under any formula, OPEC was already doing more than its share.[16]

The commission's solution was "another major act of cooperation between the Trilateral countries and the OPEC countries" for long-term development financing. By 1975, Kissinger had largely abandoned this course, choosing to focus on outmaneuvering the G-77 at their preferred forums—the UN Conference on Trade and Development (UNCTAD) and the upcoming Conference for International Economic Cooperation (CIEC)—but the prophets of interdependence at the Trilateral Commission remained optimistic. Their "wholly new approach" involved recycling OPEC's financial surplus, sitting in commercial banks in New York, London, and Paris, through a "third-window" facility in the World Bank. This third window would lend funds on terms between those of the World Bank's regular lending operations (the "first window") and those of the International Development Association (the "second window"). Basically, the third window's managers in the World Bank would borrow the estimated $3 billion from OPEC at 8 percent interest and lend it to the Fourth World at 3 percent; the $3 billion would be raised by bonds in OPEC governments and trilateral capital markets where OPEC funds were held.[17] The World Bank established the third-window facility in 1975, and it began operations once sufficient funds were received from the Netherlands, Canada, Britain, and France in the North and from Saudi Arabia, Kuwait, and Venezuela in the South, but the Ford administration declined to contribute. By 1977, it appeared not to be lending at all.[18]

This substantial but low-key focus on technical financial issues in US-dominated institutions, rather than confronting the South head-on at the UN and CIEC, matched the recommendations of other Trilateral Commission task forces. A report on the reform of international institutions, authored by Carter's future assistant treasury secretary C. Fred Bergsten, advocated this approach for the International Monetary Fund (IMF) and General Agreement on Tariffs and Trade (GATT). International economic upheaval, the report began, had brought a "renewed emphasis throughout the world on national sovereignty," especially in the South but also in the North. Reducing this tension—"between the imperatives of interdependence and the quest to retain adequate degrees of national autonomy"—required committing more political and economic resources to institutions that, though multilateral, were also weighted toward US thinking.[19] The UN had a "quite different role to play"—that of "legitimizing broad concepts" about international economic reforms and arrangements. In other words, the General Assembly could call for a New International Economic Order, but it would not be allowed to legislate one. Only by downgrading key global forums operating as a "committee of the whole" (such as the UN General Assembly and UNCTAD) and focusing resources on Northern-dominated multilateral institutions and arrangements (such as the IMF and GATT) could the trilateral countries meet the commission's ambitious task: "to make the world safe for interdependence."[20]

It is unlikely that the technical details of commodity agreements and petrodollar recycling contained in these and other commission reports would have been of great interest to Governor Carter. However, the commission was interested in him. "We wanted a forward-looking Democratic governor who would be congenial to the trilateral perspective," Brzezinski explained, and he invited Carter to an early meeting. Both left impressed. "I became an eager student," Carter recalled, "and took full advantage of what Brzezinski had to offer. . . . We got to know each other well."[21] Brzezinski remembered discussing Carter's membership with Gerard Smith and George Franklin, the commission's secretary for North America. Carter's interest in expanding trade between the state of Georgia and the Common Market, as well as his reputation for being "courageous on civil rights and reportedly a bright and upcoming Democrat," made him an attractive candidate for membership. "Well, he's obviously our man," Brzezinski told Franklin, and Carter accepted the offer.[22]

Brzezinski became the single most important influence on Carter's foreign policy both as a candidate and as president. His intellect and ability to "express complicated ideas simply," especially the "broad historical trends affecting the industrialized nations," helped Carter understand and speak about interdependence in a way that distinguished him from Kissinger, whose own strategy emphasized short-term measures to diffuse conflict with OPEC over long-term North-South collaboration.[23] As Kissinger explained his strategy for the World Food Conference: "What we would be saying" to OPEC "is that if you cooperate [on oil], we won't have to talk about food."[24]

After Carter declared his candidacy, Brzezinski reached out to offer him advice, and Carter accepted.[25] While still directing the Trilateral Commission, Brzezinski worked as Carter's main foreign policy adviser and speechwriter throughout the Democratic primaries and then in the race against Ford. During the campaign, Carter recalled, "I would study [Brzezinski's] position papers on foreign affairs in order to develop my answers to those questions all candidates had to face." Brzezinski became "a frequent visitor to Plains" and accompanied Carter to his national security debate with President Ford.[26]

Carter's association with the Trilateral Commission was also a powerful signal to the foreign policy establishment that the Georgia governor was to be taken seriously in foreign affairs. He accompanied Brzezinski to a commission meeting in Kyoto in June 1975, after which he asked Brzezinski to appear with him at an upcoming press conference. "I was a little surprised at the time," Brzezinski said, "but concluded that he probably wanted to show the newspapermen that his candidacy was being taken seriously and that he could count on expert advice in the campaign." As president, Carter downplayed his association with the commission, which became an obsession of the Far Right and Far Left for its globalist rhetoric and Wall Street connections, but during the campaign, Carter played up this connection. "Service on the Trilateral Commission," he insisted in a widely publicized 1976 autobiography promoting his candidacy, "gave me an excellent opportunity to know national and international leaders in many fields of study concerning foreign affairs."[27] His association with the commission also gave Carter the support of its other prominent members. Cooper, Gardner, and Bergsten were widely recognized and respected in foreign policy circles for their scholarship on international economics and interdependence; it made sense to bring this brain trust into the State Department, the Treasury Department, and the National Security Council (NSC) after the election. There, these men could (and did) attempt to implement their recommendations in commission reports to make the world safe for interdependence, with Brzezinski filling in the big picture.

Brzezinski crafted the big picture's frame in December 1975, when Carter asked him "to develop for me the outline of a basic speech/statement on foreign affairs. . . . I agree with your order of priorities." Brzezinski replied with three interrelated priorities:

(1) as the first priority a stable inner core for world affairs, based on closer collaboration among the advanced industrial democracies (open-ended trilateralism); (2) secondly, to shape on the above basis more stable North-South relations, which means (i) more cooperation with the emerging Third World countries (the richer and more successful), through such devices as the tripartite Paris conferences,[28] etc.; (ii) compassionate aid to the Fourth World, which the U.S. should grant as a matter of conscience as well as interest, but in which it ought to also engage other states on a multilateral basis; (3) thirdly, to promote détente with the Soviet Union and to court China.

These priorities matched the hierarchy developed by the Trilateral Commission during the 1973–74 crisis. Brzezinski placed the greatest emphasis on trilateral cooperation; from that could come better North-South relations, which would require making some concessions but would also be different from past relations. "Compassionate aid" would be directed toward the poorest countries with the worst humanitarian problems, while the United States' standing in the North-South dialogue would be improved by cultivating bilateral ties with "the richer and more successful" developing countries, which had the greatest stake in preserving international economic stability. Because they were relatively stable and not as much of a threat to interdependence, US-Soviet and US-Chinese relations were downgraded. "Détente, of course, is desirable but it ought to be more reciprocal," Brzezinski concluded. "Moreover, since the element of rivalry remains a reality, it cannot be the basis for coping with global problems."[29]

Carter approved this "skeleton," and Brzezinski and Gardner went to work on a speech that Carter would deliver to the New York Foreign Policy Association on June 23, 1976, where Kissinger had spoken on North-South relations two months earlier. "The speech was Carter's major statement on foreign policy," Brzezinski wrote, "and it foreshadowed many of his actions and concerns as President."[30]

Aside from a few personal additions—Carter insisted on the phrase "'Lone Ranger' foreign policy" to describe the Nixon-Ford administration, and Brzezinski apologized for his opposition after it received a positive response from the press—the speech matched Brzezinski's initial framework, progressing from trilateral to North-South to East-West relations. Carter also included the Trilateral Commission's plans for OECD-OPEC cooperation on increased multilateral aid, as well as a world development budget inside the World Bank, which would become a feature of G-7 discussions in his administration.[31]

The reorientation of aid toward the poorest countries—those in direct need—was also a feature of Brzezinski's framework, but elaboration of this idea came from elsewhere. The basic human needs approach to development was the contribution of another influential group advising Carter during his campaign: the Overseas Development Council. Emphasizing aid for food, shelter, health, and education channeled directly to the "bottom half" in developing countries allowed Carter to call for increased foreign aid while also countering public and congressional criticism that US aid rarely reached those for whom it was intended. As Carter was fond of saying, "I'm not in favor of taxing the poor people in our rich country to send money to the rich people in poor countries."[32] A focus on basic human needs promised a multilateral solution that would avoid both politics in the donor country and rent seeking in the recipient country; the reality, of course, was much more complicated.

Carter and Development: The Overseas Development Council

The Overseas Development Council (ODC) was founded in Washington in 1969 by James P. Grant, a former US Agency for International Development

(USAID) administrator. Its mission was to increase support among the public and Congress for more multilateral development aid at a time when US contributions were in steep decline. The ODC was well connected with the liberal internationalist establishment: like the Trilateral Commission, it was supported by the Ford and Rockefeller Foundations, and it counted David Rockefeller and other notable internationalists as board members.[33]

The ODC began its work at a hinge moment in international development. In 1961 President Kennedy announced a "decade of development" at the UN; new institutions such as the UN Development Program, Inter-American Development Bank, Alliance for Progress, USAID, and Peace Corps soon followed. These and other aid programs were informed by modernization theory, an intellectual paradigm that prescribed an evolutionary path to liberal capitalism through investment in large infrastructure and industrial projects, importation of foreign technology and capital, and strengthening of the bureaucratic apparatus of the state, as well as the encouragement of Western cultural values, standards of behavior, and modes of thought. Countries would proceed through the stages of development toward a gradual withering away of economic controls, more varied economic activity, the creation of a consumer society, and full participation in the international economy. Equally important, its proponents in the Kennedy and Johnson administrations believed that modernization would prevent Third World societies—in the throes of a revolution of rising expectations—from turning to communism, which promised its own accelerated path to industrialization. It mattered that the theory's most important text, *The Stages of Growth*, written by MIT economist and Johnson adviser Walt Rostow, was subtitled *An Anti-Communist Manifesto*.

Although this approach dominated thinking inside the World Bank and the White House throughout the 1960s, it also had a critical Third World corollary: dependency theory. Dependency theorists did not reject modernization theory per se; in both cases, the state drove economic growth through investment and subsidies. Their criticism focused on the West's overemphasis on domestic factors of production and lack of appreciation for external (or structural) barriers to development, which, they held, rich countries created and maintained for their own benefit. Inspired by the writings of Argentine economist Raúl Prebisch and German economist Hans Singer, they saw an international economic system, or division of labor, rooted in centuries of unequal political relationships set against the interests of commodity producers (largely in the South) and in favor of the interests of industrial producers (largely in the North). In the terms-of-trade debate, dependency theorists alleged a secular decline in the prices of commodities and a rise in the prices of manufactured goods, meaning that as the industrial countries got richer (benefiting from cheap imported commodities), the developing countries got poorer (receiving less for their exports and paying more for industrial imports). Third World development would never succeed, dependency theorists argued, until the rules of global trade and finance were renegotiated on an even playing field.

Many elites in newly decolonized countries were attracted to dependency theory's implicit anti-imperial message and emphasis on global structural barriers to development. Support for its basic tenets was widespread in governments across countries with wildly different capital endowments (some had oil, others had valuable minerals, and still others had neither), labor forces (some had relatively high levels of education, while in others the majority was illiterate), and historical ties (some had endured hundreds of years of colonialism, and others had remained independent). The leaders of these countries also spoke the language of dependency theory in the United Nations, where decolonization had changed the balance of the General Assembly and other UN forums. Dependency theory dominated the politics of the developing countries' UN caucus, the Group of 77, which argued on their behalf at UNCTAD (Prebisch was its founding secretary-general, serving from 1964 to 1969).

Dependency theory's international agenda included various measures to reform global trade and finance, ranging from support for commodity prices and debt forgiveness to increasing the economic decision-making powers of the UN General Assembly. Domestically, many of the theory's supporters urged import substitution industrialization (ISI), essentially a more statist form of modernization theory that promised reduced dependence on imported industrial goods through heavy state investment and high tariffs in select industries. It was expected that these industries would eventually become cost-effective and internationally competitive, but as various ISI experiments (particularly in Latin America) would show, high government subsidies protected inefficient firms and other rent seekers, accelerated inflation, and prompted excessive foreign borrowing to meet current account deficits.[34] ISI was not supported by all dependency theorists; Prebisch himself warned against taking ISI too far, which, as he correctly speculated, would leave Latin American countries in massive debt.[35] Nevertheless, in one form or another, modernization theory—in its Northern liberal or Southern statist variant—defined international development for most of the 1960s.

By 1968, the core premise of modernization theory—that national economic growth would alleviate poverty, lessen inequality, and promote stability—was under attack from many sides, but especially in the North. Attitudes toward the aid programs that funded these efforts were one indicator: in the United States, support for foreign aid remained consistently high in the first half of the decade, with well over half the country in favor; a few years later, that support, along with the US foreign aid budget, had significantly declined.[36] There are many explanations, including tight government budgets and inflation due to President Johnson's War on Poverty and the war in Vietnam. Congress, frustrated with the failure of aid to produce foreign policy results, demanded cuts, and many Americans questioned, perhaps for the first time, whether "they" really wanted to be just like "us." US forces in Vietnam were winning battles but not the war; US economic development and aid programs seemed capable of winning neither.

Vietnam was an especially potent example of modernization theory's weaknesses. The Johnson administration's development programs, such as plans for a "TVA [Tennessee Valley Authority] on the Mekong," were taken straight out of Rostow's playbook, promising to save Vietnam from communism in the same way the New Deal had saved US capitalism from itself. Thus, when the most important nonmilitary effort in the United States' most expensive war failed, it was, in one scholar's words, "a body blow to the consensus on development."[37] Public disillusionment with aid was matched by scathing critiques from conservative economists such as P. T. Bauer, who attacked modernization theory's statist premises and susceptibility to corruption.[38] Modernization's unintended consequences for population and the environment produced additional critiques, with the Green Revolution in agriculture coming under particular fire. At the UN, developing countries united against the developed countries' inattention to external barriers to development, amplifying their arguments in the General Assembly, UNCTAD, and the International Labor Organization. In the mainstream development community, there was a pervasive sense of crisis—in the words of development officials at a 1967 meeting, "a clear and present danger, an emergency," and a "paralysis of leadership."[39]

Robert McNamara stepped into this paralysis when he became president of the World Bank in April 1968, two months after his painful resignation as Johnson's secretary of defense. Surveying the hostility toward aid among Congress and the public, the criticism and confusion in development circles, and a growing economic and political divide between developed and developing countries, McNamara advised the bank's Board of Governors that the will to provide aid "was never lower."[40]

Two contrasting initiatives emerged during McNamara's first year in office. One was the publication in 1969 of the Pearson Report, named for the committee's chairman, former Canadian prime minister Lester Pearson. Shortly before McNamara joined the World Bank, his predecessor, George Woods, had called for a "grand assize" to assess what had gone wrong in the Development Decade. The report acknowledged new problems—it recognized that growth had limits for a society's overall welfare and that developing countries faced certain external constraints to development—but offered no novel solutions.[41] "The Pearson Report," *Business Week* commented, "is neither very dramatic nor very fresh. Its primary recommendations are for a doubling of the amount of aid funneled through such multinational organizations as the World Bank, and for developed countries to boost their infusions of official and private capital to the developing lands to 1% of their Gross National Product by 1975."[42]

A second initiative came from outside the World Bank. Two years before the Pearson Report was published, concerned members of the US foreign aid community had proposed the formation of a "Development House" that would be formally independent from the US government and international organizations.[43] The Ford and Rockefeller Foundations took the lead in funding the new organization, which was soon incorporated in Washington, DC, as the Overseas Development Council. The ODC board was filled with members of the development establishment, including former TVA administrator David Lilienthal, former World Bank president (1948–63) Eugene Black, former USAID director David Bell, Harvard economist Edward Mason, and David Rockefeller.[44] Father Theodore Hesburgh, president of the University of Notre Dame, was the board's first chairman (until he left to serve as Carter's ambassador to an important North-South event, the UN Conference on Science and Technology for Development), and James P. Grant, a high-ranking USAID administrator with extensive on-the-ground experience in China and Southeast Asia (his last job was leading USAID's failing programs in Vietnam) was president.

"Authoritative, widely respected," Hesburgh's biographer writes, "the ODC was one of the most effective institutions in the United States as a source of information about Third World countries."[45] It used its status to critique the development consensus that was being upheld by US government and World Bank policies, regardless of widespread acknowledgment of its failure. McNamara "really believes that aid promotes economic growth which promotes stability, democracy, and good international behavior," one critic of the Pearson Report observed. "None of the links can be proved."[46] Despite rapid economic growth in developing countries, by the end of the 1960s, income inequality between North and South had widened; despite large increases in food production thanks to the Green Revolution, most developing countries were still highly vulnerable to price shocks. "If we are to develop a firm deterrent to anarchy and subversion in two-thirds of the world seized by the revolution of rising expectations," Grant wrote in 1971, "something more fundamental than [US]AID is required."[47]

Grant and the ODC argued for a rethinking of development policy that looked beyond gross domestic product, industrialization, and other measures of modernization and toward more basic, people-oriented indicators such as access to health care, education, shelter, and food. In doing so, the ODC boosted other critics, largely outside of the World Bank, who were beginning to push for a basic human needs (BHN) approach to development. Advocates believed that a BHN approach not only would benefit a larger share of the population than traditional development projects but also would enable greater overall productivity by freeing individuals from the burden of meeting their immediate social and economic needs. Sussex University's Institute of Development Studies was one new group that debated the meaning of development, and it collaborated with the International Labor Organization on a series of country reports from 1970 to 1975 in which the BHN idea was refined.[48] That project also included prominent development economists Amartya Sen, Dharam Ghai, and Hans Singer (half of the Singer-Prebisch terms-of-trade hypothesis), and their recommendations became the basis for the International Labor Organization's definition of BHN at the 1976 World Employment Conference in terms of food, clothing, housing, education, and public transportation.[49]

The ODC did not invent basic human needs, but it distinguished itself through its powerful network in US political, business, and academic circles. "[Grant] used his post at the ODC to cultivate ideas gaining credibility internationally," David Ekbladh explains.[50] The ODC enlisted support from a variety of critical development experts, promoting Barbara Ward's essay "A 'People' Strategy of Development," and according to the World Bank, the ODC "engineered" the collaboration between Edgar Owens and Robert Shaw, authors of the influential 1972 book *Development Reconsidered*.[51] "A major rethinking of development concepts is taking place," Grant observed, "compelled by a single fact: the unparalleled growth rates achieved by most developing countries during the 1960's had little or no effect on most of the world's people, who continue to live in desperate poverty." By favoring large landowners, civil servants, and skilled industrial workers, he argued, the development process empowered interests with a disincentive for large-scale redistribution, and countries that had introduced massive welfare programs could no longer pay for them. A new development strategy would increase the participation of the poorer half of the population in the development process by supporting small farmers and entrepreneurs, making the best use of scarce capital and technology, and ensuring the availability of basic education and health care.[52]

The ODC carefully cultivated members of Congress. Minnesota liberal Donald Fraser attended several ODC meetings in the early 1970s while serving as chairman of the House Subcommittee on International Organizations.[53] (Arvonne Fraser—Donald's wife and future Carter administration official—edited an ODC publication on women and basic needs.)[54] With the ODC's help, Fraser introduced the "New Directions" legislation for US foreign aid in 1973.[55] Also known as the "Basic Human Needs Mandate," the legislation intended to redirect aid toward rural development, nutrition, family planning, health, and education. Though initially hailed as a significant departure from the 1960s development consensus, its long-term impact is unclear, with successive administrations (Carter's included) dipping into BHN funds when bilateral aid was needed for security objectives. The authors of a comprehensive 1989 review of US foreign aid since New Directions concluded: "The Carter administration and the Congress soon began to reallocate resources away from BHN to more U.S. security-dominated interests; and they regarded with skepticism the value to the United States of multilateral development assistance."[56]

As they did for the Trilateral Commission, the events of 1973–74 transformed the ODC's conceptualization of development and interdependence. Both groups saw those years, in the words of one ODC report, as "a point in time when actual choices will shape the future of relations among states and peoples for years to come."[57] In its first few years, the ODC pressed for people-based development, but in the absence of a global organizational framework, most of its recommendations involved immediate changes to the administration of development policy within Northern governments and institutions. Its first *Agenda for Action* in 1973 "had as its central theme the growing interdependence of nations"; its second "evaluated the economic shocks of 1973–74—energy, food, and inflation—and foretold their tragic toll on . . . the 'Fourth World.'" The authors "urged [the developed] nations not to set aside long-term work on the root problem of human poverty" in the face of mounting economic difficulties at home and "outlined a series of measures to repair the damage done by the economic crises of the moment."[58]

When the ODC published its 1975 *Agenda*, the evolving North-South dialogue had already transformed the stakes of the crisis and the possibilities for action. "It is only within the past 18 months [since the NIEO's announcement]," Grant and Hesburgh explained, "that a new search for economic equality has opened in earnest." With economic prospects in the North worsening and confrontation with the South increasing, "the world [is] on the verge of one of the great economic, social, and political discontinuities in history . . . it is as if the molecular structure of the world order were changing." In contrast to its first two reports, this one stated that the "greatly intensified efforts of the nations of the South to secure more equality" demanded a rethinking of interdependence that "includes, but goes beyond [its] immediate consequences" for US foreign policy. Interdependence could not be managed by the trilateral countries alone; the South's challenge, and the global inequalities motivating it, required a serious and sustained joint response. Implementing a BHN strategy would have to proceed together with North-South collaboration to redesign international institutions and agreements *"with such ingenuity that all parties gain."* The "too frequent U.S. view of that challenge as a 'zero-sum game,'" Grant and Hesburgh wrote, "must be laid aside in favor of a broader vision."[59]

During these crucial years for international development, the ODC expanded its ties to the Democratic Party, particularly to the new chairman of its 1974 Congressional and Gubernatorial Campaign Committee, Jimmy Carter. At Carter's request, Georgia lawyer Stuart Eizenstat (later Carter's chief domestic policy adviser) compiled a list of position papers critical of Nixon for use in the 1974 midterm elections. "I collected a small file cart box-full of names of people like Brzezinski and Henry Owen and people that later came into the administration who agreed to do papers for us," Eizenstat recalled.[60] In addition to supplying papers from Trilateral Commission members, Owen reached out to the ODC's Jim Howe, lead author of the annual *Agenda* series, for a lengthy report on current US development policy after the NIEO announcement in May.[61] By the time Carter announced that he was seeking the Democratic nomination for president, he had already developed a close friendship with the ODC's Father Hesburgh. Shortly thereafter, Hesburgh sent Carter his correspondence with President Ford regarding US policy at the 1974 World Food Conference.[62]

Not surprisingly, the charismatic clergyman exerted a pronounced influence on Carter and, arguably, the country. Probably the most visible US theologian of the 1970s, Hesburgh was also the ODC's political executive, giving speeches, writing articles, and going on television to explain the stakes and scope of global economic inequality. Hesburgh translated the ODC's policy objectives into a moral language that Americans could understand and relate to, while also inspiring them to demand action from their representatives. When asked on the *Today Show* why Americans should give aid to poor countries, he replied simply, "[We] ought to do it because it's the right thing to do. It's being human; it's being Christian. . . . [It's] doing the kind of thing that human beings ought to do, being compassionate toward one another." Contrasting the South's food crisis with the North's energy crisis, he said in another well-publicized speech, "If you run out of gas, you can't go on a picnic in the country, but if you run out of food, you die." Hesburgh's moralism— he asked Americans for "a little moral leadership" on the food crisis, calling it "the moral imperative of our day"—appealed to Carter's own emerging emphasis on morality in foreign policy, as well as his desire to get Americans to realize that the world's resources—and the United States' right to them—were not unlimited. When asked in the spring of 1976 what he would like the two presidential candidates to say, Hesburgh responded, "I'd like them to speak to the idealism of the American people and demand some sacrifices." He then cited a study noting that in 1974 Americans had spent $3.3 billion on flowers, seeds, and potted plants and just $3.4 billion on foreign aid.[63]

The ODC's work for the Carter campaign accelerated in 1976, as Grant worked with Trilateral Commission members Gardner and Owen to write Carter's speeches on interdependence, North-South relations, and human rights. On this last subject, Hesburgh was particularly influential. "He was preaching the need for international human rights long before Congress or President Jimmy Carter discovered it," Hesburgh's biographer argues, "and he strongly endorsed Carter's human rights campaign."[64] At the Ford-Carter foreign policy debate in October 1976, less than a month before the election, Gardner and Grant urged their candidate to connect Ford's North-South and human rights records, characterizing both as interrelated consequences of Ford-Kissinger amoralism. Their long statement, adapted by Carter at the debate, echoed Hesburgh's persistent linking of human rights and development. They accused Ford, Kissinger, and secretary of agriculture Earl Butz of a "lack of morality" and "moral leadership" in failing to commit to more food aid at the World Food Conference, while also alleging that Ford was willing to "help out his friendly dictators in Chile, South Korea, and the Southeast Asian countries."[65] Instead of being the "arms merchant of the word," Carter insisted during the debate, US "strength derive[s] from doing what's right—caring for the poor, providing food, becoming the breadbasket of the world."[66]

Hesburgh saw human rights as inseparable from development, and he saw development through the morally inflected paradigm the ODC had been pushing since its founding: basic human needs. His combination of liberal idealism and modern, politically engaged Christianity was immensely appealing to Carter. As the leader of an elite but non–Ivy League university, Hesburgh possessed intellectual authority without the risk of snobbishness. Yet as a progressive and charming priest, Hesburgh carried a moral authority that Carter lacked. Indeed, Hesburgh was just as likely to chastise Americans for their intellectual and moral parochialism as he was to celebrate their innate virtues. Throughout the 1976 presidential election and after, Hesburgh was a valuable and reliable defender of Carter, calling his critics "cynical" and insisting that the United States had always been a country of idealists. "And for the first time in ages," Hesburgh explained to the press, "Americans are giving young people around the world a new ideological choice they cannot get from Communism—mainly freedom and respect for human rights. It may be troublesome at times, but so was the Declaration of Independence."[67]

It was for good reason, then, that Carter delivered the first major human rights speech of his presidency at the commencement ceremony for Notre Dame's class of 1977. Carter explained to the new graduates how the end of colonialism had "transformed . . . the daily lives and aspirations of most human beings," who, "freed from traditional constraints . . . have been determined to achieve, for the first time in their lives, social justice." The developed countries could not ignore these demands, for both strategic and moral reasons: interdependence meant that "traditional issues of war and peace" were inseparable "from the new global questions of justice, equity, and human rights."[68] After reaffirming "America's commitment to human rights as a fundamental tenet of our foreign policy," Carter laid out his position toward the developing countries, which combined the approaches of the ODC and the Trilateral Commission. First, Carter downgraded the developing countries' emphasis on global structural inequalities in favor of addressing the immediate (and less political) problems of basic human needs. Second, Carter brought back the Trilateral Commission's optimistic plans for joint OECD-OPEC funding for development, which had largely failed when Kissinger tried it. Third, Carter promised to transcend the North-South dialogue by rejecting slogans and instead improving regional and bilateral relations, especially with the richer countries in Latin America. In short, Carter's approach at Notre Dame was basically the Brzezinski-Gardner speech for the New York Foreign Policy Association, plus the Grant-Hesburgh material on basic human needs for the Ford debates.

Governor Jimmy Carter pitched himself as an outsider to the foreign policy establishment, but it was a certain wing of that establishment that gave him the background and support he needed to win the 1976 presidential election. When Carter announced his candidacy, both the world and the United States' place in it were undergoing their most profound transformations since World War II. Carter cast the "Nixon-Kissinger-Ford" administration not only as unable to deal with the strategic complexities of interdependence but also as lacking in its moral dimension. "In food, population, freedom of the seas, international trade, stable monetary systems, environmental quality, access to commodities and energy and so forth," Carter told a crowd in Louisville, Kentucky, "we've got to be part of [the solution]." Instead of "military might . . . political power . . . [or] economic pressure," he insisted, US foreign policy "ought to be based on the fact that we are right and decent and honest and truthful and predictable and respectful; in other words, that our foreign policy itself accurately represents the character and the ideals of the American people."[69]

Zbigniew Brzezinski and the Trilateral Commission provided Carter with a comprehensive hierarchy of foreign policy imperatives intended to distinguish him from Ford but especially from Kissinger, the real target of his charges. "Our neighbors in this hemisphere feel that they've been neglected; the Japanese feel that we've ignored their interests; the European nations feel that our commitment to them is suspect," Carter told *Time* in May 1976, "plus there's no attitude of respect or natural purpose toward the developing nations." The Ford administration's foreign policy "is primarily comprised of Mr. Kissinger's own ideas, his own goals, most often derived and maintained in secrecy," he repeated. "I don't think the President plays any substantial role in the evolution of our foreign policy."[70]

Carter's charges of cynicism and amoralism had weight, but they also obscured Kissinger's actions over the last two and a half years, which had more or less adhered to the Trilateral Commission's guidelines. Against the objections of Ford's economic advisers (and with Ford's support), Kissinger led efforts to establish and institutionalize the G-7 summits among transatlantic leaders; encouraged fiscal stimulus and the locomotive theory for world recovery; attempted to organize OECD-OPEC multilateral aid; pushed for a greater US aid commitment at the World Food Conference; publicly accepted that the NIEO voiced legitimate concerns, if illegitimate demands; recommitted the United States to the CIEC after talks broke down in the planning stage; and became the first cabinet official to address UNCTAD, where he rejected minority rule in South Africa and linked human rights to development. Carter's NSC admitted as much in a February 1978 review of the administration's North-South policies. Kissinger's "conciliatory" speech at the UN's Seventh Special Session on Development in September 1975, the NSC's Guy Erb (a former ODC official) conceded, "ended the rhetorical fireworks at the UN, led to the creation of [the] CIEC, and, in effect, bought nearly three years for the beleaguered OECD countries."[71]

A genuine belief in human rights was where Carter most distinguished himself from Kissinger. Kissinger could talk about human rights in the Third World, which he did only in the last year of the Ford administration, but his reputation and record made it impossible to take him seriously. In 1975 the State Department established a new Office of Humanitarian Affairs—the consequence of a 1973 resolution introduced by Congressman Fraser—but Kissinger made it clear to subordinates that human rights would remain largely at the level of rhetoric.[72] "Tell Popper to cut out the political science lectures," he remarked upon learning that the US ambassador to Chile had raised human rights concerns with Augusto Pinochet's defense minister.[73] In June 1976, shortly before Kissinger was scheduled to speak on human rights at a meeting of the Organization of American States (OAS), he assured Pinochet in private, "Your greatest sin was that you overthrew a government that was going communist. . . . We wish your government well."[74]

For Carter, this was exactly the lack of "respect or natural purpose toward the developing nations" that sowed distrust in North-South relations. Even more important for Carter, it was a betrayal of basic American values and unworthy of a country destined to lead the world by example. Like Hesburgh, Carter frequently boiled the pursuit of human rights down to individual conscience and basic Christian principles. "You don't plot murder and I don't plot murder," Carter told the *Atlantic* one month after Kissinger lightly admonished Pinochet in his OAS speech, "so why should our government plot murder against some foreign leader?" "We have set a different standard of ethics and morality as a nation than we have in our own private lives as individuals who comprise the nation," he said on another occasion, "and that ought to be changed."[75] While Carter also insisted that his human rights policy would not be governed by "rigid moral maxims," statements like the ones just quoted defined the public's perception of that policy during the campaign—as well as fueling criticism when strategic concerns overrode human rights with allies such as Indonesia, Iran, the Philippines, and South Korea.[76]

Carter's commitment to trilateralism was never controversial, but the tension between moral maxims and strategic imperatives ensured that his human rights policy would be. Congressional supporters of human rights such as Donald Fraser and Tom Harkin introduced legislation requiring the United States to use its power in international financial institutions to vote against loans to "serial abusers." Though not necessarily endorsing those abusers, many developing countries objected to what they viewed as the politicization of development aid—a fair point when the administration inconsistently applied the new guidelines and sought to water them down in Congress.

Further, Carter was not the only one connecting human rights and development. For years, Third World leaders had been advancing their own conception of economic rights in conflict with Carter's prioritization of basic human needs. In December 1974, half a year after the NIEO's announcement, Third World states voted overwhelmingly in the UN General Assembly for the Charter of Economic Rights and Duties of States (CERDS). The charter was presented as a legal foundation for the NIEO by G-77 leader and Mexican president Luis Echeverría, who had helped draft it two years earlier at UNCTAD III in Santiago, Chile.[77]

In contrast to Carter's emphasis on the individual, CERDS and the NIEO were "a competitor vision of universal justice" in which "the central object was an augmentation of the southern state, deploying the internationalist language of rights and solidarity to enhance the status not of the citizen but of the sovereign." To the dismay of feminists Gloria Steinem and Arvonne Fraser, Third World representatives turned the proceedings of the 1975 World Conference for the International Women's Year into a pro-NIEO rally. Echeverría asked the delegates "to look at the true origin of the problem," which was not governments' disrespect for the individual rights of women but the international system's disregard for the economic rights of states. He and other delegates employed their own interdependence logic, arguing that "the problems of the role of women in society, food, population, environment, human settlements, health and education are not single problems. . . . Each is a component part of the complex system." In other words, ensuring economic sovereignty—and through that, economic development and modernization—was the precondition for ensuring political and social rights and meeting the basic needs of citizens. "It is not possible to postulate in realistic terms the universal triumph of human beings," Echeverría charged, "as long as we do not give form to a New International Economic Order." A US diplomat summarized the G-77 position: "Problems of women are the problems of society . . . problems of society . . . are caused by [an] unjust world economic order; therefore to improve the situation of women we must first achieve . . . [a] new, more just and equitable economic order."[78]

Competing conceptions of justice and rights—political or economic, the citizen or the sovereign—would play a major role in determining the content and direction of North-South politics during Carter's presidency. The equity issue proved particularly divisive, as the Carter administration emphasized the equal opportunity of individuals via basic human needs over the equal opportunity of states via the global structural reform pushed by the G-77. The South "ridiculed" this approach, Roger Hansen, an NSC official and contributor to ODC reports, explained in 1980, "as an attempt to interfere with developing country sovereignty, to limit the process of Southern industrialization by stressing such goals as rural development, basic education and preventive medicine and to dismiss further consideration of the need for the broader structural reforms desired by the South." In turn, the North "caricatured the Southern stress on structural reform as nothing but an attempt to rig markets and mechanisms."[79]

Problems emerged early in Carter's term, as the NSC and the State Department found themselves working at cross-purposes to define Carter's North-South, human rights, and Latin America policies for the next four years. Success in the North-South dialogue was increasingly equated with watering down the South's proposals—such as the limited version of a Common Fund for Commodities agreed on at UNCTAD V in 1979—thereby defining progress in mostly negative terms. Some administration officials, especially those from the ODC, found the lack of momentum frustrating after so much buildup during the campaign. It was one thing to declare that the world and its problems were interdependent; it was another to put together a coherent response while also attending to numerous bilateral and regional initiatives. Ultimately, the Carter administration defined its North-South policy in the context of its most public priority: reshaping the United States' relationship with Latin America, where human rights, democracy, development, and the North-South dialogue intersected more directly than anywhere else in the world.

CHAPTER 5

Debt, Development, and Human Rights

The Dialogue in Latin America

Jimmy Carter was not the first president to rethink US–Latin American relations in the 1970s. In 1969 Richard Nixon told the Inter-American Press Association that the time had come for a "more mature partnership" between the United States and Latin America "in which all voices are heard and none is predominant." Drawing from the recommendations of Nelson Rockefeller, who had a longtime interest in Latin American affairs, Nixon called for reducing trade barriers, increasing multilateral aid, and elevating Latin America's importance in the State Department's portfolio.[1]

The Nixon approach was short-lived. New treasury secretary John Connally opposed giving Latin America any kind of preferential treatment in trade and blocked efforts by National Security Council (NSC) staff to send the required legislation to Congress. Matters were made worse by Connally's abrupt introduction of Nixon's "New Economy Policy" in August 1971, which called for a 10 percent reduction in foreign aid and a 10 percent surcharge on imports. Like the United States' allies in western Europe, Latin Americans were angered at the administration's failure to consult them before announcing the policy, as Nixon had promised in his speech two years prior.[2]

The twin crises of 1973–74—OPEC's oil embargo and the New International Economic Order (NIEO)—sparked a major rethinking of US global power in foreign policy circles. The first energy crisis showed that the United States could no longer assume developed country solidarity in the face of the

Third World's economic demands. During the Yom Kippur War, France and Germany declined to allow US planes to land there and refuel on their way to resupply Israel; by the end of 1973, Britain, France, Germany, and Japan had each signed or promised separate oil deals with Saudi Arabia, Iran, Iraq, Kuwait, Abu Dhabi, and Algeria.[3] As a consequence, restoring the unity of the developed countries was Kissinger's top priority following his promotion to secretary of state.

Kissinger also sought to improve the United States' other "special relationship"—that is, with Latin America. One reason, Kissinger wrote in his memoirs, "was the growing insistence of developing countries on bringing about a redistribution of the world's wealth by votes in international forums."[4] Latin Americans had been at the center of these efforts throughout the 1950s and 1960s. The UN Economic Commission on Latin America (ECLA) had been established in 1948 as a mechanism to encourage regional cooperation on trade and development. Argentinean economist Raúl Prebisch—whose terms-of-trade hypothesis formed the basis of dependency theory—was the ECLA's executive secretary from 1950 to 1963, when he departed to head the UN Conference on Trade and Development (UNCTAD), the General Assembly's new forum to address development issues from a Third World perspective. These efforts culminated in the adoption of the Charter of Economic Rights and Duties of States, completed at UNCTAD in 1972 and presented to the General Assembly by Mexican president Luis Echeverría shortly after the NIEO's announcement in May 1974.

Latin American countries played leading roles in the NIEO's intellectual and institutional generation. Those same countries also had long but troubled economic relationships with the United States. Both the Nixon-Ford and Carter administrations argued that reforming the United States' relationship with the South should start with Latin America—especially Mexico and Venezuela, whose pro-NIEO leaders preached and promised global cooperation over confrontation. Although Kissinger had some success on noneconomic issues—most notably the Panama Canal negotiations—it was Carter who introduced the most ambitious goal. With help from the Overseas Development Council, Carter and secretary of state Cyrus Vance advanced a vision of human rights for the continent centered on the promotion of economic and social rights, or basic human needs. For this and other economic measures, Carter required the consent of not just Latin American leaders but also the US Congress. In the end, Carter's failure to achieve either undermined both his relationships with Latin American leaders and his ambition to put US–Latin American relations on a more equal footing.

Kissinger: The Special Relationship, Reconsidered

Kissinger's strategy toward the NIEO was to use targeted concessions and bi-lateral appeals to break the unholy alliance of developing countries with oil (namely, OPEC members) and developing countries without. Latin America represented this nexus better than anywhere else. Venezuela—one of the most advanced, democratic, and cash-rich Latin American countries—used its sta-tus to promote the South's agenda for trade and development in both global and regional forums. Finance minister Manuel Pérez-Guerrero had been a del-egate at both the Bretton Woods and San Francisco conferences and served as secretary-general of UNCTAD (replacing Prebisch in 1969) and cochair of the 1975–77 Conference on International Economic Cooperation (CIEC).[5] Others, such as Mexico and OPEC's newest member, Ecuador (which joined in 1973), also used their status as oil price crisis beneficiaries to promote solidarity be-tween OPEC and the less developed countries (LDCs) on issues of trade and finance.[6]

On September 24, 1973, two days after being sworn in as secretary of state, Kissinger pledged to the UN General Assembly that the United States would "give new vigor to our policy of partnership in the Western Hemisphere."[7] A week later, he informed Latin American foreign ministers of his desire to fos-ter "a new dialogue . . . based on equality and on respect for mutual dignity." Kissinger made clear the reason behind his sudden attention to Latin Amer-ica, citing the "revolution of [the world's] patterns" of trade, energy, and food that brought the problems—and thus the demands—of developing countries to the front of the developed countries' agenda. The future of North-South relations—or, more specifically, the potential for the South to win concessions from the North—Kissinger suggested, would depend in large part on how co-operative Latin Americans were with the United States in international fo-rums. "So if the technically advanced nations can ever cooperate with the developing nations," Kissinger reiterated, "then it must start here in the West-ern Hemisphere."[8]

The following day the State Department's Bureau of Inter-American Af-fairs provided an outline of its "new conceptual approach" to Latin America. A policy of "Pan-Americanism," the report explained, "has guided U.S. policy towards the countries of Latin America for over a century." This system had worked well into the postwar period by providing "a philosophical rationale as well as a juridical basis for what was in fact a hegemonic power system with the U.S. at its head."[9] The problem, the bureau argued, was regionalism: whereas bilateral relations were still "quite satisfactory," multilateral relations had sharply deteriorated to the point where even the friendliest of Latin American countries sided with the "radicals" against the United States in the UN and elsewhere. This was exactly the kind of regionalism that Zbigniew Brzezinski described in *Between Two Ages*, in which he predicted that the increasing unity of the European Community (EC) would spread to other regions.[10] "Farthest along in Europe," the State Department explained, "the regional bloc concept is taking hold in Latin America as well," where the "Latins . . . slavishly attempt to imitate Europe and form a common market." As with the EC, the United States had to accept the "inevitable"—that is, it could no longer seek to participate in Latin American multilateral politics "on an equal footing with all of the other countries." Only by limiting paternalistic assumptions of diplomatic compliance and mutuality of interests, which had harmed both US–Latin American relations and North-South relations more broadly, could the United States hold on to a diminishing regional hegemony, the deterioration of which was having global consequences. "There would be 'linkage' but not 100% membership," the report concluded. "The relationship would not be unlike the one we are seeking to establish with Western Europe."[11]

There were some similarities between US–Latin American relations and transatlantic relations. Both regions had taken on a new importance at the outset of the Cold War, and in both cases the United States had developed new mutual defense treaties—in Europe, NATO; in Latin America, the Rio Treaty—intended to deter foreign (namely, communist) attacks on the signatories. The United States claimed a special relationship in each instance that justified greater involvement in domestic and regional political developments, and it used economic and military aid to foster a firm anticommunist consensus and discourage Soviet interventionism.

However, the State Department's comparison obscured crucial differences dating back to the 1820s. "Of the 50 times the United States sent troops outside North America during the nineteenth century," one scholar notes, "43 instances were in Latin America and the Caribbean." The US economic presence expanded side by side, so that by the end of World War I more than half of all US foreign investment was in Latin America and the Caribbean—as well as more than 60 percent of US diplomats stationed abroad.[12]

Due in part to president Franklin Roosevelt's Good Neighbor policy, most Latin American countries were reliable partners during World War II, supplying commodities to the Allied powers.[13] However, the outbreak of the Cold War quickly brought a reassertion of US power throughout the region. The 1947 Rio Treaty applied NATO's Article V mutual-defense obligation to Latin America, and it was formalized the following year with the establishment of the Organization of American States (OAS). Socialist governments and even electorally competitive communist parties were tolerated in western Europe, but in the case of Latin America, their presence led to CIA interventions (Guatemala, 1954; Cuba, 1961) and even the landing of US troops (Panama, 1964; Dominican Republic, 1965–66).[14]

As the United States claimed extraordinary powers for intervention, it also pledged a special obligation to Latin America's economic development. A first step was the establishment in 1959 of the Inter-American Development Bank, a sort of mini–World Bank for Latin America; like at the World Bank, the United States retained an effective veto power. In 1961 President Kennedy proposed a ten-year development program for Latin America, the Alliance for Progress, designed to prevent the spread of "Castroism" by promoting economic growth, social and institutional reform, and democracy.

The alliance's high hopes for economic growth and democratic stabilization ran into the same contradictions as other US development projects. By 1963, Kennedy administration officials predicted that the goals of development and democracy would prove incompatible in several alliance countries; the Johnson administration confirmed this in 1964 when it sent US naval support to right-wing military officers in Brazil seeking to overthrow the left-leaning nationalist government of João Goulart.[15] The contradiction was obvious: "The U.S. had promised change through another democratic revolution while training the armies to prevent it."[16]

The economics of the Alliance for Progress was subject to its own inconsistencies. The focus on foreign investment was not lost on the US business community, which convinced Congress to place strict limits on any competitive imports and ensure that those countries could use alliance funds only to buy US-made capital goods.[17] Further, despite meeting the alliance's target of 2.5 percent annual growth in regional output per capita, social indicators such as income distribution, land reform, and wage levels were relatively unaffected.[18] Because the majority of alliance investment was channeled through US corporations, only $1.9 billion of the $7.1 billion in income received through private investment between 1961 and 1968 was reinvested in Latin America; the remaining $5.2 billion was repatriated to the United States. Other aid was used to pay off growing public debts, which by 1966 had climbed to more than $12 billion; servicing those debts amounted to about 90 percent of total public and private grant disbursements. At the same time, due to congressional restrictions on competitive imports, US merchandise imports from Latin America *fell* from 27.2 percent in 1960 to 15.8 percent in 1968, lending support to claims by Latin American economists in ECLA and UNCTAD about North-South terms of trade. "When you look at net capital flows and their economic effect, and after all due credit is given to the U.S. effort to step up support in

Latin America," US ambassador to the OAS William T. Denzer confessed to Congress in 1969, "one sees that not much money has been put into Latin America after all."[19]

These unbalanced and heavy-handed efforts to foster a Pan-American consensus on security and trade contributed to the regionalism identified by Kissinger's State Department. US governments had always asserted a natural harmony of interests with Latin Americans, and indeed, US markets were essential to Latin American producers, and vice versa. However, the United States resisted lowering its own tariffs on Latin American–made industrial goods, the production of which had picked up rapidly under the import substitution industrialization policies of the 1930s and 1940s. Merwin L. Bohan, a member of the US delegation to the 1945 conference establishing the Inter-American Economic and Social Council, admitted at the time: "The United States has promoted the industrialization of Latin America not only as a matter of general policy, but specifically through lending capital and technical assistance. However, when the governments of Latin America take measures to protect the industries thus created, there is a disposition to frown on all forms of protectionism."[20]

Thus, contrary to the State Department's analysis, regionalism was not simply the consequence of paternalistic rhetoric or a desire to imitate the EC. Informed by the theories of the ECLA and its leader Prebisch, 1950s Latin American governments understood economic union as the only way to continue industrialization in the face of US and European protectionism. In 1960 the Latin American Free Trade Association (LAFTA) was established with seven members and was soon expanded to eleven; the same year, five countries created a Central American Common Market to promote free trade and establish a uniform Central American tariff. Seven years later, Latin American leaders pledged to establish a full Latin American Common Market by 1985, which would integrate LAFTA and the Central American Common Market. Further efforts at Caribbean integration followed in 1968, and the Andean Common Market (or Andean Pact) was formed in 1969 by Chile, Colombia, Ecuador, and Peru.[21] Regional economic integration gained an international component in 1971 when the Latin American members of the Special Latin American Coordinating Commission—established in 1969 to form collective bargaining positions in external economic affairs—joined with the EC to announce a "permanent dialogue" to coordinate bilateral and regional trade relations, as well as to consult on Latin American economic policy in international organizations.[22] "Either we must achieve the integration of Latin America," Carlos Andrés Pérez announced after committing Venezuela to the Andean Pact in 1973, "or the transnational companies will do it for us."[23]

Despite several setbacks—in 1968 LAFTA was "deadlocked" over intercountry trade disputes, and in 1969 the Central American Common Market was "wrecked" by conflict between El Salvador and Honduras—integration continued alongside Kissinger's "new dialogue" discussions.[24] On October 17, 1975, all twenty-five Latin American and Caribbean governments announced the creation of the Latin American Economic System (SELA). SELA was intended to bring together Latin American regional and international economic objectives, which had suffered from the proliferation of subregional organizations during the 1960s. The establishment of SELA in 1975 was critical because, as the North-South dialogue developed, pro-NIEO leaders Pérez and Echeverría could use it to foster regional and global solidarity in new negotiating forums such as the CIEC.

SELA's formation was also a reaction to the US Congress's 1974 Trade Reform Act, which included a provision excluding *all* OPEC members from the generalized system of preferences granting developing nations special tariffs—even though Venezuela had continued to ship oil to the United States during the 1973–74 OPEC boycott. Throughout 1974 Pérez had been defending OPEC against Ford's charges at the UN that wealthy oil producers were gouging consumers, including developing countries, for their own benefit.[25] In response to Ford's remarks, in September 1974 Pérez took out a full-page ad in the *New York Times* to explain the developing countries' position: "Each year we, the countries which produce coffee, meat, tin, iron, copper, or petroleum, have been handing over a larger amount of our products in order to obtain imports of machinery and other manufactured goods, and this has resulted in a constant and growing outflow of capital and [the] impoverishment of our countries. . . . Great countries have created the economic confrontation by denying equal participation to developing nations who need to balance their terms of trade."[26]

Regardless of the actual economic impact of the Trade Reform Act's anti-OPEC provision—90 percent of Venezuela's exports already entered OAS countries tariff free, the US delegate to the OAS remarked—Pérez quickly organized a regional response. At a special OAS session in January 1975, delegates from twenty Latin American countries denounced the measure as "discriminatory and coercive," and several even said that the issue was serious enough to call off Kissinger's new dialogue, about which there had been much talk but no specific policy changes. The final resolution, approved by all delegations except the United States', expressed "deep concern over the deterioration of inter-American solidarity cause[d] by the [act's] provisions . . . [which] run counter to the fundamental provisions of the charter of the OAS."[27] Inspired by this act of unity, two months later Echeverría hosted Pérez in Mexico City, where they agreed on the need for an omnibus organization—SELA—to represent Latin American regional interests within the context of global solidarity with the developing countries.[28]

After the OAS resolution, Venezuela and Ecuador announced that they would not attend Kissinger's proposed foreign ministers' meeting in Buenos Aires; Mexico and Chile dropped out shortly thereafter, and the meeting was canceled. With one fell swoop, the new dialogue—never on firm ground anyway—was over. "Ironically," Kissinger concluded, "the Trade Act had managed to unify Latin America to a far greater degree than the New Dialogue."[29]

Kissinger's main goal in the new dialogue was to diffuse Latin American regional support for the NIEO, organized primarily by Pérez and Echeverría and supported by left-leaning governments in Peru, Ecuador, and elsewhere. Rhetoric aside, Kissinger's proposal was unacceptable to Latin Americans mainly because there was nothing new about it. "The Europeans are forming blocs," Kissinger insisted to Treasury Department officials. "We are the only multilateralists left and that plays into the hands of the countries that are forming blocs." The new dialogue pledged to recognize Latin America as an independent bloc, but Kissinger refused to abandon the concept of a natural hemispheric community with mutually compatible interests, an idea that US policymakers had been asserting all the way back to Henry Clay. Was it a proposal for a new institution, Venezuela's foreign minister wondered at the February 1974 meeting in Mexico City, or was it a new word for existing arrangements?[30] It was, in fact, the latter: as Winston Lord, head of policy planning at the State Department, put it to Kissinger in January 1975, the new dialogue was simply "old wine in new bottles."[31]

After the fallout from the OAS resolution, the State Department examined the failure of its regionalist strategy. One problem was the fundamental ambiguity of the special relationship. Another was the growing economic diversity of Latin American countries. Despite the proliferation of subregional and regional efforts at economic integration, a few Latin American countries had incomes matching or exceeding some of those in western Europe. These countries were also the most vocal and influential supporters of Third World economic demands in international organizations. Yet, because of their new wealth and a protectionist US Congress, the United States lacked bilateral leverage just where it was needed the most. "The three countries where our interests are greatest: Brazil, Mexico and Venezuela, are rightly no longer eligible for concessional [US]AID programs, just as they have received no grant military equipment since 1968," Lord and William P. Rogers, assistant secretary of state for inter-American affairs, wrote to Kissinger in September 1975. Nor had the United States been responsive "to their clamor for 'trade, not aid,'" due to "competing domestic and international pressures."[32] In other words, if the United States could not or would not lower its trade barriers, why would Latin Americans endorse Kissinger's emphasis on reciprocity and give up the regional and international influence they possessed as some of the South's lead economic negotiators?

Kissinger had more success on another long-standing problem in US–Latin American relations. Ever since its signing by an unauthorized representative of the Panamanian government, the 1903 Hays-Bunau-Varilla Treaty, establishing permanent US rights over the Panama Canal Zone, played a major role in defining US–Latin American relations. US control over the Canal Zone was a powerfully enduring example of Yankee imperialism and was consistently opposed not just by successive Panamanian governments but also by virtually all Latin American governments, friendly or otherwise. After violent riots over the canal in 1964, the Johnson administration began negotiations with Panamanian representatives to reach a mutually acceptable agreement on a continued US presence. Talks fell apart in 1968 following two changes of government—one through elections, and the next, eleven days later, through a military coup.

The new government was led by General Omar Torrijos, a Panamanian military officer who had received training at the notorious School of the Americas, an anticommunist US military institute. Torrijos, who positioned himself as a left-leaning nationalist, soon expressed interest in reopening negotiations. In 1973 Richard Nixon appointed Ellsworth Bunker, a respected diplomat who had served as US ambassador to the OAS under Lyndon Johnson, to represent the new US position, which was to ensure permanent US use of, rather than control over, the canal.[33]

Kissinger placed great emphasis on the negotiations and established a personal relationship with Torrijos based on their mutual interest in reaching a new agreement. In 1974 few Americans had any knowledge of the Panama Canal; the "small minority" who did, he explained to Torrijos, was "violently opposed to the agreement, but no group is really for it."[34] But because the canal was tremendously important to Latin Americans, it was central to Kissinger's goal of reducing Latin American support for developing countries' strategy of confrontation at the UN. "If these [canal] negotiations fail," Kissinger explained to Ford in 1975, "we will be beaten to death in every international forum and there will be riots all over Latin America."[35] Torrijos also had to tread carefully. "There is a large group of people [in Panama] whose mission it is to see to it that there is no agreement," he told Kissinger. "They live off this problem."[36] Nevertheless, negotiations proceeded slowly throughout 1975, and it was clear that even if the two sides reached agreement on a new treaty, neither would risk bringing it to the US Senate during an election year. The final negotiations and signing of the treaty would have to wait for the next president, Jimmy Carter, whose administration had its own idea of what Latin Americans really needed from the United States.

The Carter Approach: A Global Policy for Latin America

Kissinger's private efforts could not prevent Panama Canal negotiations—a relatively bipartisan if low-key issue up to that point—from playing a part in the 1976 presidential election. Ronald Reagan, Gerald Ford's challenger for the Republican nomination, used opposition to the negotiations to fire up the Republican base. "We built it, we paid for it, it's ours, and we're going to keep it!" Reagan thundered in Florida during the Republican primary. Even Carter was unwilling to take a strong stand in favor of a new agreement. "The Panamanian question is one that's been confused by Mr. Ford," Carter alleged during their foreign policy debate in October 1976. "He had directed his diplomatic representative to yield to the Panamanians full sovereignty over the Panama Canal Zone at the end of a certain period of time."[37] Here, Carter was confused. Although neither wanted to admit it, both candidates supported—and Carter eventually signed—an agreement to return sovereignty of the canal to Panama at a later date, in exchange for a guarantee of permanent US access: the same conditions under which Bunker had begun negotiations in 1973.

Despite Carter's reticence during the campaign, concluding the Panama Canal treaties was the first official policy decision to emerge from his National Security Council's inaugural meeting. Just as Kissinger had emphasized to Ford, secretary of state Cyrus Vance and national security adviser Zbigniew Brzezinski both stressed to Carter that settling the negotiations was the necessary first step in reshaping US–Latin American relations.[38] The implications were especially important for US relations with "regional influentials" such as Brazil, Mexico, and Venezuela, which, in addition to their role in the North-South dialogue, together accounted for almost 70 percent of all US trade with Latin America and more than half of all US investment in the hemisphere.[39] "Latin America has become our primary LDC market for machinery, consumer goods, and chemical products—almost as large, in fact, as the entire European Common Market, and larger than Japan," the State Department wrote in early 1977. "Venezuela (for its huge financial reserves) and Brazil (one of the world's largest economies) have global roles that match or exceed many of the Western European countries."[40] The treaty's urgency was confirmed during the transition by a joint cable sent from the presidents of

Venezuela and Mexico describing it as "the crucial test of the degree of sincerity of a good inter-American policy of the United States." "The Panamanian cause is no longer the cause of that nation alone," they insisted. "Its intrinsic merits have made it the cause of all Latin America."[41]

Carter was also urged to make the Panama Canal a priority by the conclusions of the independent Commission on United States–Latin American Relations, also known as the Linowitz Commission. Its chairman, Sol M. Linowitz, had left his job running the Xerox Corporation to replace Bunker as US ambassador to the OAS. Other members included future Carter administration officials W. Michael Blumenthal, Richard Gardner, Samuel Huntington, and Father Theodore Hesburgh, as well as several former US government officials and scholars.[42]

The Linowitz Commission issued two separate reports in 1974 and 1976, both of which called for an end to the "paternalism and so-called 'special relationship'" that had guided US policy in the past. The authors of the second report recognized that Kissinger had initiated a "more appropriate and effective policy" but determined that its largely defensive nature missed the point: "This Commission believes *the new administration should focus early attention on improving U.S. relations with Latin America not because of hidden dangers but because of latent opportunities.* Latin America presents the United States with a good chance to fashion a coherent and constructive approach to the fundamental issues of North-South relations more generally." Instead of a regional approach that sought to co-opt a Latin American bloc in global forums, the authors recommended a new strategy that focused on pressing global issues with regional implications, such as commodity policy, debt, food, technology, arms sales, and human rights. "The primary aim of United States policy in the Western Hemisphere," they explained, "should be to work with Latin American countries in dealing with this broad global agenda." First, however, the United States had to resolve the "smoldering dispute" over the canal, "unquestionably . . . the most urgent issue" in Western Hemisphere relations.[43]

After Carter's election, Linowitz sent a copy of the report to Vance, and Vance brought it to Brzezinski and the president. In early December Brzezinski asked the twenty-nine-year-old executive director of the commission, Robert A. Pastor, to join the NSC staff as head of Latin American affairs. (Linowitz was also brought on as Bunker's conegotiator.)[44]

Pastor's first task was to draw up two presidential review memorandums (PRMs) on Panama (PRM-1) and Latin America (PRM-17). Pastor finished PRM-1 quickly, and Carter signed it on January 21, 1977. PRM-1 was essentially a refinement of the original US negotiating terms pursued by Kissinger and Bunker. It specified that US negotiators should seek to retain control of the canal for "the longest possible period, to terminate not earlier than December 31, 1999," and to obtain a "right in principle" to continue defensive operations for fifty years (though negotiators were permitted to go down to twenty). Additional terms were set for possible expansion and access to certain water and land areas along the canal. The negotiations were to remain confidential, but the State and Defense Departments would be in regular consultation with congressional leaders to build support for ratification of a treaty.[45]

Negotiation was difficult on both sides, but Linowitz and his Panamanian partners reached a final agreement on August 10, 1977, six months after Linowitz's appointment. Two separate treaties resulted from the negotiations. The first treaty required the United States to eliminate the Canal Zone, its "state within a state," and to transfer all property and responsibility for the canal by the year 2000, when Panama would be in full control. The Treaty on the Permanent Neutrality of the Canal, meanwhile, gave the United States and Panama joint responsibility to defend the canal and keep it open.[46]

Carter was determined to put his own stamp on the canal treaties. He decided that the signing ceremony would be held not at the White House, as Torrijos preferred, but at OAS headquarters. And instead of inviting representatives of the four democratic governments that had advised Torrijos during the negotiations, as Pastor and Brzezinski recommended, Carter decided to invite all Latin American heads of state, including dictators Augusto Pinochet and Anastasio Somoza. "The point of the ceremony," Carter explained, "was for the American people to see that the treaties enjoyed complete support by all the countries in Latin America and the Caribbean."[47] He stressed this in his speech at the treaty's signing. "This opens a new chapter in our relations with all nations of this hemisphere," Carter declared. "We do not have to show our strength as a nation by running over a small nation."[48]

Pastor's second task was PRM-17. He quickly ran up against the State Department bureaucracy, which was eager to protect the powers and interests of its embassies. "The main conceptual issue," Pastor recalled, "was whether the United States should assert a 'special relationship' with Latin America or adopt a single global policy for the developing world that could be adapted to the unique characteristics of the region's past relationship with the United States." Pastor and the NSC advocated the global approach recommended by the Linowitz Commission, while the State Department's Bureau of Inter-American Affairs favored the special relationship.[49] When Brzezinski wondered whether "we need a Latin American policy," Pastor said "No . . . Your question struck at the heart of the issue. *The idea of 'Latin America' as a region is a myth.* It is composed of extremely diverse economies and polities, which can manage to form a collective negotiating position only when there is a symbolic need to confront the U.S., such as in the Trade Act of 1974 (GSP/OPEC provision). The most important business of the governments of this hemisphere is dealt with bilaterally or globally." He went on to explain, "The policy that we should seek is one which will help us move *from a special policy toward the region to a global North-South policy.*" Regardless, Pastor conceded that because of Carter's special emphasis on the region, any new approach would reflect in part the language and assumptions of the old one. "We cannot move from our current policy—which is indeed a 'special one,'" Pastor acknowledged, "to no policy in a single step."[50]

Pastor's analysis shared important similarities with that of Kissinger's State Department following the failure of the new dialogue. In September 1975 Lord and Rogers recommended to Kissinger that in place of the new dialogue, "*we should approach individual countries and groups of countries in Latin America in a differentiated fashion, placing greater emphasis on bilateral and sub-regional relationships, and attempting whenever possible to implement our global economic policies in a way that will engage Latin America's new middle powers in productive commercial relationships and contain the inevitable conflicts their global emergence will entail.*" Although vague on specifics—two of their three recommendations involved stressing the importance of Kissinger's initiatives at the UN Seventh Special Session to Latin America—their main conclusion could have been lifted straight from a Trilateral Commission or Linowitz Commission report: "interdependence and trade rather than special relationship and aid."[51]

Pastor later admitted that a truly global policy was wishful thinking. "The debate had an unrealistic, theological quality," he recalled, "because one could argue that in the postwar period the United States always tilted global policies to favor Latin America, and this did not change." Nevertheless, he recommended that Carter place economic issues at the forefront of his approach to Latin America, so that all the major concerns of the developing countries— "trade, finance, investment, science and technology, aid, human rights, arms transfers and nuclear proliferation"—would be addressed "according to global criteria." At the same time, the United States should pledge noninterventionism in Latin American affairs and tolerance of political diversity, except in the case of gross violations of human rights; then, Carter should seek to isolate the worst offenders through bilateral and multilateral pressure. But because "North-South economic issues are [Latin America's] principal preoccupation," Pastor recommended global trade policies that reflected the existing economic diversity of the so-called Third World: "This means concessional assistance for the poorest countries, and increased trade prospects and improved and coordinated debt management for the middle-income developing countries, which are most of the Latin American countries. *Trade, not aid.*"[52]

Carter consolidated Pastor's initiatives in a speech to the OAS on Pan-American Day, April 14, 1977. After an introduction in Spanish, Carter acknowledged Latin America's role as a "driving force" in North-South relations, citing as examples Prebisch's work at ECLA and UNCTAD and Pérez-Guerrero's current role as cochair of the CIEC. In place of Kissinger's attempts to separate Latin America from the G-77, Carter pledged "not [to] seek to divide the nations of Latin America one from another or to set Latin America apart from the rest of the world." His three-point approach included respect for Latin American sovereignty, support for human rights and democratic governments, and progress on the North-South dialogue through "global policies [that] are of particular interest to other American states." As recommended by Pastor, those policies included supporting the creation of a Common Fund for Commodities, redirecting bilateral aid to the poorest countries, increasing contributions to multilateral lending institutions for more advanced developing countries, flexibility on new rules for foreign investment, support for regional and subregional economic integration, and special treatment for developing countries in General Agreement on Tariffs and Trade (GATT) negotiations. Carter also stressed reductions in conventional weapons and arrangements for nuclear fuel sharing as an element of North-South cooperation, the latter issue being of particular concern to Brazil.[53]

Almost by definition, the most important economic initiatives of Carter's global approach to Latin America would take place outside of specifically inter-American forums. The developed countries formally consented to negotiations for the Common Fund during the CIEC, which concluded in June 1977; subsequent Common Fund negotiations were carried out over the next two years by a special committee of UNCTAD. Support for basic human needs became enshrined in the State Department's definition of human rights, which Secretary Vance announced in speeches throughout 1977; however, effective implementation would be held up by both Congress and the administration when political developments in Africa, South Asia, and Latin America led to a reassertion of Cold War priorities. The administration had its greatest success in the conclusion of the Tokyo round of trade negotiations in 1979, where the generalized system of preferences was formalized in the GATT charter.

The Carter administration's North-South policy played out in Latin America largely as Kissinger had predicted in 1975: through bilateral, subregional, and occasionally multilateral diplomacy. Carter used bilateral relationships with key Latin American countries—namely, Mexico, Venezuela, Brazil, and

Jamaica—to encourage a common position on human rights, economic development, and the Panama Canal. Carter and Vance gave new purpose to the multilateral OAS—which both Pastor and Kissinger had declared essentially dead—to enhance the positions of the region's most advanced economies (as well as its few emerging democracies, which were often one and the same) and to isolate its worst human rights offenders. First lady Rosalynn Carter traveled to Jamaica, Peru, Ecuador, and Brazil to reiterate the themes of the president's OAS speech, and Carter met several times throughout 1977–79 with the presidents of Mexico, Venezuela, and Jamaica to solicit their cooperation in cooling North-South tensions. Additionally, President Carter gave special attention to the Caribbean. In a sign of good faith, he surprised Caribbean governments in May 1977 by meeting with the region's major sugar producers before taking any action to protect domestic sugar producers; the following day he announced that the United States would pursue new international sugar agreements.[54] Carter's ambassador to the UN, Andrew Young, also became personally involved in the creation of the Caribbean Group for Cooperation in Economic Development, a subregional development bank launched in 1977 with World Bank support.

Human Rights and the North-South Dialogue in Latin America

A real human rights policy was the Carter administration's most visible legacy in Latin America and, arguably, the world. "Nothing the Carter Administration has done has excited more hope, puzzlement, and confusion than the effort to make human rights a primary theme in the international relations of the United States," historian Arthur Schlesinger Jr. wrote in 1977.[55] Time has hardly cleared this confusion. Historian Tony Smith reflects an enduring and conflicting consensus on Carter's human rights policy. While Carter's "abiding concern for human rights abroad" was his "finest legacy to the post–cold war world," Smith writes, his moralism and "naïve failure to understand" the realities of global politics ensured his ultimate failure.[56]

Not everyone who backed Carter during the campaign embraced human rights as much as he did. For most of Carter's interlocutors at the Trilateral Commission, including Brzezinski, human rights was just one aspect of the new interdependence, and even then it ranked below the need for trilateral economic coordination, energy cooperation and conservation, and moderation of the North-South dialogue. Brzezinski shared Carter's belief in human rights "up to a point," he explained. "Indeed, later on, when a choice between the two had to be made, between projecting U.S. power or enhancing human rights (as, for example, in Iran), I felt that power had to come first."[57]

For Carter, a human rights policy implied not only ending the "Nixon-Kissinger-Ford" policy of supporting anticommunist governments regardless of their human rights records but also actively using the United States' bilateral leverage to push its nondemocratic partners toward openness and reform. His predecessors' policies, Carter believed, had contributed to developing countries' dissatisfaction with a US-led world order, causing an otherwise false coalition of Third World states to unite around the common denominator of US hypocrisy. Kissinger's conciliatory speech at the UN Seventh Special Session in 1975 had been a start, but such gestures were undermined by the rest of the Ford administration's policies toward the Third World, including its intervention in Angola and its approval of Pinochet's regime in Chile. Here, Brzezinski agreed. "I was concerned that America was becoming 'lonely' in the world," he explained in his memoirs. "I felt strongly that a major emphasis on human rights as a component of U.S. foreign policy would advance America's global interests . . . [in] the emerging nations of the Third World."[58] In other words, the United States could not have it both ways: to credibly align itself with progressive and democratic reform in the Third World, it had to match its criticism of other states' human rights records with improvements to its own.

The task of defining a human rights policy fell to an interagency commission chaired by deputy secretary of state Warren Christopher. The group worked largely from the template Carter had laid out in his Notre Dame speech, and the results reflected the importance he had placed on meeting basic human needs. PRM-28 defined three areas of human rights: (1) "the right to be free from governmental violations of the integrity of the person," such as torture and a lack of fair trials; (2) "economic and social rights," including "the right to be free from government action or inaction" that inhibits individuals' access to "basic needs" such as health care, education, and shelter; and (3) "the right to enjoy civil and political liberties." There was unanimous support for inclusion of the first group of rights, Christopher wrote, but "considerable discussion" about the second and third. However, Carter and Vance "expressly included them" because of their relevance for North-South relations. "A policy which subordinated these rights would not only be inconsistent with our humanitarian ideals and efforts," Christopher explained, "but would also be unacceptable in the Third World where the tendency is to view basic economic and social rights as the most important human rights of all."[59]

Although PRM-28 defined all three groups of rights as central to Carter's human rights policy, the administration suggested giving priority to the first set of violations. Civil and political liberties were a "long term goal" that required building strong democratic institutions, while social and economic rights were "primarily a matter of helping to stimulate economic development." However, "in countries where the first group of rights is denied or threatened, the protection of those rights has obvious priority."[60] This was especially relevant for US policy in Latin America, home to both the most advanced developing economies, which no longer qualified for the basic assistance provided by USAID, and the most blatant and well-publicized violations of "the integrity of the person" prioritized in PRM-28.

There were other important reasons why a human rights policy was implemented first—and pretty much exclusively—in the Western Hemisphere. The two countries in which the United States had the greatest economic stake, Mexico and Venezuela, were functioning if imperfect democracies, and despite their support for the NIEO, the United States retained good bilateral relations with both of them. In the military dictatorships of Chile, Argentina, and Uruguay, the United States had few interests beyond shared anticommunism, and the only real admirers of these regimes were other sitting or aspiring military dictators. "Venezuela's interests are not the same as ours," the State Department noted, "but they are closer to ours than any other regional power." Among Pérez's goals, only "high prices for oil and OPEC solidarity . . . directly conflicts with our own." Pérez had "a much larger role to play" than other Latin American heads of state in issues ranging from Panama Canal negotiations to human rights to regional economic development. Cooperation with Pérez—the leader of the most important developing country in the most important region of developing countries—on human rights and development, State decided, "would be a model for similar projects in other developing countries."[61]

Carter's goal of creating inter-American solidarity around human rights received an early victory at the June 1977 meeting of the OAS in Grenada. Intent on sending a signal, within months of taking office Carter reduced military aid to Argentina and Uruguay, two of the worst violators of the first category of human rights. Two weeks later, Vance traveled to the OAS meeting with the intention of multilateralizing what was still only bilateral pressure. With the support of the democratic governments of Venezuela, Costa Rica, and the Caribbean, the OAS passed a resolution declaring that "there are no circumstances that justify torture, summary execution, or prolonged detention without trial contrary to law." Attempts by Argentina and Chile to include an amendment justifying extreme actions in the face of terrorism were rejected by the other members.[62]

The State Department viewed this OAS session as a major step forward. "We now have hard evidence that human rights concerns have genuine support in Latin America," with "half of Latin America, including the entire Caribbean, lined up behind us." However, there was a caveat: "The Grenada Assembly put us clearly on notice that we cannot escape the economic dimension of human rights." Although the human rights resolutions narrowly passed, a resolution from Colombia calling for the promotion of human rights through economic development was "carried by acclamation" from all delegations. The rhetoric on development had been delivered by the president, the first lady, and Vance; now, action was needed to ensure that human rights was not seen as a smoke screen for avoiding "the aspect of human rights emphasized most in Latin culture, socio-economic well-being." "Progress on economic issues," the State Department concluded, "will be critical to allay fears that we are defining human rights narrowly to divert attention from basic North-South issues of growth and equity."[63]

That action would be hard to carry out. In fact, it would have been easier if the administration's slogan—"trade, not aid"—were reversed. "A decade ago," the State Department pointed out, "aid was our major tool, and the Executive Branch could take most of the decisions." But now the president had less authority, explicit or otherwise, to negotiate on trade and finance. "Decisions on trade are shared with Congress and critically influenced by domestic pressure-groups," while for capital and technology transfers, "which come right after trade [in terms of importance] for the Latins . . . private firms and banks call the tune, not the U.S. government."[64] In the age of interdependence, US foreign economic policy was stuck between Congress, beholden to corporate and labor lobbies, and capital, beholden to profit. Of course, the same criticism could be made of the corporate- and interest group–dominated Alliance for Progress in the 1960s, which benefited US firms far more than Latin American ones. But that was the point: post-Bretton Woods capital mobility, aided by petrodollar recycling, transformed banks into supranational entities capable of dictating terms to poor and rich governments alike. As Carter would learn in his meetings with Latin American leaders, they would find this defense self-serving at best.

Debt, Development, and Human Rights: Venezuela

Venezuela had long occupied a unique position in Third World politics. "At minimal risk of inciting U.S. retaliation," one scholar explains, "Caracas could express a Third World solidarity and sometimes defy cold war policies." During the Alliance for Progress, the progressive Romulo Betancourt was the

Kennedy administration's chosen partner, sharing a commitment to both social and economic reform and regional anticommunism. Like other US allies,
Betancourt condemned Cuban guerrillas and defeated his own country's in-
surgents by force, but he also allowed Marxist political parties to operate
freely, believing "from experience . . . that a policy of tolerance and flexibility
could divide and weaken the communist left." Pérez continued Venezuela's
policy of resisting Castro's adventurism in the hemisphere, but he also pursued a cautious rapprochement, opening diplomatic relations with Cuba in
1974. He expanded Betancourt's democratic progressivism into a strident
Third World internationalism, though he distrusted the Non-Aligned Movement due to Castro's ambitions for pro-Soviet leadership. Pérez preferred to
use the United Nations to advocate for developing countries, where they had
the best chance to achieve both solidarity and credibility.[65]

Pérez also used his international advocacy to build support for his government at home. Venezuelan television networks carried his UN speeches live,
and newspapers celebrated Venezuela's outsized role in global politics. However, unlike many other countries in a Third World leadership position—
especially its OPEC brethren—Venezuela abstained from the infamous 1975
UN resolution equating Zionism with racism. Instead, Venezuelan diplomats
Pérez-Guerrero and Simon Alberto Consalvi were widely respected for their
approach to international economic issues in UNCTAD and the General Assembly.[66] Venezuela's insistence on a link between the arms race and global
poverty also matched the beliefs of Jimmy Carter and many other liberal internationalists in the West. Pérez received support for his efforts from the leaders
of several Christian Democratic and Social Democratic parties, including West
German chancellor Willy Brandt, who made the link a main theme of the 1980
Brandt Commission report titled *North-South: A Programme for Survival*.[67]

Pérez had been elected president in March 1974, just as human rights abuses
in Latin America were becoming the focus of concerted international attention and activism in the United States and especially western Europe.[68] He welcomed Carter's focus on Southern Cone dictators such as Pinochet, whom he
held responsible for the death of his friend Salvador Allende. Following Pinochet's seizure of power, Pérez "opened his country to a flood of [Chilean] ex-
iles," turning Caracas into "a central meeting place for UP [Unidad Popular]
and Christian Democratic leaders, some of whom moved clandestinely back
and forth from Chile."[69]

From the beginning of his administration, Carter wrote to Pérez regularly,
describing him as his "counselor" on North-South and Latin American issues.
Pérez, impressed with Carter's sincerity and commitment to human rights,
praised his counterpart as "a voice [rising] from a great nation to tell the world

that human values are paramount."[70] In their first official meeting in Washington, two weeks after the OAS resolution against the Southern Cone, Pérez joked to Carter that "coordination of policies might be too easy," given their mutual interest in human rights, democracy, and development. Indeed, as they ran through bilateral and regional issues—human rights, terrorism, Caribbean development, Cuba—Carter and Pérez were mostly in agreement. Where disagreement existed, such as Pérez's decision to reopen diplomatic relations with Cuba, both sides appeared to be understanding about their varying domestic and international pressures. Pérez proposed that they issue a joint declaration and take additional measures to strengthen the Inter-American Human Rights Commission of the OAS following the resolution at Grenada.[71]

Pérez continued to support Carter's human rights policy throughout 1977. He publicly endorsed Carter's nonproliferation and arms control agendas, increased contributions to the Inter-American Human Rights Commission, and backed a Carter administration proposal to grant the commission the authority to conduct "automatic, on-site investigation[s] of alleged abuses in individual countries."[72] Yet State Department fears about the economic dimension of human rights persisted, for good reason. In past years, the United States had failed to meet the 0.7 percent of GDP target for official development assistance recommended by the UN; in fact, it rejected the target as unfair because the United States gave more aid in absolute terms than any other country.[73] Most important, in June 1977 the much-hyped CIEC, cochaired by Pérez-Guerrero, concluded with only modest results.

As Kissinger had done at UNCTAD IV,[74] Secretary Vance delivered a well-received opening speech at the CIEC committing the United States to a new era of North-South cooperation. The US delegation generally held to the positions advocated by the Overseas Development Council and Trilateral Commission during the campaign—which were not far off from Kissinger's stance in 1975. US officials agreed to a Common Fund but left its content and capitalization ambiguous; they supported a special action program for the Fourth World worth $1 billion, with a US contribution of $375 million (subject to congressional approval); and they pledged to increase official development assistance to multilateral agencies, with Vance promising to double bilateral and multilateral assistance within five years (also subject to congressional approval). No substantial agreements were reached on energy—the most important issue for the United States—and debt—the most important issue for developing countries. "At the Conference's last plenary meeting," an executive director of the International Monetary Fund (IMF) reported in *Foreign Affairs*, "a hastily drafted, and uncommonly bland, report was presented for adoption to a glum and exhausted audience." The report was "approved but not applauded by the delegates."[75]

The State Department was "reasonably satisfied" with the CIEC's results, in that blandness, not acrimony, dominated its concluding resolutions. The real failure was the persistence of bloc politics, "on which the state of bilateral relations between the U.S. and particular countries has had only a rough bearing." For instance, Iran and Saudi Arabia were "helpful" at the CIEC, largely because any major plan for debt relief would negatively impact their own status as creditors. Mexico and Venezuela, two countries especially attuned to the growing debt problem in Latin America—the result of excessive lending of Arab petrodollars by the Washington, London, and Paris banks that held them—"were not [helpful]."[76]

In fact, CIEC discussions had been postponed near the end of the Ford administration for this very reason. "Brazil, Venezuela, Argentina," and others, the NSC remarked, "all indicated that their support for postponement was based on expectations that the new Administration will soften the U.S. position on LDC debt."[77] By 1977, the debt problem had eclipsed the Common Fund as a priority for not only the oil-importing developing countries. In the 1970s Washington banks saw oil-rich Venezuela as a safe bet, and under Pérez, the country's external debt expanded from just $700 million in 1974 to $6.1 billion in 1978.[78] Venezuela, Nigeria, and other indebted oil exporters argued that action on debt at the CIEC would greatly improve the climate of future North-South discussions at UNCTAD, the UN Convention on the Law of the Sea, and the GATT.[79]

However, instructions from the State Department guaranteed that no substantial agreements would be reached at the CIEC. "Because of its temporary nature and restricted membership," State explained, "it is not a forum for negotiating binding commitments. It should not be expected, therefore, that CIEC will provide final answers to any of the outstanding North/South issues." The CIEC could provide "general guidelines" on issues under discussion in other forums, such as commodities (UNCTAD), basic human needs (World Bank), external financing (IMF), and trade (GATT), but on debt, negotiators had no instructions beyond opposition. The State Department concluded, "We see no prospect of action in CIEC or elsewhere on generalized debt relief."[80]

In March 1978 Carter made his third official trip to Venezuela to consult on human rights and the North-South dialogue. After a series of press conferences, Carter gave a major speech to the Venezuelan congress in which he recommitted the United States to the (limited) agreements reached at the CIEC, emphasized basic human needs, and proposed new cooperation on the sharing of science and technology for development.[81]

North-South issues again dominated Carter's private meeting with Pérez. Despite their harmony on human rights, a serious divide had emerged on the future direction of the dialogue. "Since [the CIEC] virtually nothing has happened," Pérez complained, noting that he felt "pessimistic" about the future. "What worries us is that the North-South dialogue has stagnated." Pérez-Guerrero, former UNCTAD secretary-general and CIEC cochair, explained why: "We have the impression . . . that even the U.S. at times was more inclined to defend the status quo than create new solutions. There seemed to be at times those who looked to poverty as the problem rather than to structural changes. But while poverty and the need for aid should be attended to, a change in the rules of the game to permit nations to develop more equitably was also important." Pérez added: "Concern over the poor is understood, but poverty is a symptom not a cause."[82]

Venezuela's criticisms of the United States' emphasis on basic needs and poverty rather than the developing countries' structural agenda for trade and finance put Carter on the defensive. He blamed the G-77 for wanting "all or nothing" in the North-South dialogue and accused it of being unaware of the "practical limitations that exist," especially in the US Congress. In a way, Carter's criticisms of the Nixon-Kissinger-Ford style of foreign policy had painted him into a corner. Kissinger and Ford had been "prepared to cooperate more with the developing world than [with] Congress," Carter explained, whereas he had pledged closer cooperation and consultation with Congress on foreign policy. Carter also blamed the lack of progress on the diversity of the developing countries' coalition, which led to an "inability . . . to negotiate with any semblance of order or mutual understanding with 90 different nations." He and Vance recommended smaller groups to work out proposals on issues such as commodities and debt, and UNCTAD did establish a body to work through the Common Fund, as agreed to at the CIEC. But without a commitment from the United States to back a specific forum for dealing with debt, nothing substantial could occur. On debt, the United States was prepared to do exactly what Pérez-Guerrero suspected and what Vance had indicated behind the scenes at the CIEC: defend the status quo.[83]

The Carter administration's decision on debt would have profound consequences for Latin America and for the South in general. Not exactly blameless, Pérez was the first to fall. He had entered office with an unprecedented 48.7 percent of the vote, a plurality not seen since Betancourt's victory in 1958, and his Acción Democrática Party controlled both houses of the Venezuelan congress. Pérez used this mandate to nationalize the country's oil and iron industries, giving his government control over the massive revenues flowing in from a global commodity boom.[84]

As part of his "Great Venezuela" program, Pérez embraced a populist social policy, subsidizing education and health care, and a nationalist industrial policy involving large subsidies to existing and new state-owned enterprises. By 1978, Pérez's government had managed to reduce the poverty rate to 10 percent and the unemployment rate to 5.5 percent, and Venezuela had a per capita income equaling that of West Germany.[85] With an eye to rising inflation, Pérez established the Venezuelan Investment Fund to reinvest oil profits in various regional development projects and to provide aid to Latin American and Caribbean oil importers.[86]

The boom did not last. Efforts to "sow the oil" through industrial policy, such as an attempt to build a Venezuelan auto industry, required far more investment than could ever be realized in profits. Pérez ended up putting more money into industry and infrastructure than into social programs, spending 15 percent less on education, health, housing, and government services than his predecessor. The focus on industrial policy left other critical sectors behind: by the end of Pérez's term, dependence on foreign food had increased to 70 percent, and food prices had risen by 16 percent, leading the government to subsidize basic foodstuffs in addition to industry.[87] His strategy also suffered from the vast web of patronage and corruption encouraged by ready money and a lack of adequate oversight. Public corruption became the focal point of opposition to his government, including within Acción Democrática, which began to block his spending proposals in congress.[88] Falling oil prices in 1976–77 did not help, leading Pérez to seek outside loans to meet his large domestic and foreign commitments.

In December 1978 Pérez and Acción Democrática were defeated by the Christian Democratic Party. The new president, Luis Herrera Campins, quickly "liberated" domestic food prices and eliminated automobile production. "I inherited a country mortgaged by debts," Herrera explained to Venezuelans on the day of his inauguration.[89] His meetings with US officials were dominated not by the North-South dialogue and human rights but by concerns about falling oil prices and new energy-based cooperation with the United States and Mexico, which had just discovered large oil and gas reserves off its coast.

Like Herrera, José López-Portillo—Echeverría's successor in Mexico—was "expected to moderate Mexico's flamboyant advocacy of Third World positions." Echeverría's leadership in the North-South dialogue had become "an irritant" in bilateral relations with the United States and had caused worry among both US and Mexican investors, Carter administration officials explained.[90] Calming investor fears was essential for the success of López-Portillo's plans for a gas pipeline to the United States, which involved a complicated interplay of inviting but also containing US influence in the project.

López-Portillo would not return to the North-South dialogue in a significant way until 1981, when he agreed to host a North-South summit in Cancún attended by the new conservative leaders of the United States and Britain: Ronald Reagan and Margaret Thatcher. That North-South summit—expected to revive whatever little spirit of generosity remained in the North after a second oil crisis, more inflation, and the return of East-West tensions—would be the last. Less than a year later, López-Portillo's finance minister announced that Mexico was defaulting on its foreign debt, kicking off a regional debt crisis culminating in La Década Perdida—the lost decade of development for Latin America.

Security Crises and the End of the Global Approach

Changes of government in Venezuela and Mexico were one reason why North-South issues virtually disappeared from the United States' Latin America strategy by 1979. Another was a series of global and regional security crises that would overturn fundamental assumptions about human rights and democracy central to the Carter administration's post–Cold War vision.

Many scholars have described a second half of the Carter administration, in which a series of international crises overtook its lofty goals for world order and cooperation.[91] Much of this transition is centered on a Vance-Brzezinski split, in which Carter sided with the hawkish cold warrior Brzezinski over the more dovish Vance.[92] In fact, most of the impetus for a tougher stance on security came from Carter. Frustrated with the State Department's failure to speak out on Soviet-Cuban interventions in Angola and Afghanistan, the president instructed Brzezinski to take the lead.[93]

The first and most serious crisis in Latin America involved Nicaragua, which had been run as a family dictatorship since the 1930s. By the mid-1970s, the Somoza family had alienated virtually every group outside of its inner circle with its blatant corruption and repression. In September 1977 Anastasio Somoza, under pressure from the Carter administration, permitted a more open political atmosphere, but he soon reversed course when he realized the full scope of the opposition to his regime, which included not just the lower and middle classes but also the leaders of the Nicaraguan business community. Following the assassination of Pedro Joaquín Chamorro, a prominent opposition leader and newspaper editor, members of the business community called for a general strike that shut down the capital. However, their leadership during the strike was eclipsed when the Sandinista National Liberation Front (FSLN), a Cuban-inspired group of guerrillas founded in 1961, seized control of the palace in August 1978, signaling the end of nearly five decades of family dictatorship.

"Caught between a dictator it refused to defend and a guerrilla movement that it would not support," the Carter administration sought a multilateral solution through the Organization of American States. After Somoza rejected OAS calls for a national plebiscite, the Carter administration imposed sanctions on his regime but declined to support the FSLN, which, despite representing an increasingly broad coalition, proclaimed a revolutionary Marxist ideology. However, the administration's allies in Panama, Costa Rica, Mexico, and Venezuela supported the FSLN, as did Cuba, which supplied the guerrillas with much-needed arms. With help from Panama, Mexico, Venezuela, and others, the OAS rejected a US proposal designed to limit the FSLN's representation in a transitional government. Lacking the support of his democratic friends, Carter decided against a unilateral solution, and a Marxist government took power in Managua on July 19, 1979. With his country's fortune in tow, Somoza fled to Miami, but unlike the ailing shah of Iran—who spent his final days in Minnesota receiving treatment for cancer—the Carter administration denied him entry. Somoza eventually took up residence in Paraguay, where he was assassinated one year later.[94]

The crisis in Nicaragua marked a turn back toward Cold War worries in the Western Hemisphere and away from the global approach urged by Pastor and the Linowitz Commission. When the Marxist New Jewel movement seized control in Grenada in March 1979, Carter again asked the Latin American democracies for advice. This time, they recommended neither helping nor confronting the increasingly pro-Cuban, pro-Soviet regime. Instead, the United States supported democratic governments in the Caribbean by increasing its aid programs, including the Caribbean Group for Cooperation in Economic Development, promoted by UN ambassador Andrew Young. Support in Congress for Carter's Caribbean development policy was never on firm ground, and it took another hit when the United States discovered a Soviet brigade off the coast of Cuba during the 1979 Non-Aligned Summit in Havana. According to Pastor, "Castro thought the United States had concocted the entire incident to embarrass him at the Summit, but the incident was more embarrassing and politically costly to the Carter administration. As with each of the strategic confrontations in Cuba, the Soviet brigade issue had almost nothing to do with Cuba and almost everything to do with the perceived balance of power between the Soviet Union and the United States."[95]

There was one bright spot in the Caribbean. Since the "quite successful" start to the Caribbean Group for Cooperation in Economic Development, a hopeful Brzezinski reported to Carter, "the political winds in the Caribbean are definitely blowing in a moderate direction."[96] But this was too little, too late. According to Pastor, there was "no question" that the greatest failure was the administration's economic policy. "We have been criticized most vigorously not for what we have failed to do, but for what we have done," including doubling sugar duties, dumping tin, holding back funds from development banks, giving Australia and New Zealand but not Latin America preferences on meat, and imposing countervailing duties against Brazilian exports. "These decisions do not seem terribly important to us, but each has provoked a bitter response in Latin America, and they have a cumulative effect."[97]

Mexico was one example. The United States had failed to reduce trade barriers against Mexico during the negotiations over López-Portillo's proposed gas pipeline. The conflict on trade expanded to disputes over border policy and weapon sales, and Carter's unfortunate public comment about contracting "Montezuma's revenge" while visiting Mexico in March 1979 compounded López-Portillo's sense of disrespect, unnecessarily prolonging the important gas negotiations and straining US-Mexico relations.[98] When López-Portillo refused to admit the shah of Iran into Mexico after his operation in the United States, reasoning that it would hurt his standing in the Third World, Carter was "outraged." "By the end of 1980," Pastor concludes, "the relationship that Carter had hoped to build with Mexico had become a casualty to miscalculations, divergent perceptions, and some policy differences."[99]

All the economic policies listed by Pastor had one thing in common: they had been determined primarily by Congress. There was scarce public or congressional support for liberalizing US trade with developing countries when Carter entered office, but as Kissinger had learned with the 1974 Trade Act, the one factor uniting the diverse governments of Latin America—Marxist, leftist, democratic, capitalist, liberal, nationalist, or authoritarian—was US trade policy. Outside of GATT negotiations, the only real tool the president had to change trade policy was to convince Congress and the American people that it was in their interests to do so. But the domestic effects of interdependence—in the form of surging energy prices, stagflation, and unemployment—contributed to support for protectionism not seen in the United States since the 1930s. And considering the strong precedent of US corporate influence over economic legislation affecting Latin America, even a direct appeal to the American people probably would have had little positive effect (and almost certainly would have caused a great deal of backlash).

Carter's call for increased economic and political cooperation with the Third World proved persuasive enough in 1976, but his seeming inability to deal effectively with multiple security crises in Latin America, the Caribbean, the Middle East, and Central Asia—as well as a stagnant economy impervious to the tools of the old Keynesian playbook—exhausted public support for development before his administration could really get started. Nor did he continue to make the case for Third World development to *Americans* after the first few months of his presidency, a fact not lost on officials in the NSC's North-South cluster.[100] As two public opinion analysts put it, the American public "felt bullied by OPEC, humiliated by the Ayatollah Khomeini, tricked by Castro, outtraded by Japan, and out-gunned by the Russians." When the second oil shock hit in July 1979, the same month the Sandinistas took control of Nicaragua, Carter's popularity was lower than Nixon's had been two months before he resigned.[101]

Despite claiming to take a global approach, the Carter administration's strategy in Latin America never really extended beyond regionalism. It was not without its successes: the number of human rights violations related to the integrity of the person declined significantly in the Southern Cone, and Carter would leave a powerful legacy in US foreign policy that both Republicans and Democrats would draw on, sometimes for opposite purposes. However, a global approach based on changing US trade policies for advanced developing countries and a basic human needs strategy for poorer developing countries was impossible without support from Congress, which Carter neither had nor sought.

Instead, as the NSC's Thomas Thornton explained, congressional protectionism was running opposite to "the open trade policies that the situation requires." As for the basic needs approach, it was "seen as patronizing, if not interventionist, by most of the poorer countries with whom we deal," and it "reflected a condescending American attitude and was therefore especially ill-suited to mesh with a key aspect of our North-South strategy—the attempt to cultivate regional influentials."[102] Key developing countries remained unconvinced that Carter's emphasis on basic needs was not a tactic to avoid a discussion of structural issues. Thus, Pérez characterized poverty as a symptom of international economic relations rather than a cause in itself.

If the global approach never really happened, the bilateral or regional approach failed to translate to other areas—namely, functionally specific forums such as the CIEC and UNCTAD. According to the NSC, these forums constituted the "soft" plane of North-South bargaining and were the only places where the United States confronted the South as a whole. Despite warm relationships with several Third World leaders, "there is no effective link between our bilateral concerns with specific developing countries and the implementation of international economic policy on the one hand," Guy Erb wrote to Brzezinski, "and [soft] 'North-South' encounters on the other."[103] This made sense when considering the generally conservative position taken by the United States in each of the soft forums; as Pérez-Guerrero told Carter, developing countries saw the United States as "more inclined to defend the status quo than create new solutions." These contradictions—between Carter's rhetoric and bilateral relationship building and his diplomats' conservatism in UNCTAD and the CIEC—produced a strategy that was "fragmented and limited," causing division in both North-South and North-North relations.

Nowhere was division more likely than on debt. From the beginning of the North-South dialogue, US proposals on debt focused almost exclusively on the poorest Fourth World countries. But since then, official debts had skyrocketed in the fourteen "upper-tier" developing countries. Their annual interest payments were estimated at $7 billion, and their annual payments on principal were expected to reach $16 billion by 1979, a 45 percent increase from 1976 and nowhere near the modest amounts the United States had pledged for the Fourth World.[104]

If the United States was not prepared to act on debt, it would at least have to allow more exports from debtors—but it was not prepared to do that either. "Without an adaptation to that need," Erb foreshadowed, "we run the risk of threatening the viability of the international financial system." The outlook for UNCTAD V in May–June 1979 was not good: "The US position for the forthcoming UNCTAD meeting on international debt is currently so modest that strains within the OECD group and a confrontation with the developing countries appear inevitable." Within the OECD, France, Britain, and Germany viewed the United States "as a conservative force whose defense of economic principles will prevent the adoption of measures that some European countries are willing to accept," and progressive countries such as Sweden and the Netherlands considered it "an obstacle to real progress in the North-South Dialogue."[105]

Erb then outlined three strategies the United States could take. One, it could continue to "muddle through" soft forums, with the hope that G-77 disunity would prevent confrontation. Two, it could "buy some time" with "a long list of initiatives," as Kissinger had done in his speech at the UN Seventh Special Session: "Such a policy might buy some time, but our credibility would be immediately questioned, and we would be correctly perceived as retreating from stated objectives." Three, the United States could embrace the theme of shared cooperation from Carter's speech to the Venezuelan congress. Such an approach would include stressing the "hard choices" limiting US policy, such as congressional pressure and other domestic concerns, "coupled with a serious effort to move toward mutually beneficial policy initiatives wherever possible," especially in the areas of science and technology, food, and energy. This approach would also emphasize US actions in the UN and functional entities such as the IMF, World Bank, GATT, and especially UNCTAD, where the

United States was farthest apart from both the G-77 and the OECD. Option three would not resolve the North-South divide by itself, but it "could break the deadlock in which the OECD countries and Group of 77 now find themselves," while also helping to "clear the air" in US bilateral or regional relationships.[106] However, it would require a substantial change in the State Department's conservative position in soft forums. "We approach these economic negotiations individually without any grand strategy," Thornton elaborated, "What we need to do is find some areas where we need not be defensive. The only way to force [undersecretary of state for economic affairs Richard] Cooper and Company to do this is to make them show their entire hand on the full range of North-South negotiations. They have a very good case to make on each individual point. The poverty of their position seen as a whole, however, will be so evident that Vance or the President will tell them to do something."[107] "Firm implementation of this option would entail some bureaucratic upheavals," Erb concluded, "but without a commitment to take that risk I see little prospect that our North-South policies will be any different in 1980 than they are now."[108]

Brzezinski approved option three and put Pastor, Erb, and Thornton to work on an outline for a new US strategy for the North-South dialogue. But would they succeed against bureaucratic resistance, a hostile Congress, and a skeptical public at a moment of economic crisis and foreign policy reversals?

CHAPTER 6

Basic Needs and Appropriate Technology

National security adviser Zbigniew Brzezinski liked to tell reporters that, in contrast to Henry Kissinger and Gerald Ford, he and Jimmy Carter sought "architecture" over "acrobatics" for managing the United States' global responsibilities.[1] As he informed Carter in April 1977: "Your [foreign] policy . . . places emphasis not so much on maneuver, but on building new structures—new relationships with friends, with adversaries, with the developing world, even with the whole world—that we hope will have a measure of permanence. It is, therefore, an optimistic policy—we hope to build a better world—not simply survive in a hostile one. *It is a policy of constructive global engagement.*"[2]

Carter's team entered office determined to move US foreign policy beyond Cold War binaries, and North-South relations immediately became its most ambitious—and scattershot—area of policymaking. In its first year the administration successfully pursued its political goals in the Third World, the most important being resolution of the Panama Canal negotiations, but it failed to secure an agreement with developing countries on energy at the Conference on International Economic Cooperation (CIEC). Outside of North-South economic negotiations (the North-South dialogue), Carter and secretary of state Cyrus Vance devoted significant attention to reforming US foreign assistance: evangelizing the concept of basic human needs at home and abroad, working with Congress to redirect aid away from large-scale development projects and toward antipoverty programs, and setting up a world hunger initiative that declared US policy to be a "basic minimum level of health, nutrition, and family planning services . . . available to the world's poor, whether they live in rural areas or urban slums."[3]

Carter was equally ambitious with transatlantic relations. At the G-7 summits in London (May 1977) and Bonn (July 1978), Carter and his counterparts pledged to increase world development budgets and resist protectionism at home, but low growth and rising unemployment left summiteers unwilling to commit to numbers. Carter's desire to work with Europeans on reducing the global arms trade and the spread of nuclear technology ran into firm resistance from France and West Germany, both unwilling to risk offending Third World countries with which they had signed major arms and nuclear fuel agreements. For example, when Carter proposed joint action to restrict the sharing of nuclear technology at his first G-7 summit in London, West German chancellor Helmut Schmidt balked, insisting that countries on a "'have not' or 'must not'" list would be less inclined to cooperate on North-South economic issues.[4] According to one scholar, this "showdown between the German Chancellor, Helmut Schmidt, and the US President widened into one of the deepest trans-Atlantic rows of the cold war."[5]

Administration officials were well aware of this conceptual incoherence. "We have not devised an overall economic or political strategy," the National Security Council's new North-South cluster concluded in its first annual report. "Much of our policy has appeared to be in the form of isolated initiatives rather than part of a more general perspective."[6] Staffed by academics on loan from the Overseas Development Council (ODC) and other institutions, the North-South cluster stressed the need for a comprehensive and balanced response—one that included not just antipoverty relief (basic needs and appropriate technology for development) but also structural reforms, including major changes in US trade policy. The State Department, in contrast, dug in. At the fifth meeting of the UN Conference on Trade and Development (UNCTAD V) and the UN Conference on Science and Technology for Development (UNCSTD), both held in 1979, US negotiators insisted that the only offer on the table for the South was new money from old institutions—the US Agency for International Development (USAID) and the World Bank—specifically earmarked for poverty relief and the transfer of appropriate technology.

PRM-8: Toward a North-South Strategy

The White House spent the better part of 1977 working through Presidential Review Memorandum (PRM)-8. An attempt to set medium-term (twelve-month) and long-term (four- to eight-year) policies for reforming North-South political and economic relations, PRM-8 was one of the first studies called for by the National Security Council (NSC) in January 1977. A CIA analysis noted: "Of the first 24 PRMs assigned by the NSC . . . fully 15 dealt at least in part with 'southern' matters—e.g., human rights, military base rights in key LDCs [less developed countries], Southern Africa, and nuclear weapons proliferation prospects in such countries as India, Pakistan, Brazil, Argentina—an indication of the importance accorded issues affecting U.S. relations with the LDCs by the new administration."[7]

Group morale was low. Roger Hansen, an expert on North-South relations at Johns Hopkins and ODC senior fellow threatened to quit due to bureaucratic turf wars and personality clashes among the State Department, the Economic Policy Group (EPG) headed by the Treasury Department, and the North-South cluster. "It has taken three weeks to get thoughtful people from key agencies to believe that this was a serious exercise," Hansen wrote to a Brzezinski aide in a desperate memo titled "My 'Resignation.'" "There *is* deep skepticism, much of it stemming from the fact that the EPG is seen as the 'operative' group on the issue."[8] Hansen was not alone. The same day, Robert Pastor wrote to Brzezinski's deputy on "The Atomization of the North-South Cluster," complaining that "[it] is a unit only in name."[9] "I have wasted your time and mine," Hansen despaired to Brzezinski in July 1977, after he had in fact resigned, "and it appears that no constructive purpose has been served."[10]

In October 1977 Carter finally signed a presidential directive for North-South relations that declared, "trade, access to capital markets, and foreign assistance [constitute] the leading edge of our strategy, since these policies maximize the role of market forces and most efficiently promote development." The document also pledged to "pursue multiple objectives in the Third World relating to our security, economic, and humanitarian concerns," including "policies which restrict arms transfers and control nuclear technology," encourage communist countries "to make a more constructive contribution to the amelioration of poverty," and address "the basic human needs of poor people in developing countries." In terms of the North-South *dialogue*—that is, discussions in the UN General Assembly and UNCTAD, which would hold its fifth meeting in May 1979—the administration's position was dismissive if not hostile. "We will make an effort to channel negotiations, particularly on technical issues, in more specialized, functionally specific institutions where the environment is less politicized," the directive emphasized. "Other issues—such as commodities and official debt—are of political importance to LDCs frequently out of proportion to their potential economic significance."[11]

Southern leaders did not hesitate to register their disappointment at the administration's less than forthcoming stance on global negotiations. At the CIEC's conclusion in June 1977, US negotiators had replayed the Kissinger card of accepting a Common Fund "in principle" while resisting proposals for a new forum to deal with developing countries' rising sovereign debts.[12] "Since [the CIEC] virtually nothing has happened," president Carlos Andrés Pérez of Venezuela told Carter when the latter visited Caracas in March 1978. "What worries us is that the North-South dialogue has stagnated. We have talked about ways of moving the dialogue forward in the UN. The G-77 has pressed for an open forum. No decisions have been made to carry out the limited agreements of [the] CIEC."[13]

Carter received similar feedback that summer when he, Brzezinski, deputy secretary of state Warren Christopher, and UN ambassador Andrew Young met with the heads of several Latin American countries to discuss, in Jamaican prime minister Michael Manley's phrase, the "primordial issue of the North-South dialogue." Speaking for the group, Manley listed the Common Fund, resource transfers, International Monetary Fund (IMF) reform, and debt rescheduling as the "four components" necessary to move the dialogue forward. Without renewed attention to the dialogue, Pérez added, "the President is likely to hear screams instead of rhetoric" from the South.[14]

Two months after those meetings, the Carter administration underwent its second major North-South strategy review. The most consistent observation was that the administration's progressive but disparate actions had done no more to change the dialogue's agenda than had those of its predecessors. "Since 1974 we have been on the defensive," undersecretary for economic affairs Richard Cooper wrote to Vance. "To a great extent this is inherent in the character of the debate, since the G-77 are the demandeurs, and we are the defenders, if not of the status quo at least of the essentials of the existing international economic system."[15] North-South cluster member and ODC fellow Guy Erb described the administration's "defensive" position another way: "containment." The United States was trying to contain not only "leading developing countries" and their support for the New International Economic Order (NIEO), he explained: "We seek to contain first those developed countries that wish to adopt more forthcoming approaches to negotiations with developing countries."[16] Rather than a leader, all too often the United States was the rich countries' lowest common denominator.

Another problem, the NSC's Thomas Thornton pointed out, was that the administration lacked, if not the capital for "a different distribution of the world's resources and power," as the South insisted, then any "strong base of public and Congressional support for [such] policies."[17] But that support had to be cultivated—and in a sustained and realistic way. The Common Fund was one prominent example. "The developing countries see the Fund as the touchstone of industrial countries' attitudes toward their aspirations and our support for it as an important indication of our commitment to a constructive North/South dialogue," Vance told Carter in August 1978. Reminding Carter of his commitments at the London and Bonn summits on that issue, Vance urged the president to begin a strategy to secure the fund's eventual ratification by the Senate.[18] *"Even this modest version (with a provision that excluded mandatory U.S. contributions),"* treasury secretary Michael Blumenthal warned Carter at the time, *"may not be acceptable to the Congress without your heavy personal involvement."*[19] However, Carter never spoke to Congress in support of the Common Fund agreements, and after the conclusion of negotiations in July 1980, he would not risk sending them to the Senate during election season. To no one's surprise, the Reagan administration declined to submit the agreements signed by Carter to Congress for ratification, and the Common Fund finally became operational in 1989 without any US support.

In August Cooper proposed to Vance "A Possible Orientation for North-South Strategy in 1979" that focused on two unique US strengths: "our leadership in moral and humane values (in particular, our commitment to freedom of the individual and our defense of his rights against the state and other large impersonal entities) and our technological prowess."[20] Unlike strategies related to the transfer of resources and power, such as the Common Fund—which US officials had a difficult time selling to one another, let alone to Congress and the American public—new proposals for combating poverty and sharing scientific knowledge could be promoted as examples of US leadership consistent with individualistic values about markets and human rights.

Carter was fond of biblical logic—and technology transfer was like teaching a man to fish and leaving him with the rod and reel. Further, Carter and Vance had already done a good deal of legwork, getting the word out that the basic needs approach was official US policy in several speeches throughout 1977, including Vance's landmark address at the University of Georgia, where he declared that "the right to the fulfillment of such vital needs as food, shelter, health care, and education" is an essential human right.[21] "The President's early emphasis on the importance of human rights as an element of American foreign policy, and the shift of emphasis in our aid program to basic human needs, have both helped us to regain the initiative in the area of moral and humane values," Cooper stated. "Not all developing countries will like this position, but in my view it provides the only possible basis for building and sustaining broad-based support for foreign assistance with the American public."[22]

Negotiating the Stalemate: UNCTAD V

The year 1979 was a fateful one for world order. The People's Republic of China began opening its economy to the West, while the Soviet Union pursued a strategy of outright aggression in Afghanistan. Communist Vietnam invaded communist Cambodia, where the United States and others ignored genocide until the last minute. In Nicaragua, a right-wing dictator fell to leftist revolutionaries; in Iran, a pro-Western autocracy was turned into an anti-Western theocracy practically overnight. The developed countries' oil bill spiked again, as did inflation and unemployment. Economic growth suffered, and so did Carter's approval rating.

It was also a fateful year for the North-South dialogue. With the exception of ongoing Common Fund negotiations, North and South had not returned to the table since the failed CIEC in 1977. The conferences scheduled for 1979—especially the fifth meeting of UNCTAD in May and the UNCSTD in August—were highly anticipated by both sides. However, in their expectations of what the dialogue could—or should—achieve, North and South could not have been farther apart.

In September 1978 representatives from the three G-77 groups (Latin America, Africa, and Asia) began meeting to prepare an agenda for UNCTAD that reflected shared priorities and reinforced group solidarity. In their first presentation in December, the ministers made it clear that they expected movement on the proposals for global structural reform that the North and South had been kicking back and forth since 1974. "The North-South dialogue has moved from the era of declaration to the era of negotiation," they announced in a group statement to the press. Indeed, this was why UNCTAD V was being held three (rather than four) years, after UNCTAD IV: the G-77 wanted to ensure that the United States' negotiating capacity was not constrained by election year politics.[23]

In February 1979 the G-77 ministers met for the fourth time in Arusha, Tanzania, after which they released to the press their agenda for UNCTAD V. In addition to a comprehensive "Framework of Negotiations,"[24] which would be used at UNCTAD V more or less verbatim, the lengthy "Arusha Programme" contained a strongly worded "Plan for Collective Self-Reliance." This action plan called for, in effect, the establishment of a set of alternative international trade agreements designed by UNCTAD experts and governed by and for the South.[25]

The action plan was, on its face, unrealistic. It involved the creation of dozens of new organizations and agreements that the Group B developed countries could not possibly support. But like many bold proposals associated with

the NIEO, its logic becomes clearer in light of developed countries' resistance
to more moderate reforms to the existing system. A good example is the generalized system of preferences (GSP), a plan to grant poorer countries special
nonreciprocal trade concessions with the North that would otherwise violate
the rules of the General Agreement on Tariffs and Trade (GATT). First proposed in 1964 by UNCTAD founding secretary-general Raúl Prebisch, the GSP
had been affirmed by both sides at UNCTAD II in 1968 and once again at
GATT negotiations in 1971. However, Northern countries demanded their *own*
concessions in return, including "the right not only to decide the products to
which to extend GSP but also to withdraw the preference if domestic problems required it," thereby nullifying the GSP's full power.[26]

In contrast, efforts at Southern regional and subregional organization required
only the support of interested states. In response to the 1974 US Trade Act,
which removed special preferences for Venezuela because of its OPEC membership (despite its nonparticipation in OPEC's anti-US boycott), Latin American states formed their own regional trade pact excluding the United States and
oriented toward Europe.[27] In any case, the Arusha Programme demonstrated
the G-77's profound frustration with the course of the dialogue, following Kissinger's laundry list of promises in 1975–76 and the Carter administration's inability (or, as many in the South saw it, unwillingness) to follow through on its
own renewed pledges to increase official development aid, open US markets to
Southern competition, and provide financing and loans on better terms.[28] "The
phase of petition is over," the G-77 ministers reiterated in their joint statement.
"That of organized practical action must begin."[29]

In its own preparations, the Carter administration effectively declared the
negotiations over before they began. "We believe that by UNCTAD V, if agreement on the Common Fund can be reached, commodity and debt issues will
move off center stage," the State Department predicted in late 1978. "New issues, however, will emerge to fill the agenda. We want to be in a position to
guide the selection of issues and shape the way in which they are addressed."[30]

In the meantime, US officials developed a list of alternative proposals for a
post-UNCTAD North-South agenda. The objective was to move the dialogue
beyond the South's persistent emphasis on international economic structures
and resource transfers—basically, what Northern states could do for Southern
states—and toward "the alleviation of the worst physical aspects of poverty
[and] the promotion of self-sustaining growth with equity"—what Southern
states, with Northern states' targeted assistance, could do for their own citizens. For the State Department, the South's adherence to the NIEO's structural
agenda and unenthusiastic reception of basic needs was the dialogue's "central
irony"; although "it ostensibly centers on development, development per se is

almost never discussed." More important, a basic needs or development-focused approach to the dialogue would be "politically appealing, economically sound and domestically supportable," in a way that the previous strategy of limited concessions to G-77 institutional demands—for example, the Common Fund—had not been.[31]

Vance introduced the new US policy in a March 1979 address titled "America's Commitment to Third World Development." The speech contained the usual nods to the necessity of international cooperation in an interdependent world, the United States' commitment to working with developing countries toward a more just economic order, and so on. Vance also listed several accomplishments of Carter's first two years, including expansion of the IMF's lending capacities; new individual commodity agreements for coffee, tin, and sugar; easing of the debt burdens of some least developed countries; and Carter's proposed International Development Cooperation Authority (IDCA), intended to streamline the administration of US foreign assistance.[32]

However, two features stood out. First, Vance made it clear that the United States would no longer pretend to accept the NIEO's premises, dismissing "alterations in the international system and resource transfers among nations [as] ends in themselves." In other words, the United States would not affix its name to any more new institutions controlled by the South. Second, Vance indicated that the United States' UNCTAD V agenda would be just as one-sided as the Arusha Programme. From that point on, he declared, US policy would address only "practical ways to meet human needs" in the areas of energy, food, health, and technology. Vance stopped short of saying that the US government opposed more multilateral development assistance (i.e., official development aid) in principle. Instead, Vance blamed that on the "American people," who "will never be convinced that there is an inherent value only in resource flows among nations." He added, in a line straight from Carter's 1976 campaign: "They want to know, and have a right to know, how their taxes are being used to better the lives of people abroad."[33]

One month after Vance's speech, five thousand delegates and officials from more than two hundred states and international organizations met in the brand-new Philippine International Convention Center in Manila for UNCTAD V. The Manila program (adapted from Arusha) was complex, even by UNCTAD standards. The conference agenda listed more than a dozen categories, including interdependence, trade, monetary and financial issues, technology transfer, economic cooperation among developing countries, and measures for the least developed countries, with numerous subcategories for each.

At UNCTAD IV, in a major policy reversal, Kissinger had endorsed the G-77's Integrated Programme for Commodities, establishing a path toward the

Common Fund. The developed countries would drag their feet in subsequent negotiations—as the developing countries did not hesitate to point out—but at least in theory, the G-77 had made real progress toward its long-standing goal of giving UNCTAD an actual mandate in international economic policy.[34]

The South's hope for Manila was to extend this mandate and bring about structural change in other areas controlled by developed countries, ranging from trade and finance to food and technology. This was the reason for the proliferation of agenda items, UNCTAD's secretary-general Gamani Corea explained: "In fact, structural change was not only the theme of each agenda item: it was also the subject of a separate agenda item which was intended to provide a conceptual frame for the Conference and in the context of which the international community was invited to confirm its conviction that structural changes were needed and to set up a mechanism for keeping issues in this field under review, particularly issues arising out of the interdependence of problems in the field of trade, money, and development."[35] This affirmed the UNCTAD leadership's commitment to the NIEO's most basic objective: the redistribution of *political* power in international economic relations.

Per Vance's speech, US negotiators pursued the opposite. A State Department official involved in the negotiations summarized the US position: "The specifics varied from issue to issue, but the policy remained the same: no funds, no institutions, no expansion of UNCTAD, no change in the present system, no impairment of U.S. autonomy, no increased international management, no invasion of the private sector." On commodities—which accounted for more than 80 percent of developing countries' exports (95 percent for the least developed countries)—the United States rejected G-77 proposals for new "comprehensive frameworks" for marketing and distribution (though true to Vance's promise, it remained committed to completing Common Fund negotiations). On debt, the United States rejected G-77 proposals for a separate commission that included creditors, still insisting that there was "no generalized debt problem" among developing countries (although it did agree to retroactive term adjustments for seriously indebted countries). Where they could, US negotiators stressed Washington's hope that "the North-South dialogue would address the real issues of development [i.e., basic needs] rather than engage in sterile rhetoric." Thus, the United States supported the comprehensive new program of action for least developed countries, based on the mutual recognition that most of the development programs of the 1960s had neither grown their economies nor improved their living standards. The final resolution matched the US commitment to double its level of official development assistance in three years (the same proposal Vance had made at the CIEC) with a pledge for aid to meet "social objectives," apparently a reference to basic needs.[36]

Considering that both sides expected conflict, the State Department equated stalemate with success. "Sweeping resolutions demanding major restructuring of the world's economy went nowhere," one official reported to Vance, and the conference "ended on a quiet note with no strong recriminations on the part of the G-77."[37] However, this had less to do with Southern satisfaction with the conference's results than with Southern disunity over the topic of energy.

Oil prices had been a source of tension within the Southern coalition since 1974. Both the Ford and Carter administrations maintained that OPEC's actions hurt poor countries even more than rich ones. Energy was so controversial that, despite its obvious importance for global development, it appeared nowhere in UNCTAD V's official agenda. However, UN secretary-general Kurt Waldheim made the energy-development link in his plenary address. A few days later, Ambassador Young argued that "global development had been seriously retarded" by high energy prices and noted the "cruel irony" for "the most underdeveloped countries who are least able to bear it."[38]

Meanwhile, oil-importing developing countries were losing patience. In 1975 the Tanzanian minister of commerce accused OPEC of "appearing to turn their backs on the developing countries, particularly the least developed," after another 10 percent price increase. OPEC *had* promised hundreds of millions in aid through several new multilateral agencies, but these entities were just beginning to function. Further, there was a hierarchy: the first round of aid went almost exclusively to countries with Muslim majorities, while the rest had to wait for a second wave of funds.[39] This explained in part other UN activities, such as the infamous November 1975 General Assembly resolution equating Zionism with racism: African states with large Islamic populations voted for the resolution, and most of the others abstained, were absent, or voted against the resolution. The State Department wrote at the time: "The Africans had been led to believe that they would receive far more aid than they actually have from the Arabs, in return for breaking relations with Israel and voting sympathetically on Arab causes. In fact, the Arabs have done very little at all in the area of aid to Africa, and that has not been lost on the Africans."[40]

The first Southern delegation to bring up energy at UNCTAD V was from Latin America. At the plenary session of the Interdependence Commission, the head of the Colombian delegation insisted that energy be brought under UNCTAD's mandate. Other Latin American delegations soon joined Colombia, placing Venezuela, which had positioned itself as a leader of both OPEC and the G-77, in the uncomfortable role of mediator. The resolution was squashed, as Venezuela promised to discuss the energy-development relationship at OPEC's next meeting (which it did), but this crack in the Southern front was visible and undeniable.[41] Indeed, two months after UNCTAD V, the Organization of African Unity expressed its frustration with OPEC by refusing to condemn Egypt's rapprochement with Israel and giving Anwar Sadat a standing ovation.[42] "Manila may mark the end of discussing this issue [energy] in North-South fora," the State Department noted optimistically, "although industrial countries will have to approach this issue with great caution."[43]

In the Carter administration's defense, its open rejection of further structural reforms through UNCTAD was more honest than Kissinger's announcement of dozens of initiatives without the political capital, time, or interest to back them up. But UNCTAD V was the first of several important conferences that would determine which direction the dialogue would take in the future. The State Department believed this would largely depend on how well the United States delivered in the areas in which it *had* promised new things. At a minimum, State explained, this meant "doing everything possible within the Executive Branch and on the Hill to keep development assistance and food aid at respectable levels, to fight trade protectionism, and to secure legislation implementing commodity agreements."[44]

It also meant a strong US performance in August at the UN Conference on Science and Technology for Development—the second half of Cooper and Vance's strategy for "sustaining broad-based support for foreign assistance with the American public."[45]

UNCSTD: A Case Study

The UNCSTD was not the most important component of the North-South dialogue, but its status as the last large global conference of the 1970s—and there had been many—conferred special significance. "Like the Vienna SALT [Strategic Arms Limitation Talks] II summit," explained one writer in *Science News*, "UNCSTD . . . culminates years of planning and many rounds of preliminary discussions between the nations involved. And like SALT, issues for the UNCSTD summit have been brought into focus only after years of growingly contentious rhetoric—much of it with little common ground in sight."[46]

In spite of the North's conference fatigue and the South's past disappointments, there were good reasons to see promise in the UNCSTD. First—and this is easily overlooked in the battles over the Common Fund, debt, and energy—technology was the first point listed in the NIEO declaration: "The benefits of technological progress are not shared equitably by all members of the international community. The developing countries, which constitute 70 per cent of the world's population, account for only 30 per cent of the world's income."

The South's paucity of qualified scientists and engineers and its dependence on multinational corporations were explicitly linked in that first full paragraph to colonial and postcolonial underdevelopment. In fact, as one study of the history of sustainable development argues, in the 1960s "the power of large-scale technologies to increase productivity, generate wealth, and overcome persistent material scarcity" was one of the few postwar development "faiths" shared by Western and Third World leaders.[47] Thus, the NIEO called for "giving to the developing countries access to the achievements of modern science and technology, and promoting the transfer of technology and the creation of indigenous technology for the benefit of the developing countries."[48]

Second, US officials had been telling the Third World for years that concrete actions on specialized economic topics (including technology transfer) were best left to small, focused gatherings rather than the UNCTAD and General Assembly meetings covering a dozen or more issues simultaneously. Although the UNCSTD would be a political conference in the sense that the developing countries saw it as part of the NIEO (it originated at the 1975 UN Seventh Special Session), the focus on technology and support of the scientific community suggested that grandstanding might be kept to a minimum. Nor would there be the intractable issue of energy, which had so divided North and South at the 1974 World Food Conference and the 1975–77 CIEC and the South itself at UNCTAD V.

Third, the idea of sharing scientific ideas with developing countries—as opposed to merely sending more US taxpayer dollars—was arguably the most domestically attractive North-South policy Carter could have. It fit neatly with one of his favorite lines about development from the campaign trail: "I don't think it's right to tax the poor people in our rich country and give the money to the rich people in the poor countries." This position had a long presidential pedigree beginning with Democrat Harry Truman, who, the State Department noted approvingly, "is the President . . . [Carter] admires most." In fact, State argued, Truman's 1949 "Point Four" program for technology transfer "represented the beginnings of our development-oriented foreign aid program."[49] More important, given the economic climate—the UNCSTD would convene just a few weeks after Carter's "Crisis of Confidence" speech and in the midst of soaring domestic energy costs and inflation—it was probably the only foreign assistance measure that could gain bipartisan support in Congress.

Finally, technology transfer had long been a priority for the politically influential but diplomatically elusive Southern countries the Carter administration referred to as "regional influentials." Also called the "advanced developing countries," these countries "were expected to play key roles in leading the other

100 or so Third World nations to a fuller, more just, and more cooperative membership in the much-discussed interdependent world."[50] Integrating (or co-opting) members of this group by granting them a more prominent position in the existing international order was an important part of North-South strategy as outlined in PRM-8, and in September 1977 Carter made a much-publicized tour of Brazil, Nigeria, India, Iran, and Venezuela—the original regional influentials—to signal this priority. Although Carter's actions on the Panama Canal, Middle East peace, and apartheid helped, the United States had less to offer these countries on the economic side. "These are countries which do not need our financial assistance and for which we find it increasingly difficult to justify financial assistance," the State Department explained. "We can, nonetheless, emphasize our willingness to engage in technological collaboration, to help train people, and to help establish applied research facilities in those countries, provided they are willing to bear much of the cost. At the same time, this approach complements well our emphasis on basic human needs—food, health, education—in our foreign assistance programs."[51]

The Carter administration had a strong scientific bent, and some of its most important members sought to link science and technology to foreign policy in new ways. It began with the president himself, a trained nuclear engineer who believed nuclear weapons were the greatest threat to world peace. Carter tasked Gerard Smith, his chief delegate to SALT, with "finding a way of using the U.S. hegemony in nuclear technology to impose conditions on the use of this technology by other countries." Harold Brown had been a government research scientist and president of Cal Tech, and as Carter's defense secretary he led a massive increase in the Pentagon's funding for research in microelectronics, computers, and jet engines to modernize the US military.[52] Brzezinski, Carter's most trusted foreign policy adviser, had earlier envisioned a new "technetronic era" in which intergovernmental collaboration on science and technology would strengthen ties among advanced capitalist nations and with influential members of the developing world.[53] In fact, technology played an important role in the establishment of official diplomatic relations between the United States and China. After visiting Beijing in May 1978, Brzezinski was convinced that the sale of advanced technology could break the negotiations logjam, and a number of visits by leading US scientists followed. On January 31, 1979—thirty days after the United States officially recognized China and seven months before the UNCSTD—the two countries signed a major science and technology agreement that paved the way for China's rapid industrial takeoff and global economic integration.[54]

One of the Americans Brzezinski sent to Beijing was not a scientist but a Catholic priest. In addition to serving as president of the University of Notre

Dame (1952–87), Father Theodore Hesburgh had been an active member of the liberal establishment for decades. Director of the US Commission on Civil Rights, chairman of the Rockefeller Foundation, and director of the Council on Foreign Relations and Chase Manhattan Bank were just a few of his other roles. In 1977 Carter asked Hesburgh to lead the US delegation to the UNC-STD. Hesburgh had shown a long-standing interest in science and foreign policy as the Vatican's permanent representative to the International Atomic Energy Agency (1957–70) and as a board member of the National Science Foundation (1954–66). However, in the 1970s the activity that took up most of Hesburgh's time outside of South Bend—and one that he managed well as a highly organized workaholic—was chairman of the Overseas Development Council.

The ODC was the most prominent and visible proponent of a basic needs approach to development.[55] "A major rethinking of development concepts is taking place," ODC president James Grant explained in 1971, two years after the group's founding, "compelled by a single fact: the unparalleled growth rates achieved by most developing countries during the 1960's had little or no effect on most of the world's people, who continue to live in desperate poverty." By favoring large landowners, civil servants, and skilled industrial workers, he argued, the development process empowered interests with a disincentive for a large-scale redistribution of wealth, while countries that had introduced massive welfare programs could no longer pay for them. A "new development strategy," Grant insisted, would increase the poorer half of the population's position in the development process by supporting small farmers and entrepreneurs, making the best use of scarce capital and technology, and ensuring the availability of basic education and health care.[56]

Grant's observations matched those of other development experts, such as British economist Barbara Ward, who championed "participatory development" from the International Institute for Environment and Development in London, and Pakistani economist Mahbub ul-Haq, a senior adviser at the World Bank who was selling basic needs to the bank's president Robert McNamara. (The ODC engineered collaborations with both scholars.[57]) Their ideas received a major public relations boost from the 1973 international best seller *Small Is Beautiful* by British economist E. F. Schumacher. His argument that the one-size-fits-all development model of the 1960s had major social and ecological consequences found a wide following among the nascent environmental movement, which applauded his call for intermediate (or appropriate) technology that was localized, participatory, and environmentally sustainable.

Hesburgh's job was to make the case for new development assistance to the American public, whose support for foreign aid had been in steady decline since the Johnson administration's escalation of the Vietnam War. "You are probably the most influential Churchman on the American scene at the present time," ODC director Martin Bordelon wrote to Hesburgh in May 1971, when the priest replaced the relatively orthodox former World Bank president Eugene Black as the ODC's chairman of the board. (Hesburgh was succeeded in 1980 by McNamara.) "Given your base, and your performance, you are one of the most influential citizens of the U.S." But there was another way Hesburgh could help the ODC's cause: the decision to decline government funding meant that it was heavily dependent on corporate contributions from Bank of America and Bechtel to United Fruit and Xerox. "ODC has too much of the image and identification with American big business," Bordelon explained, "and you would help give it a different orientation."[58]

Hesburgh did just that, appearing frequently on television news and radio programs, authoring op-eds, and staging high-profile media events around the ODC's *Agenda for Action* releases.[59] He testified to Congress in support of the 1973 "New Directions" legislation, a bill introduced by Minnesota congressman Donald Fraser that included a "Basic Human Needs Mandate" in foreign aid appropriations. A few weeks after the NIEO's announcement in May 1974, Hesburgh appeared on NBC's *The Today Show* with Pakistan's ambassador to the UN, where he informed Barbara Walters that the "fourth world of about a billion people . . . are going to starve to death if we don't do something about it."[60] When the World Food Conference convened that November, Hesburgh and Grant organized their own press conference with representatives from religious and food advocacy groups and called the Ford administration's proposals inadequate. Congress agreed to publish Hesburgh's correspondence with Ford, and Walter Cronkite devoted the last six minutes of his newscast to Hesburgh and the ODC conference, making them both household names—as much as a development NGO and a Catholic priest could be.[61]

The ODC and the Carter administration were a natural fit. Their official collaboration began during the 1976 campaign, when Grant started working with Brzezinski and Richard Gardner to write remarks critical of Ford's approach to food aid for the candidates' foreign policy debates in October. After Carter's election, ODC senior fellows Roger Hansen and Guy Erb joined the NSC's new North-South cluster, and several other members of the administration, including Brzezinki, Gardner, Cooper, and Samuel Huntington, attended the ODC's ongoing series of development seminars for "selected individuals who are not development specialists."[62]

The ODC's impact was particularly visible during the reorganization of the United States' North-South strategy through 1977. In fact, Hansen was the first in the administration to argue that basic needs "should become the centerpiece of our North-South strategy" and should "not only be a natural complement but also an integral part of a *global stress* on human rights." He wrote in a memorandum to Brzezinski in July: "North and South have long feuded over the divergent emphases in the Universal Declaration of Human Rights: the North emphasizing personal, civil and political rights; the developing countries, basic economic rights (needs). The US can take a major step toward closing this 'values gap' by embracing *jointly* the concepts of human rights and basic human needs, and by proposing a major development program to see that the fulfillment of basic human needs is achieved throughout the world by the end of the century."[63] This concept was endorsed by Secretary Vance at the next meeting of the interagency North-South Policy Review Committee, which concluded, "The fulfillment of basic human needs should be considered as an integral element of the fulfillment of human rights. The two closely related concepts can and should form a central core of US foreign policy."[64] It made sense that Carter chose Notre Dame's spring 1977 commencement to give the first major outline of his foreign policy, with human rights and development as central themes.

Hesburgh offered the same utility to Carter as he did to the ODC: he was the United States' most prominent clergyman, with the connections, charisma, intellect, and moral authority to give complicated development issues the clarity and urgency necessary to make Americans care. Both the State Department and the NSC had been arguing for Carter to take his foreign aid agenda to the American people—the same mission the ODC had been engaged in since 1969. "The Overseas Development Council and others are working on 'basic human needs' approaches to foreign assistance which could call for very large increases of aid from the industrial world, targeted for nations that agreed to concentrate efforts against hunger, local endemic diseases, lack of housing, etc.," the State Department explained in an early PRM-8 meeting around the same time Hesburgh was chosen to lead the US delegation to the UNCSTD. "The emphasis on serving the poor could help sell the increases in spending necessary to have the kinds of effects that the new Club of Rome report and the World Bank claim are possible."[65] If Hesburgh could not help Carter sell his vision of development—to Americans *and* to the G-77—could anyone?

Accounts of the US performance at the UNCSTD vary widely. Robert Olson, a former State Department official who attended UNCTAD IV, writes that the Carter administration "quite possibly provided more support to the Vienna conference [UNCSTD] than to any of the other UN megaconferences." Although the United States opposed most LDC demands, Olson notes that its own proposals demonstrated a genuine effort to respond to the needs of both poor and middle-income countries and to improve the North-South dialogue in a meaningful way.[66] In contrast, David Dickson argues that Hesburgh delivered a "corporate sermon that directly reflected the corporate community's input into the State Department's preparations"; as at UNCTAD V, the primary US goal was to contain the South's demands for structural reform and political redistribution.[67] In Stephen Macekura's account, the US delegation quickly downplayed its focus on basic needs and appropriate technology when the G-77, fearing the loss of technology transfers for industrial capacity building, reacted negatively. Appropriate technology "became only a small part of the conference, with few policy makers believing that it was a silver bullet capable of reinventing the development process. . . . It ended up as just another method to draw upon from the ever-growing pool of development approaches."[68]

A closer look into the preparations—based on the newly accessible Hesburgh papers[69]—reveals more complicated interactions between development and appropriate technology, between the United States and the G-77, and between Hesburgh and Carter. US planning began early, in October 1977, and the first issue of contention was location. Mexico wanted to have the conference in a developing country, for which, according to UN ambassador Young, there was little support. "Delegates of developing countries who want our candidacy to succeed . . . have told us—straight out—that this Mexican effort can be headed off," he wrote to Vance. "They believe that even the Latin American Group, theoretically committed to Mexico, contains many lukewarm supporters who are interested in hearing from us."[70]

Initial conversations between the US delegation and the White House were also encouraging. After meeting with Peter Bourne, the new head of Carter's ill-fated World Hunger Working Group, US delegation coordinator Jean Wilkowski gushed to ODC president Grant, "There is now less question in my mind regarding whether B[asic] H[uman] N[eed]s and the subject matter of this Conference will 'soar' under this Administration. The evidence of ODC influence and talent were strong."[71] Grant was more skeptical, writing to Wilkowski that Carter had yet to "pursue aggressively the address of basic needs." However, Grant believed that Carter had a unique opportunity to connect with Americans on the issue. In 1977 Schumacher embarked on a US tour for his best-selling book, and Carter received him at the White House for a well-publicized visit. "'Small is Beautiful' was written originally to meet the needs of poor people in developing countries, but obviously has touched a major-felt need in this country," Grant explained. "There is something potentially very exciting here. It was this 'nerve' that Schumacher touched."[72]

Still, at that time, few leaders of developing countries had openly embraced the United States' efforts with regard to appropriate technology. Tanzania's Julius Nyerere, whose struggling *Ujamaa* plan also focused on community building, was an exception. Their skepticism was not unwarranted: by 1980, USAID's efforts in Tanzania—contracted out to a private firm called Development Alternatives Inc., over which it exercised little oversight—had run into major problems, from excessive billing and internal compensation to flat-out inattention to appropriate technology's sustainability mandate.[73] The complicated relationship was well illustrated by a December 1977 exchange in Washington between State Department officials and Third World scientists. "With only a little prompting," the report described, scientists from Afghanistan to Zaire set forth their views on technology transfer, appropriate technology, and the UNCSTD for four and a half hours. Scientists from poorer developing countries endorsed appropriate technology, but their overwhelming focus was on attaining better training and administration. "Technology transfer without competence is useless," explained an engineer from Kabul University. "If the developed countries really want to help us, they should raise our technical competence." Yet sending citizens to study in US universities was not enough. "We have trained many countrymen in S&T [science and technology] in the United States, but they bring back knowledge that cannot be applied in our undeveloped state," a scientist from Ghana noted. There were also problems with US projects on the ground; an Indonesian professor criticized the makeup of USAID project budgets as "70% administration." Nor were project managers as attentive to local knowledge and needs as they purported to be. The Trinidadian director of the Caribbean Industrial Research Institute explained how USAID workers had recently installed rural power systems for farmers who could not afford the electricity costs; in another case, they built a highway on a rain-swept mountain slope that washed away three times. "In the future," said the head of Zaire's Ministry of Planning, "the U.S. should not spend 80% of its training money in the U.S. It should spend some money for training in third [world] countries. We could learn a lot in some middle income countries."[74]

As expected, scientists from richer developing countries emphasized technology transfer for industrial development. "Although we are still very much a developing country," an Indian scientist explained, "we have the third largest body of trained scientists in the world. We can put the imported technology to work." Perhaps less expected was an emphasis on sustainable growth, which, according to conventional wisdom, industrializing Third World states were opposed to or uninterested in. "U.S. science and technology is losing its position as the leader to be followed," said a South Korean engineer, "because U.S. science and technology is used to support an economy which wastes resources. Developing countries need S&T that can be applied to conserve resources needed to produce for export."[75]

Their criticisms of actual US policies notwithstanding, the scientists' comments revealed several areas of practical compromise. More effective aid administration, better technical training, and encouragement of local participation and self-ownership were all declared goals of US aid policy since the 1973 Foreign Assistance Act. However, the US would be negotiating with G-77 diplomats, not scientists, and its own strategic efforts were off to a dismal start.

Carter had muddied the waters with a new organization he championed: the Institute for Scientific and Technical Cooperation (ISTC). The seeds for such an initiative had been planted before Carter; Kissinger had proposed a US-funded International Industrialization Institute at the 1975 UN Seventh Special Session. However, there were two important differences. First, Carter's ISTC would focus on transferring alternative technology and knowledge, instead of the more conventional technology transfers Kissinger (and the wealthier G-77 leadership) had in mind. (Kissinger's International Industrialization Institute had also pledged to address the "brain drain" resulting from US-educated students remaining in the States—a concern of developing countries regardless of income.)[76] Second, instead of an independent body open to "all interested countries," the ISTC would exist as a semiautonomous agency within USAID, which was still struggling with its own Carter-induced reorganization pains.[77]

It was never really clear where the ISTC fit. The administration's intense courting of private-sector support worried USAID workers, who feared they would lose control of the ISTC's funding and purpose; at the same time, many corporate leaders were skeptical of backing yet another new government program for the Third World. The scientific community distrusted both the State Department and the private sector, believing that any new organization should be free from both politics and profit to the extent possible. Still, in the summer of 1979, shortly before the UNCSTD, Congress passed legislation approving the new institute. Importantly, no decision was made on its funding.[78]

While the administration promoted the ISTC to Congress, planning for the UNCSTD suffered. The official PRM on the subject was not launched until February 1978; in July, Grant called it a "roof without a house." PRM-33 made the ISTC—a program based in and controlled by Washington—the only new card in the US delegation's hand. Although the ISTC could be useful, Grant explained, the current US proposal "provides no sense of urgency" for what was supposed to be the most compelling social objective of Carter's approach to the South: the elimination of absolute poverty by the end of the century. Nor did it address the concerns of the influential middle-income countries at the conference, whose own proposals for industrial technology transfer the United States could not simply ignore. Gone, too, was any talk of interdependence or Northern countries' responsibility to avoid protectionism and pursue growth amid the global economic slowdown.[79] "There is general USG[overnment] consensus that the Conference contains several very contentious issues which are not and would not be sufficiently responded to by the US if we only presented the ISTC and the ongoing programs," the NSC's Erb warned special representative for economic summits Henry Owen on July 20, less than two months before Vienna. "If the Conference is to avoid a total collapse the US must be prepared to respond to the contentious issues in a moderate fashion."[80]

The most contentious issue was the G-77's proposal for a $2 billion to $4 billion UN science and technology fund.[81] This was not an insignificant sum, but the effect would have been to raise the Third World's share of the global research and development budget from 5 percent to 7 percent.[82] However, the G-77 insisted that this fund be governed by a committee of the whole, which would operate on the "one country, one vote" rule. Against the advice of the Treasury Department and the Office of Management and Budget (which favored no fund at all), on August 3, less than three weeks before the UNCSTD convened, Vance and Owen suggested a modest counterproposal: US funding of $25 million annually, or 20 percent of a two-year, $250 million fund administered through the UN Development Program (UNDP), where the United States had greater say.[83] However, before Hesburgh could sell this package to the G-77, he had to sell it to the rest of Carter's cabinet.

Enthusiasm was in short supply. "It will not embarrass the Administration," Owen assured Hesburgh when questioned on PRM-33's lack of concrete North-South goals. "Its weaknesses as a North-South political document are its strengths in avoiding domestic controversy."[84] A meeting with Brzezinski was more encouraging but noncommittal on getting anything more from the White House. Hesburgh's discussion with Secretary Blumenthal went nowhere, though it may have been the most honest. "In a nutshell," the treasury secretary said bluntly, "the President [is] 'broke.'"[85]

Hesburgh was in an awkward position. Chosen for his ability to sell the greater good to the self-interested, he now faced the prospect of going to the conference armed with little more than a homily. In July 1979 Carter went on national television to address the energy crisis, inflation, unemployment, and what he called a "crisis of confidence." That same month, White House staff scrubbed Carter's proposed address to the UNCSTD, replacing strong language on North-South relations and global poverty with, in Hesburgh's description, "banalities."[86]

On August 14 Hesburgh met with Vance to make one final plea for Carter's support. He began by recalling Vance's North-South address in March, in which

the secretary had committed the United States to focusing on "concrete development problems which we can tackle together and which directly affect
people's lives." The North-South dialogue was "prickly," Hesburgh conceded,
but he warned against "wishing the subject would go away by trying to avoid
references to [it]." This was why, in addition to the "limited [and] bilateral"
ISTC, the United States needed to fully support the UNDP plan. Not only was
it "ammunition" for the conference, Hesburgh explained. It also "would allow
us to do things that could not be done through bilateral assistance alone," such
as the UN-funded census project Hesburgh had witnessed while in China for
Brzezinski. Vance was sympathetic, agreeing with Hesburgh on the need for
"real leadership" and promising "that during the next year he intended to de-
vote much more time to North-South issues, which he felt he had been forced
to ignore because of higher priority subjects."[87] It was a fair enough answer.
While Carter and Brzezinski wooed the People's Republic of China with promises of Western technology and investment, Vance spent the first half of 1979
struggling to conclude the difficult and unpopular SALT II negotiations with
his Soviet counterpart. In December the Soviets shocked the West with their
brazen invasion of Afghanistan. For Brzezinski, "a major watershed had been
reached in the American-Soviet relationship." He told Carter that the invasion
was "the most direct case of Soviet military aggression since 1945, and that we
needed to mount a broader strategic response." Carter agreed, and he and
Brzezinski quickly redirected NSC resources toward the development of a new
Carter Doctrine that promised to do for the United States' autocratic allies in
the Middle East what the Truman Doctrine (Carter's favorite president) once
did for anticommunist allies in Greece and Turkey.[88]

As détente continued to deteriorate, the decline in Iran's oil output after
the shah's abdication had set off a panic in oil markets. Starting in April, the
price of global crude oil steadily increased for the next twelve months until it
hit an unprecedented $42 per barrel. Nor was trilateralism faring any better.
In Tokyo, G-7 leaders blamed one another for failing to reduce energy consumption and OPEC for "severely increas[ing] the problems facing developing countries without oil resources as well as the difficulties for developed
countries in helping them."[89] This provided a valuable lesson for the North-
South dialogue: even when the oil question was not immediately present, it
was never far away.

The last UN megaconference of the 1970s—and, as it turned out, the last
new negotiating conference of the North-South dialogue—proceeded like
many others before it. On August 20 four thousand delegates from 150 countries convened in Vienna for a fourteen-day conference on global poverty, at a
total cost of $50 million. Hesburgh deployed his moral argument for action

on technology for development, asking whether "we can really call ourselves a civilization when one-fourth of this earth's population lives in abject poverty, starving, idle, and numbed by ignorance." No one disagreed. A familiar pattern followed. The G-77 presented its main, NIEO-centric proposals for structural change: an international code of conduct for technology transfer, a universal science and technology information system within the UN, and a $2 billion research fund. The United States swatted these proposals down, and the Europeans followed suit. The United States did agree to an enlargement of the UN Economic and Social Council's (ECOSOC's) Committee on Science and Technology for Development into a committee of the whole. This gave the South equal representation on the UN's primary science and technology advisory committee, but to what end was unclear in the absence of a new fund.[90]

Predictably, the G-77 kept up the discussion of its $2 billion fund, giving the United States little space to argue the ISTC's merits. The G-77 accused the United States of not wanting any new fund; not denying the charge, the United States complained to the press that "the developing countries had been slow in making their own preparations for the conference."[91] Days later, Sweden proposed the UNDP fund as a compromise, and the US delegation "clarified" its position in support. However, it rejected the G-77's call (backed by some European countries) that the newly enlarged ECOSOC committee have a role in administering the UNDP fund. This was important, as the UNDP did not operate as a committee of the whole and thus was weighted toward the developed countries. In other words, the G-77 was granted a voice—the enlarged ECOSOC committee—with no money, and it was granted some money—the UNDP fund—with no greater voice. The G-77 decried the "serious blow" dealt to the conference by "one major power," but on August 29, two days before the conference ended, it accepted the proposal as is—the best it could get.[92] Once again, the United States seemed to be the rich countries' lowest common denominator, forced into offering only qualified support for what was supposed to be the conference's main achievement.

The US delegation did not exercise real leadership at the UNCSTD, as Hesburgh had hoped, but it was hardly equipped to. For two years the White House's main offer had been the ISTC, which Congress approved in July but without any promise of funding. In a final options paper sent to Carter on August 2, Vance promised a new presidential directive for him to sign that "could be cited by our delegation at the Vienna Conference as further evidence of our commitment to doing more for the developing countries in this area." Either Vance never sent the directive or the president never signed it. Carter approved the reiteration of calls at the Tokyo summit for an increase in bilateral aid to assist in energy production and expanded bilateral and multilateral aid for agricultural research, but with no specific budget commitments. Vance also relayed Hesburgh's concerns about the UNDP and cited the recommendation of representative Clement Zablocki, a key congressional ally for Carter's foreign aid proposals, that the United States immediately begin consultations with the House Appropriations Committee. Carter left that line of the options paper blank.[93]

This too was a mistake. The UNDP fund actually had many supporters on Capitol Hill. Nearly two dozen US senators and representatives, including Adlai Stevenson, traveled to Vienna as part of the US delegation, far more than had attended the 1974 World Food Conference. The UNDP's administrator, Bradford Morse, was a liberal Republican former congressman from Massachusetts and UN undersecretary-general. The United States should be doing more than "just reacting," lamented one member of the House Science Committee on the eve of the delegation's departure. "We should be bold. We should be leading the way."[94] But the White House was never really behind the UNDP fund, even with the provision limiting the Third World's expanded committee to an advisory role. Thus, it was no surprise when Congress rejected the (even lower) $15 million in Carter's 1981 budget request.[95] With the ISTC's funding still held up in Congress (it never materialized, and the project languished in USAID until it officially folded in the early 1990s), the United States spent more on its delegation's travel and lodging for the UNCSTD than it did on its own initiatives.

The importance the Carter administration placed on North-South relations, particularly in its first two years, was part of an attempt to transcend the postwar Cold War framework for US foreign policy. "The U.S. has to help in the shaping of a new international system that cannot be confined to the developed countries but must involve increasingly the entire international community of more than 150 nation states," Brzezinski informed Carter in April 1977.[96] "We can no longer have a policy solely for the industrial nations as the foundation of global stability, but we must respond to the new reality of a politically awakening world," Carter repeated in his famous Notre Dame speech a few weeks later. "It is a new world, and we should help to shape it. It is a new world that calls for a new American foreign policy—a policy based on constant decency in its values and on optimism in our historical vision."[97]

There were some notable successes. Carter earned the support of Latin American democrats by concluding the Panama Canal treaties and shaming human rights abusers; he brokered a peace between Egypt and Israel that continues to hold more than forty years later; and he enabled China's global economic integration through official diplomatic recognition and a major economic treaty. There were glaring inconsistencies too. Carter was silent on human rights abuses in Iran, South Korea, and China, and his administration repeatedly intervened when congressional restrictions on loans and arms sales threatened important bilateral objectives. For instance, in November 1979 Vance and Cooper convinced Congress to "eliminate outright or ease a number of constraints on our use of development and security assistance in areas where Soviet and Cuban activity is growing," including several restrictions on the president's ability to use peacekeeping and development funds for military aid.[98] Still, that Carter looked to the Third World as more than a staging ground for Cold War proxy battles was a qualitative change from his postwar predecessors.

Carter administration officials expected that this reformed approach to the Third World would also improve the North-South dialogue. It did not. "Unfortunately," the National Security Council admitted in October 1978, "there is very little feedback among these realms, except to the extent that the broad atmosphere of trust and confidence has probably reduced somewhat the bitterness our economic 'shortcomings' would otherwise have evoked."[99] In fact, in some important cases, the pursuit of global North-South objectives related to human rights and nuclear nonproliferation worsened bilateral ties with regional influentials such as India and Brazil.[100]

The administration's flagship North-South economic initiatives fared even worse. Expectations were already high when Carter entered office, evidenced by the fact that in mid-1976 developing countries had delayed the conclusion of the Conference on International Economic Cooperation until after January 1977. But there was a flip side to the Carter team's mock-superhero pledge to "make the world safe for interdependence," and it involved changing the terms of the North-South dialogue itself. "The CIEC is an early phase of our attempt to refashion the North-South dialogue along our preferred lines," the State Department explained in February 1977. "Our long-term objective is to modify the North-South dialogue and move it away from [an] emphasis on restructuring the international economic system to a pragmatic search for ways to improve it."[101]

In the lull between the end of the CIEC in June 1977 and the opening of UNCTAD V in May 1979, "pragmatic" came to mean basic needs–oriented development assistance. "Far from being a moralistic glint in campaigner Jimmy Carter's eye," proclaimed the Washington Post, "the idea has progressed to becoming routine rhetoric in his administration's pronouncements on foreign aid."[102] Carter drew from a swell of support for basic needs in Congress and the development and scientific communities. He made intentional gestures to influential advocates such as E. F. Schumacher and Mahbub ul-Haq, and the administration's North-South cluster incorporated both ideas and personnel from the Overseas Development Council, the United States' leading basic needs–focused think tank. In meetings with influential G-77 leaders such as Venezuela's Carlos Andres Pérez and Jamaica's Michael Manley, he emphasized basic needs as a common goal in the North-South dialogue. To underline his commitment, Carter also announced a sweeping reorganization of US aid efforts.

The problems with this new strategy began at home. The International Development Cooperation Authority, Carter's flagship proposal to reorient foreign aid around long-term and shared objectives, was as ambitious as it was unpopular with the thirty-one agencies scrambling to retain influence over their respective areas of US aid policy. "The president's recent proposal to reorganize U.S. foreign assistance is weak as a result of bureaucratic distrust and 'turf protection' and requires strengthening if U.S. efforts to combat hunger and poverty are to be taken seriously," complained the head of the President's Commission on World Hunger, a separate initiative launched around the same time as the IDCA.[103]

The two soon found themselves working at cross-purposes. When the President's Commission on World Hunger recommended in December 1979 that the United States "make the elimination of hunger the primary focus of its relationships with the developing countries" and that the president ask Congress for an increase in aid for "the economic and technical aspects of development assistance and not . . . security assistance," Carter was telling Vance to do the opposite.[104] "Working closely with Henry Owen and [US]AID," Vance reported to his boss triumphantly, "we have succeeded in getting Congress to eliminate outright or ease a number of constraints on our use of development and security assistance in areas where Soviet and Cuban activity is growing."[105]

More fundamental problems awaited in the dialogue itself. It was not that there was *no* support for a basic needs approach in the South. Most Southern scientists backed this approach, as did an increasing number of Southern economists in the UN. In fact, as Samuel Moyn explains, in the years 1975–77, basic needs "took the United Nations system by storm." This was particularly true in the International Labor Organization, whose "move to basic needs occurred out of the recognition that it made little sense to adapt a strategy devised for northern industrial conflicts without recognizing the entirely different organization of labor and production" in the South.[106]

Even the G-77's Arusha Programme for UNCTAD V endorsed the analogous concept of "appropriate technology for development" for the numerically superior least developed countries.[107] The primary area of disagreement—and it was a fundamental one—concerned governance: Should new antipoverty efforts proceed through the same channels as past development assistance—that is, bilaterally through USAID and, to a lesser degree, through multilateral institutions such as the World Bank and certain UN agencies where US influence was greatest? Or should new UN agencies be formed that, by operating as committees of the whole, would enable the South to set its own priorities and determine its own needs? To put it simply: how much say should poor states have in the distribution of basic needs assistance?

Not much, Carter answered. This was consistent with his campaign line about not taking money from poor folks in the rich United States and giving it to rich folks in poor countries, and it aligned with the conservative objectives of the Treasury Department and Office of Management and Budget. It also reflected the influence of an anti-UN and anti–Third World attitude in the United States that had been growing since the first oil crisis but reached a crescendo with the infamous 1975 General Assembly resolution equating Zionism with racism. Americans had overwhelmingly endorsed UN ambassador Daniel Patrick Moynihan's naming and shaming of Third World dictators, and they supported President Ford's and Congress's threats to withdraw from the UN's politicized suborganizations.

Part choice and part political necessity, the Carter administration's basic needs package did not respond to the South's alienation from the *governance* of development. This was important beyond the North-South dialogue, for it reinforced the worst assumptions about the fundamental character of both US foreign aid and its role in fostering North-South cooperation. It affirmed the South's status as beggars and recipients of charity rather than as genuine partners in a common project, as Vance and Carter had once insisted. The argument that only the US government (and its contractors) could responsibly determine the distribution of aid was at odds with elementary basic needs objectives such as self-sufficiency, shared project accountability, and local participation and ownership.

Further, the basic needs strategy was never sufficient for negotiations with the diverse G-77 coalition. "There are plenty of poor people in regionally influential countries," one official explained, but "by definition, most of them have relatively large economies so that even very generous US aid programs make only a marginal impact of them—politically or economically."[108] Lacking some commitment to revising the institutional arrangements that affected those countries the most—in the Carter years, trade and debt—even the most generous basic needs proposals would be treated with skepticism. The NSC estimated interest payments on debt owed by the fourteen upper-tier developing countries since 1973 at $7 billion. By 1979, their annual payments on principal would rise to $16 billion, up 45 percent from 1975.[109] "I have emphasized to State that the initiatives in support of *internal* LDC development—

useful as they might be—do not respond adequately to the political dimension of the North-South dialogue," Erb told Brzezinski before UNCTAD V. "We believe that U.S. policy must also include a response to the *international* reforms that LDCs call for if we are to have a significant impact."[110] Or, as the president of (heavily indebted) Venezuela told Carter during his March 1978 visit to Caracas: "Concern over the poor is understood, but poverty is a symptom not a cause."[111]

Instead, US policy moved in the opposite direction. Separate UNCTAD negotiations to improve the ad hoc "Paris Club" arrangements for handling sovereign debt broke down over the G-77's insistence on the establishment of "an independent forum—which does not consist only of creditors—[that] could be given responsibility for supervising the negotiations."[112] At its core, the dispute over advanced developing countries' debt servicing was the same as the one over the least developed countries' basic needs: should developing countries have a greater say in matters of international economic governance that affect them most?

Again, the answer was no. At UNCTAD V, the United States rejected every G-77 proposal for new institutions or rule-making powers for developing countries. Instead of offering a counterproposal to the G-77's International Debt Commission (consisting of both debtors and creditors), the US delegation was instructed "not [to] accept any effort to study further individual proposals on debt issues (e.g., the debt commission, moratorium, indexation)."[113] By mid-1979, even the suggestion of institutional change had become controversial, as Hesburgh learned when he discovered the White House's last-minute revisions to Carter's UNCSTD address. "He [Hesburgh] would like to see included the Secretary's [Vance's] ideas on the North-South dialogue as expressed in his Seattle and Chicago speeches. Rather than disputing with the LDC's the issue of change in the international system, we should agree—as the Secretary had done in his landmark speeches—that the system needed changing and then get on with how North and South could collaborate in bringing this about. He [Hesburgh] recalled that Henry Kissinger had also de-fanged this issue [at UNCTAD IV] in Nairobi."[114]

The reference to Kissinger is instructive. The irony is that Kissinger may have been less sincere about his concern for the South's plight, yet he was much more willing to meet the South on its own terms in the dialogue. This mattered. During his 1976 trip to Africa, where he addressed UNCTAD IV—the first US cabinet member to do so—Kissinger spoke not of the social and economic rights African governments owed to their citizens but of the right of "the independent nations of Africa" to "the economic progress which will give meaning to their political independence and dignity to their struggle for equality."[115] Indeed, Ford administration neoliberals had been so opposed to Kissinger's flagship counterinitiatives—the world food reserve system and the International Resources Bank—because they appeared to legitimize the NIEO's claim that it was the global market system, not developing countries themselves, that needed to change. His political commitment to these initiatives was doubtful, and promising things the United States could not deliver was certainly a poor long-term strategy. Still, as frustrated Carter administration officials admitted in 1978, Kissinger's offers had "ended the rhetorical fireworks at the UN, led to the creation of CIEC, and, in effect, bought nearly three years for the beleaguered OECD countries."[116]

The North-South dialogue limped along in the UN for another year after UNCTAD V and the UNCSTD. Functional negotiations on a number of topics—the Common Fund, shipping, the law of the sea—continued in smaller forums, stalled by the same disagreements as before. Undeterred, the G-77 pushed ahead for a new round of "action oriented" and "global and sustained" negotiations to be launched at the Eleventh Special Session of the UN General Assembly in August 1980.[117]

Neither side budged, and on December 16, 1980, the negotiations were finally suspended "without agreement."[118] Carter had already lost the presidential election in November, and it was time for the administration to admit defeat: the South had not been persuaded that poverty within nations was more important than poverty between them, and the American public still had no convincing rationale for increasing foreign aid in the post-Vietnam, anti-UN era. "In policy terms," the NSC concluded in a lengthy and disappointed review of the administration's actions in those areas, "there is not much left beyond handling North-South issues on a case-by-case basis. This is of course how the Carter Administration—and Kissinger before then—handled them."[119]

CHAPTER 7

The Reagan Revolution and the End of the North-South Dialogue

National Security, Human Rights, and Free Markets

During the 1980 presidential campaign, Ronald Reagan and the Republicans characterized Jimmy Carter as a naïve do-gooder, handing out foreign aid to unfriendly left-wing governments while punishing reliable anticommunist allies in Latin America and elsewhere. According to the 1980 Republican Party platform, Carter's blind faith in détente had led him to dangerously underestimate the "scope and magnitude of the growth of Soviet military power [that] threatens American interest at every level." Instead, Reagan and the Republicans promised "peace through strength" by rearming the United States and its Third World allies while instituting a "bold program of tax rate reductions, spending restraints, and regulatory reforms that will inject new life into the economic bloodstream of this country."[1]

The elevation of the Soviet threat instantly transformed the South's position in US foreign policy. In a May 1981 commencement speech at Connecticut's Fairfield University, secretary of state Al Haig condemned the "recent American policy [under Carter]" that considered "economic and humanitarian assistance" enough to promote Third World development. Instead, "peaceful development" there required "security" against the constant threat of "illegal Soviet intervention"; in this way, US interventionism and support for authoritarian governments were both "task[s] of humanitarian concern" and preconditions for economic growth.[2] To that end, the administration immediately began lobbying Congress to turn back Carter-era restrictions on military assistance to regimes in Argentina, Chile, Guatemala, and Uruguay and instructed US representatives to multilateral development banks to approve new loans to right-wing governments in Latin America, South Korea, and the Philippines.[3]

Linking human rights and economic development in the South with hard-line anticommunism was representative of a larger co-option of human rights language by the administration, particularly after the appointment of Elliott Abrams as assistant secretary of state for human rights in December 1981. Americans disapproved of Carter's handling of the Iran crisis and its economic fallout, but concern for human rights remained high. According to one poll, 79 percent of respondents rated human rights somewhat or very important in 1978; in 1982, that number had climbed to 85 percent.[4] Abrams was well aware of these attitudes: before coming to the Reagan administration, he had served as chief of staff to neoconservative senator Daniel Patrick Moynihan.

Like Moynihan, Abrams had deep ties to anti-Carter neoconservatives. He had worked on senator Henry "Scoop" Jackson's unsuccessful campaign for the 1976 Democratic presidential nomination, and four years later he married Rachel Decter, daughter of neoconservative writer Midge Decter and step-daughter of *Commentary* editor Norman Podhoretz.[5] Moynihan's bombastic, moralizing attacks on the human rights records of the United States' Third World critics at the height of North-South conflict over the New International Economic Order (NIEO) proved enormously popular with Americans across the political spectrum. Reagan officials too recognized human rights' political utility for broader foreign policy goals. "We will never maintain wide public support for our foreign policy unless we can relate it to American ideals and to the defense of freedom," read a State Department memo on human rights written one week before Abrams's appointment.[6]

What was essentially a return to Eisenhower-era rollback in the Third World was therefore presented as a human rights campaign in support of prodemocracy forces opposed to the establishment of totalitarian Marxist regimes. As Abrams explained to the Council on Foreign Relations, "To prevent any country from being taken over by a communist regime is in our view a very real victory for the cause of human rights."[7] In practice, the administration's approach would continue to follow the blueprint laid out by its chief neoconservative intellectual: Reagan's 1980 campaign foreign policy adviser and subsequent UN ambassador Jeane Kirkpatrick. Her influential 1979 *Commentary* article "Dictatorships and Double Standards" justified support for right-wing authoritarian governments on the grounds that they could be reformed, while Marxist or totalitarian ones could not.

Kirkpatrick's was not a popular view. In fact, Abrams had been nominated for his post because the administration's first choice, the ultraconservative Ernest Lefever, had repeated Kirkpatrick's argument verbatim to the Senate Foreign Affairs Committee, resulting in his rejection.[8] Abrams, in contrast, was confirmed unanimously after a generous statement of support from Moynihan and Abrams's promise that "our foreign policy in general has human rights at its core."[9] Although the administration won some converts owing to its protests of political repression in Cuba, the Soviet Union, and the Eastern Bloc, its policies in the Third World were vehemently opposed by human rights groups in the United States and Europe. Ultimately, Abrams spent his tenure fighting off criticism from Freedom House (a longtime Moynihan ally) and other organizations about the administration's actions in Latin America. Abrams avoided prosecution during the Iran-Contra scandal by cooperating with federal prosecutors and eventually pleaded guilty to two charges of withholding information. He would later play a starring role in the 2003 Iraq war as a special assistant to president George W. Bush and senior director for democracy, human rights, and international operations in the National Security Council (NSC).[10]

The Reagan administration's economic policies toward the South were informed less by foreign policy concerns and more by a deep faith in the virtues of its domestic economic program. That program's goals—cutting taxes and spending, attacking inflation, and removing government regulations—were clearly, publicly, and often stated by the president, and they were epitomized in memorable quips such as, "The nine most terrifying words in the English language: 'I'm from the government, and I'm here to help'" and "Government is not the solution, government is the problem." David Stockman, in charge of the Office of Management and Budget (OMB) from 1981 to 1985, was a charismatic if controversial media figure who made "supply-side economics" a household term during debates over the signature 1981 Kemp-Roth tax cuts and Gramm-Latta spending bill.[11] Important work was also done by Nobel Prize–winning economist Milton Friedman, whose 1980 best seller *Free to Choose* was turned into a popular television series with Friedman and his wife Rose, as well as conservative "policy entrepreneurs" such as Arthur Laffer (author of the supply-side theory), *Wall Street Journal* columnist Jude Wanninski, and various individuals employed by the Heritage Foundation and other well-funded conservative think tanks.[12]

The administration's campaign against Keynesian economics at home led some critics to allege that, in one Reagan official's words, "it has no international economic policy save for carrying out its domestic program." The Reagan administration had "relegated international economics to a lower priority than any administration in the postwar period," determined political scientist Benjamin Cohen in 1983.[13] According to Paul Krugman, who served on Reagan's Council of Economic Advisers, top Reagan Treasury officials were notorious for their lack of expertise on international economic issues and were looked down on by their better-informed colleagues in the Federal Reserve.[14] These impressions were strengthened by Reagan's controversial—and to some, hypocritical—endorsement of import quotas on sugar, steel, and cars, as well as a reliance on foreign borrowing to pay for new military expenditures.

This criticism misses the point. Reagan's team may have had less experience and fewer academic credentials—the relative lack of PhDs was a striking contrast to the ultrabrainy Carter administration—but their philosophy toward international economic relations possessed a clear logic. Henry R. Nau, in charge of international economic affairs in the National Security Council from 1981 to 1983 and professor of political science at George Washington University, defended that philosophy as "domesticism," or "the simple proposition that the world economy is only as good as the national economies that compose it."[15]

According to Nau, the domesticists stood in contrast to the globalists of both parties who, in the 1970s, traced "global economic problems . . . largely to the malfunctioning of the international economic system itself." Globalists believed that external and inevitable structural factors—namely, other nations' rise in prosperity and assertiveness in the 1950s and 1960s—were to blame for declining US hegemony, leading the Nixon, Ford, and (especially) Carter administrations to look for solutions in new international economic arrangements from the G-7 summits to the North-South dialogue. For the domesticists, however, the culprit was unsound US fiscal and monetary policies in the late 1960s, which led to inflation that was first exported by increased borrowing and then compounded by the 1973 and 1979 oil shocks. In this sense, the United States was only as globally weak as it wanted to be: "Reestablishing sound U.S. domestic policies was the fulcrum for restoring the proper emphasis on price stability and market incentives in the world economy as a whole. Rather than ignoring the effects of U.S. policy changes in the world economy, domesticism stressed their global importance."[16]

For Reagan's economic officials, that importance extended to the developing world—and back. As Nau explained it, "Progress toward domestic stability and freer trade" in the South would "rejuvenate international financial flows" and give Northern investors "more predictable access to foreign markets." The expected result was the beginning of a virtuous circle of private investment and trade based on "real transfers of goods and services to be redeemed." Equally important, as direct investment in and commercial bank lending to poor countries increased, concessional lending from multilateral development banks "could then supplement these commercial flows rather than substitute for them." In this way, market reforms in the South would achieve two related goals: strengthen the legitimacy of international capital markets by making poor countries safe for foreign investment, and reduce US government funding of globalist mechanisms of North-South wealth transfer that encouraged fiscal irresponsibility and rent seeking, not unlike welfare payments to individuals.[17]

This is precisely the message Reagan delivered to the boards of governors of the World Bank and International Monetary Fund (IMF) in September 1981. The speech is mostly remembered for Reagan's insistence that what "[unites] societies which have achieved the most spectacular broad based economic progress . . . is their willingness to believe in the magic of the marketplace." The "magic" line is a trademark Reaganism, but the president also discussed several other policies with specific implications for North-South relations.[18]

First, Reagan asserted that both development and "political freedoms"—or human rights—were impossible without first establishing "economic freedom": "Those [societies] which put [economic] freedom as the first priority find they have also provided security and economic progress." This was a complete reversal of the Carter administration's formulation of basic human needs as economic rights: here, economic rights were reconfigured negatively as the ability to make business decisions free *from* government involvement, rather than the positive Carter formulation of the right *to* adequate housing, education, health care, and food. Poverty was no longer an offense to human rights if it occurred in the context of a free economy, nor was political repression if it guaranteed security against those who might impose restrictions on economic activity.

Second, Reagan argued that "the most important contribution any country can make to world development is to pursue sound economic policies at home."[19] This was a responsibility toward developing countries that the United States—"overspent, overtaxed, and overregulated, with the result being slow growth and soaring inflation"—had abnegated. The idea that a healthy North meant a healthy South was not new, having been endorsed by the developed countries since the first G-7 summit in 1975. Both the Ford and Carter administrations had advocated for some mixture of fiscal stimulus in strong economies, such as the United States and Germany, and reform in weak or underperforming ones, such as Italy and Britain. But rapid adjustment *across* the North—led by the United States—prepared the way for disaster in the South. From 1979 to 1981 the Federal Reserve issued several interest rate increases (dubbed the "Volcker shocks," after Fed chief Paul Volcker) that added, in one estimate, $41 billion to the debts of already indebted developing countries.[20] In 1981 the governments of Britain and Germany followed up with their own anti-inflation drives, further damaging the South's terms of trade. Starting in 1980, developing countries' exports as a share of world trade entered a steep decline (after a decade-long relative rise), while commodity prices—a core NIEO concern throughout the 1970s—fell "'to a level not experienced since at least the 1930s.'"[21]

Third, Reagan dismissed the value of concessional aid to all but the poorest countries, holding that, "unless a nation puts its own financial and economic house in order, no amount of aid will produce progress." Reagan recognized that the United States had a responsibility for development through the implementation of sound macroeconomic policies, but he viewed foreign aid in the same way he viewed welfare programs at home: they only encouraged dependency and stagnation. Again, the best "American contribution" to development was to ensure a "growing, prosperous United States economy" that could buy, sell, and invest overseas. To further de-emphasize aid's importance relative to private capital, Reagan added that "the financial flows generated by trade investment and growth capital flows far exceed official development assistance funds provided to developing countries."

Fourth, Reagan reversed his administration's initial hostility toward (some) multilateral institutions, specifically the World Bank and IMF. This was not out of a newfound sympathy for their missions. Rather, the idea was to use US influence in those institutions to turn them into vehicles for market reform. Thus, Reagan declared a "special responsibility to provide constructive suggestions to make [them] more effective," such as "enhancing" the role of private capital in World Bank projects and encouraging "deficit countries" to reach agreements with the IMF on "sound, comprehensive stabilization program[s]" that would "signal private markets of [their] intent to solve [their] own economic problems."

In another sign of things to come, Reagan avoided direct mention of the North-South dialogue in the United Nations, which had been suspended one year earlier due to both sides' inability to agree on an agenda. Instead, Reagan concluded his speech by calling for an "end to the divisive rhetoric of 'us versus them,' 'North versus South.' Instead, let us decide what all of us, both developed and developing countries, can accomplish together."[22]

Foreign Aid and Human Rights: Successes and Setbacks

The administration undertook several efforts in its first year to realign US development policy with its procorporate, domesticist agenda. Some activities were expanded. The Overseas Private Investment Corporation (OPIC), a US government–owned corporation with the goal of facilitating foreign investment in the Third World, was granted the authority to issue insurance to private corporations against "foreign strife," and it was instructed to reject projects that would "substantially reduce the positive trade benefits likely to accrue to the United States from the investment."[23] At the US Agency for International Development (USAID), Reagan officials created a Bureau for Private Enterprise to promote lending to small and medium-sized Third World businesses; Elise Dupont, wife of the governor of Delaware, was selected to lead the new agency, despite having no foreign affairs experience.[24] A more consequential Reagan program was the Caribbean Basin Initiative, which offered economic and military assistance to countries of Central America and the Caribbean that did not "expropriate without compensation"; it also took into account those countries' "attitude towards foreign investment and policies employed to promote their own development."[25]

Major cuts were proposed to traditional development aid, with Stockman's OMB leading the charge. Stockman truly wanted to reduce the size of government in all sectors, and he attacked the foreign aid budget with the same zeal he directed toward domestic outlays. He later stated: "I believed that the organs of international aid and so-called Third World development—the UN, the multilateral banks, and the U.S. Agency for International Development—were infested with socialist error. The international aid bureaucracy was turning Third World countries into quagmires of self-imposed inefficiency and burying them beneath mountainous external debts they would never be able to repay." To address that situation, in early 1981 Stockman worked out a budget plan with Republican senator Phil Gramm that would have cut US multilateral and bilateral aid by 45 percent, canceled Carter's $3.2 billion pledge to the World Bank's International Development Association (IDA), frozen all US contributions to other regional multilateral banks and UN agencies, and phased out Public Law 480 or the Food for Peace program.[26]

Stockman's campaign against foreign aid quickly ran up against the administration's national security strategy, exposing the limits of Reaganism's commitment to reduce spending. According to Stockman, Secretary Haig leaked the Gramm-Stockman budget to the press, sparking angry phone calls from Capitol Hill and formal protests from the European Economic Community,

OECD, and Australia.[27] While the OMB held that "every major program should take some reduction," it too had to accept a hierarchy: "bilateral aid has priority over multilateral aid programs, [and] security assistance has priority over development assistance." The result was a compromise budget that pledged to reduce overall aid by 20 percent, cut but did not cancel US contributions to the IDA, and deferred new aid obligations.[28]

In practice, aid was not so much reduced as redirected toward nations that fit into the administration's national security strategy. In fact, from 1981 to 1986, bilateral development aid rose by 22 percent, from $4.9 billion to $6 billion, while security assistance rose by more than 100 percent.[29] Aid distribution also changed, as USAID redirected funds toward those governments deemed friendly or under threat, such as El Salvador, Honduras, Sudan, and Pakistan, and away from unfriendly governments such as Nicaragua and Tanzania.[30] The jettisoning of human rights as a factor in determining aid was a foregone conclusion, but even the administration's promarket requirements could be put aside to further other foreign policy goals. According to a 1985 report by the Overseas Development Council, aid recipients were rejecting USAID conditionalities, "with the knowledge that their bureaucratic and congressional allies in Washington would block a cutoff of funds."[31]

From Ottawa to Cancún

While the Reagan administration struggled in its first year to balance commitments to reforming Third World markets and supporting anticommunist allies, it still had no explicit policy toward North-South negotiations, which had been stalled in the United Nations since the end of the Carter administration. At the June 1980 G-7 summit in Venice, the developed countries agreed "to approach in a positive spirit the prospect of global negotiations in the framework of the United Nations," scheduled for January 1981, but did not elaborate. In effect, G-7 leaders kicked the can down the road until the outcome of the US presidential election in November.[32]

Reagan officials opposed global negotiations in both form and spirit. "Ultimately, the South wants our money," complained a Treasury official. "It's a scam. Our problem is that the whole mindset of the dialogue is objectionable. It's unreal."[33] The president agreed. "The talkfests, at the UN and so on, and like Global Negotiations—no, he [Reagan] never saw any value in that," Nau recalled. One dissenting voice was Kirkpatrick, "who said, 'Mr. President, why can't we go to New York and just dance the dance of seven veils? Just take off one veil at the time—just tantalize them, but we won't give away anything. We won't arouse their anger, we won't around their opposition.' And Reagan smiled and laughed, as he usually did."[34] Reagan faced more serious pressure to show up at the dialogue from foreign leaders. Canada's Pierre Trudeau, for instance had been trying to push the United States' North-South policy in a more progressive direction for several years. In fact, when Carter first met Trudeau, Zbigniew Brzezinski advised the president to "recognize Canada's special access and credibility among third world countries, especially the poorest, and bear in mind that Canada's policy toward China and Cuba has evolved more rapidly than ours."[35] Canada was hosting the June 1981 G-7 summit in Ottawa, and Trudeau was one of the few Western leaders who was still committed to large resource transfers and institutional change. According to Trudeau's foreign minister Mark MacGuigan, the prime minister was "totally consumed by the issue" and "filled with youthful vigor and idealism." "Power sharing is at the heart of the North-South dialogue," Trudeau explained to MacGuigan and Larry Smith, assistant undersecretary for North-South affairs, "and [Western] politicians should be able to understand this readily and recognize that it is better to share power now than in the future, even though it may be easier the other way round."[36]

Trudeau also supported the activities of the Independent Commission on International Development Issues. The commission was the initiative of World Bank president Robert McNamara, who announced the idea in a speech to the bank's board of governors in September 1977.[37] McNamara had been inspired by a 1976 joint report from the Club of Rome and the Dutch Ministry for Development Cooperation, which, among other things, supported the South's calls for democratizing international institutions and criticized World Bank policies for ignoring poverty. While the Dutch report garnered little attention in the North, it was well received in the South and made a strong impression on McNamara. In early 1977 he proposed to Willy Brandt, leader of the German Social Democratic Party and former chancellor, that they convene their own commission, consisting of former heads of state from both North and South, to "determine the necessary volume of aid, especially for the poorest countries, and the required changes in the policies of developed countries, as well as [to] discuss the structural modification of the international economy."[38] McNamara had launched a similar initiative at the outset of the 1970s development crisis—a 1969 World Bank–funded project headed by former Canadian prime minister Lester Pearson—that had been criticized for its lack of new ideas and quickly forgotten. This time, the commission would not be funded by the World Bank, and a majority of its twenty-one members would hail from developing countries.[39]

The commission published its first report in February 1980. Subtitled *A Programme for Survival*, the Brandt Report, as it became known, cited global inequality as the leading threat to world peace and explored development's relationship to the global arms trade, nuclear disarmament, and the environment.[40] For Northern politicians, the report's specific policy recommendations were bold—among other things, it endorsed the Common Fund, called for larger and automatic transfers of wealth from North to South, and proposed a World Development Fund with a fully international membership. The report was popular among developing countries at the United Nations, where delegates gave supportive speeches in the General Assembly, and it was well received in Europe. In Britain alone, sixty-eight thousand copies were sold, and ten thousand people showed up when Parliament was scheduled to discuss it.[41]

Looking back, little in the Brandt Report was new. The South had been calling for most of the policies for years, and all agreed that a highly unequal world was an unstable one. Unfortunately, its main pitch to the developed countries—to fund a Marshall Plan for the South that would also stimulate the economies of the North—could not have come at a worse time. Western governments were terrified of inflation following the 1979 oil crisis and were mired in recession; one after another, they hiked interest rates and cut spending. One leader particularly opposed to the report's brand of global Keynesianism was Margaret Thatcher, who was even more determined than Reagan to reverse the macroeconomic consensus in her country. Nevertheless, given the report's popularity in Europe and the South, even the Thatcher government took a conciliatory stance. "Nowhere can the Brandt report be read with greater interest than in Britain," foreign secretary Lord Carrington insisted during a visit to Caracas. "It has been the publishing success of the year, and at the last count has sold ten times as many copies as in the United States. . . . We also know that, as a leading British newspaper put it yesterday, soft words are not enough. . . . Above all, we believe it is not rhetoric which is required, but action."[42]

That action would take the form of a high-profile North-South summit in October 1981 at the Mexican resort of Cancún. Brandt had discussed the idea of a summit with UN secretary-general Kurt Waldheim in 1979, before the report's publication, but Brandt and Austrian chancellor Bruno Kreisky wanted a smaller group of leaders modeled on the 1975–77 Conference on International Economic Cooperation (CIEC) instead of a large international gathering. The G-77 preferred an open forum, but Mexican president José López-Portillo agreed to host the summit, with Austria as a cosponsor, as a way to restart North-South negotiations.[43]

According to her memoirs, Thatcher persuaded Reagan to attend the Cancún summit during her visit to Washington in February. Although Thatcher dismissed "the whole concept of 'North-South' dialogue, which the Brandt

Commission had made the fashionable talk of the international community," she "felt that, whatever our misgivings about the occasion, we should be present, both to argue for our positions and to forestall criticism that we were uninterested in the developing world."[44] This may have been true, but it was not the only reason for Reagan's attendance. At the Ottawa summit in July, Trudeau and French president François Mitterrand "were laying in wait to attack the United States for its inaction on Third World issues," particularly Reagan's promise earlier that year to cut US contributions to the IDA.[45] To Reagan's frustration, they refused to even discuss East-West issues until the United States agreed to a more forthcoming position on global negotiations, and North-South relations became the longest section of the customary joint communiqué.[46] In the words of one American participant, the differences between Reagan and his counterparts on North-South relations were "enormous," and the United States was "the skunk at the party."[47] Yet the Reagan administration had to choose between alienating its allies and leaving the door open to global negotiations, and in the end, it chose the latter. "There is now a disposition on the part of all summit countries to pursue any opportunity for meaningful progress [in the North-South dialogue], including what are known as global negotiations," Trudeau declared at the summit's end. "That openness to the process of global negotiations represents a consensus which did not exist before our summit and seemed very remote not too many months ago."[48]

The Cancún summit on October 23, 1981, was attended by twenty-two heads of state "representing two-thirds of the world's population and controlling three-fourths of the world's wealth."[49] Despite the hype and international visibility, the summit was yet another North-South anticlimax. As in his speech to the World Bank a month before, Reagan preached the virtues of market reforms and projected a shower of private investment in the South once the United States put its own house in order. The United States was alone in opposing the creation of an energy affiliate for least developed countries inside the World Bank, although Britain joined the United States in rejecting the Brandt Report's proposal for an independent World Development Fund.[50] Thatcher recalled telling her European and Third World counterparts, "There was no way in which I was going to put British deposits into a bank which was totally run by those on overdraft."[51] The participants had agreed not to produce a joint statement, in the interests of a "free exchange of ideas," so it was left to López-Portillo and Trudeau to put a positive spin on this grim nonconclusion. One reporter described the scene: "[Few] among the approximately 3,000 journalists and staff present failed to note the decidedly opposite mood of the two men. López Portillo was cautiously optimistic; Trudeau was dejected. Cynics in attendance claimed López Portillo had no option but to act in this fashion, as the host of the conference. It was Trudeau . . . who accurately reflected the results of the conference."[52]

The 1982 Debt Crisis and the Triumph of Reaganism

Despite a follow-up attempt by the Brandt Commission in 1983, the Cancún summit marked the effective end of the North-South dialogue. This appears obvious in retrospect. As Thatcher recalled in her memoirs:

> The summit was a success—though not really for any of the reasons publicly given. At its conclusion there was, of course, the expected general— and largely meaningless—talk about global negotiations on North-South issues. . . . But what mattered to me was that the independence of the IMF and World Bank were maintained. Equally valuable, this was the last of such gatherings. The intractable problems of Third World poverty, hunger, and debt would not be solved by misdirected international intervention, but rather by liberating enterprise, promoting trade—and defeating socialism in all its forms.[53]

In its own preparations for the summit, the US State Department also believed the dialogue's days were numbered: "The October summit could mark the end, for the foreseeable future, of serious attempts to negotiate global economic bargains between North and South. It may be the last gasp of a decade-long effort at multilateral diplomacy."[54]

The State Department was correct, but such optimism had been proved wrong before. In fact, US officials had been predicting the dialogue's end since late 1974, when Henry Kissinger began his strategy of splitting the unholy alliance of OPEC and the oil-importing developing countries by making strategic concessions to the NIEO program. Promarket ideologues like treasury secretary William Simon and Alan Greenspan had charged Kissinger with abandoning the US commitment to free markets abroad and endangering their own reform efforts at home, but this "economic theology," as Kissinger put it, was overruled by the pragmatic Gerald Ford. At the same time, a growing number of neoconservatives, who were then outside of government and in between parties, organized around their opposition to what Moynihan called, in a lengthy essay in *Commentary*, Kissinger's "appeasement" of the G-77's economic and moral claims. Instead, Moynihan argued, the United States must "go into opposition" at the UN by using the Third World's human rights record to delegitimize its criticisms of the US-led liberal world order.[55] This was also tried for a time—eight months—until Moynihan too found himself isolated from both the Europeans and the consensus-driven Ford and was forced to resign.

The Carter administration placed the North-South dialogue at the top of its international agenda, and for the first time since Kissinger's 1975 speech at the UN Seventh Special Session, the outlook was genuinely hopeful. Carter was serious about responding to the South's problems and sought to turn his signature foreign policy initiative—human rights—into a global campaign to meet basic human needs in poor countries. This was an important distinction: whereas Kissinger wanted to water down the NIEO, and Simon and Moynihan wanted to reject it in form and spirit, Carter and secretary of state Cyrus Vance wanted to transform it. This too failed, for reasons made plain to Carter in conversations with G-77 leaders such as Venezuelan president Carlos Andrés Pérez. The Third World suspected (correctly) that Carter's focus on attacking poverty *within* countries was intended to end the discussion of global structural reform, however sincere Carter was about achieving the former goal.

Between 1974 and 1982 the North-South dialogue transformed US foreign policy, but *US foreign policy did not transform the North-South dialogue.* The G-77's solidarity and power had been diminished by many things—OPEC's halfhearted aid efforts in the wake of the first oil crisis, the North's coming together in the G-7 summits, the return to recession and austerity in the North, the abrupt end to détente caused by the Soviet Union's invasion of Afghanistan—but its agenda remained the same: the redistribution of both resources and power from North to South through comprehensive global negotiations. Kissinger had entertained the possibility of some redistribution of resources and power; Carter had been willing to commit more resources, but only to US-dominated institutions. Neoconservatives and neoliberals had rejected both throughout the 1970s, and with Reagan's election, they were in a position to put those beliefs into practice. It was a testament to the remarkable impact the NIEO and the North-South dialogue had on international politics in the 1970s that, long after the threat of serious economic retaliation had passed, the Reagan administration was still unable to kill, or even opt out of, global negotiations. Diplomatic norms, European concerns, and Southern solidarity all continued to mandate US participation. As a pre-Cancún Treasury Department analysis explained, there was no way Reagan could just say no to global negotiations. Even if Reagan announced his opposition after Cancún, he would "still have to come up with alternative ideas which would involve showing how all the topics to be discussed in GN [global negotiations] could more properly be discussed in other fora."[56] Shortly after the summit, the administration announced its support for a new round of global negotiations, on the condition that they "deal with specific, identifiable obstacles to development," "focus on international growth and development," and "[do] not create new institutions or weaken the power of . . . the IMF and World Bank."[57] Minus Carter's basic needs proposals—which, though significant, had come to naught through the dialogue—this had been the US position four years back.

Those global negotiations would not take place. On the evening of August 12, 1982, Mexico's finance minister flew to Washington to deliver grim news: his country was no longer able to service its debts.[58] Shortly thereafter, Mexico announced a unilateral debt moratorium of ninety days and requested a renegotiated payment schedule and additional loans to meet past obligations. Washington and London arranged a temporary loan as well as consultations between the banks and Mexican officials, but President López-Portillo balked at the banks' insistence that he accept an IMF-designed austerity program in exchange for new loans. Instead, López-Portillo nationalized the banks, imposed import controls, and condemned the IMF as "witch doctors" whose treatment plan was to "deprive the patient of food and subject him to compulsory rest."[59]

Within three months, López-Portillo was out of power. In November a new government accepted the IMF's package, but by then, the crisis had spread to Argentina and Brazil. Reagan's and Thatcher's cuts to official development aid compounded the problem, as did Reagan's own borrowing, which drove up interest rates, and Thatcher's austerity, which decreased demand.[60] The South's "lost decade of development" had begun. Even though the largest debtors were located in Latin America, the Caribbean, Asia (the Philippines), and North Africa (Morocco), the crisis hit smaller debtors in sub-Saharan Africa especially hard due to their relative impoverishment.[61] By the end of 1984, at least thirty "structural adjustment" loans had been negotiated in Latin America and other developing countries, with the banks providing the capital and the IMF enforcing the terms.[62] This "new diplomatic constellation, with the IMF and the U.S. taking on key brokerage roles between banks and debtor states," virtually ensured that the burden of adjustment would fall overwhelmingly on the citizens of indebted countries and hardly at all on foreign investors.[63] "The principal—although largely undeclared—objective of the Western world's debt strategy, ably coordinated by the IMF, was to buy time," explained Nigel Lawson, Britain's chancellor of the exchequer during the crisis. "Time was needed not only to enable debtor countries to put sensible economic policies in place but also for the Western banks to rebuild their shattered balance sheets."[64]

Those "sensible economic policies"—including privatization of government services and industry, deregulation of labor and capital markets, removal of price controls, and spending cuts—became part of a one-size-fits-all reform prescription known as the Washington Consensus.[65] Early in the crisis, there was some fear in the North about debtors forming a "debtpec" to argue collectively for better terms, but the South as a diplomatic unit had vanished: "Debtor states abandoned the mores of North-South negotiations, preferring more efficacious bilateral ties with creditors and altering global communications channels as a result. LDC interests were badly divided. Some were unaffected; others held mostly official debt, were meeting payments and wanted the issue depoliticized, or preferred continuing radical demands. This reduced coalitional opportunities. Nor was the issue suitable to bloc politics. Even the large debtors, because of the continuing need for credit and their different positions in the business cycle, have been unable to create a unified position."[66] The eight-year effort to achieve the NIEO was over, and the new neoliberal order had arrived.

The developed countries were stunned by the "historic" and "unprecedented" debt crisis.[67] US officials initially argued that it was a "temporary problem of liquidity" brought about by unsound domestic policies that could be contained by a bit of cash and structural reforms.[68] Debt relief was dismissed as encouraging moral hazard. As treasury secretary Donald Regan told Congress: "I don't think we should just let a nation off the hook because we are sympathetic to the fact that they are having difficulties. . . . You just can't let your heart rule your head in these situations."[69]

Instead, the expectation was that, once reforms were in place, private capital would have the confidence to return. The World Bank too was caught off guard; as late as 1981, researchers were "optimistic . . . about the future availability of private capital flows to already-indebted developing countries" and believed the debt problem was "manageable and would not obstruct economic growth." There was a reason for this optimism: "From the late 1960s onward, the industrial countries made substantial investments in economic research on developing countries through organizations that they controlled, such as the OECD and the World Bank."[70]

As the North-South dialogue dragged on, the self-serving conclusion in the North was that the biggest obstacle to development was not a lack of money, rich-country protectionism, or global rules but the developing countries themselves. The World Bank issued its first structural adjustment loan in 1980, one year after McNamara introduced the concept in a high-profile speech at UNCTAD V. Under McNamara's successor A. W. Clausen, a former Bank of America CEO, by the mid-1980s, structural adjustment loans accounted for one-third of the World Bank's new lending. Dissenters within the bank and other international financial institutions were either silent or ignored, as Stanley Fischer, the bank's chief economist, explained:

It was clear . . . at the beginning of 1989, as it had been clear to many much earlier, that growth in the debtor countries would not return without debt relief. But the official agencies operate on the basis of an agreed upon strategy, and none of them could openly confront the existing strategy without having an alternative to put in place. And to propose such an alternative would have required agreement among the major shareholders of the institutions. So long as the United States was not willing to move, the IFI's [international financial institutions] were not free to speak.[71]

Fischer's explanation reveals the most damaging legacy of US policy toward the NIEO and the North-South dialogue. US officials' focus on defeating the South's proposals for global reform left them blind to the global crisis brewing right in front of them. At UNCTAD IV in 1976, secretary-general Gamani Corea warned of an impending debt problem in the South; a year later, CIEC cochairman Manuel Pérez-Guerrero insisted on behalf of the Group of 19 developing countries that the participants discuss the debt problem and reach agreement on a new framework for debt renegotiation and rescheduling.[72] The Carter administration agreed to some debt relief for least developed countries on a case-by-case basis, but as late as 1979, when the issue of debt resurfaced at UNCTAD V, US officials believed that "official debt . . . [is] of political importance to LDCs frequently out of proportion to [its] economic significance."[73] By the time the debt crisis hit, the consensus on markets, the state, and development in the United States, the IMF, and the World Bank had moved decisively in favor of the NIEO's greatest critics: the neoliberals and neoconservatives who began the 1970s on the fringes of the foreign policy establishment and came to dominate it in the 1980s and beyond.

Epilogue

Global South: What's in a Name?

In 1983 the members of the Brandt Commission released a second report. *Common Crisis North-South: Cooperation for World Recovery* was just as severe in its diagnosis of the world economy as the first report but notably less optimistic about a cure. "The [first] Commission foresaw the world community in the 1980s facing much greater danger than at any time since the Second World War," it began. "The prospects are now even darker."[1]

At the Cancún summit of October 1981, world leaders had declared that they would revisit the issue of global negotiations at the next United Nations General Assembly. "Now, more than a year later, there is little sign of action. The North-South dialogue remains much where it was when the Commission [first] reported." Unlike the first Brandt Report—the similarly urgent *North-South: A Programme for Survival*—the 1983 follow-up focused on what might be done immediately. "We insist that longer-term measures of reform will be essential to the international financial and trading system, without which recovery and growth could not be sustained," its authors declared. "But our measures constitute the minimum emergency action which we believe nations must now take together."[2]

By the time the second Brandt Report went to press, the South's drive to establish a New International Economic Order (NIEO) was finished. The global debt crisis of the 1980s also meant the end of the South as a diplomatic force—or at least one that would be taken seriously by the US government and its foreign policy apparatus. Indeed, a search for the term *New International Economic Order* in available Reagan administration documents turns up nothing after 1983. By 1984, two years into the debt crisis, all mentions of *North-South* or *North-South dialogue* were in reference to the two Koreas. According to Google N-Gram, which measures a phrase's frequency of use over time, *New International Economic Order* skyrocketed after 1970, peaked in 1980, and plummeted after 1982. The term *North-South dialogue* also rose, fell and disappeared during these years, although overall, its frequency in print was less common than NIEO.

Meanwhile, the South as a category of analysis was about to undergo a major expansion. Beginning in the late 1990s, the term *global South* took off in political and academic discourse. Today, many liberals embrace the term as a politically correct or up-to-date alternative to *Third World*, which is more or less in line with the first (1980) Brandt Report's definition of North and South: "although neither is a uniform or permanent grouping, 'North' and 'South are broadly synonymous with 'rich' and 'poor,' 'developed' and 'developing.'"[3] In academia and activism, however, the global South accounts for a lot more intellectual work than the South ever did. Some political scientists still use the old term *South* when speaking of the Group of 77 countries acting in the UN, where the state apparatus issues its decree (yea or nay). For scholars working on transnational issues such as human rights, health, labor, and immigration, *global South* can denote a complex network of relationships in which the state is one of many actors (and not always the most significant one). Global South is also a major analytic concept for the multidisciplinary field of postcolonial studies, where scholars from sociology and anthropology to literary theory emphasize its fluidity and emancipatory potential for subaltern populations, including some residing in the North. "[The] 'Global South' is not an entity that exists *per se*, but has to be understood as something that is created, imagined, invented, maintained, and recreated by the ever-changing and never fixed status positions of social actors and institutions," explains the author of a 2017 article in the journal *Global South*.[4] What links these more inclusive understandings of the global South is their dethroning of the state as the central actor in politics and economics. If the South of the 1970s was a collection of poor states seeking power in the global economy, the global South of today comprises the poor peoples and cultures marginalized by the global economy. More often than not, the state is an agent of repression, not liberation.

The decline of the South in the 1980s followed by the rise of the global South in the 1990s and 2000s was no coincidence. Rather, the fall of an old state-centric South in favor of a diverse, transnational global South could not have occurred without the worldwide embrace of free markets and economic integration of the last few decades. Neoliberal globalization spread the market to every country, but it did not do so equally. Nor was it the case that each country that opened up its economy after 1980 did well, short or long term. Nevertheless, neoliberal globalization created new inequalities within the South and beyond, ones that called into question the old political and economic utility of that category.

Neoliberal Globalization: Some Major Developments

The late 1980s and 1990s saw a proliferation of both regional and global trade liberalization, if not reform. Part of this came about due to the failure of participants in the General Agreement on Tariffs and Trade (GATT) to reach a decision in the Uruguay round, which began in 1982 but soon deadlocked. In 1988 the United States and Canada signed a major free-trade agreement. With Mexico's addition a few years later, the 1994 North American Free Trade Agreement (NAFTA) created the largest free market in the world, eliminating most tariffs and capital restrictions among the three countries. At the same time, the twelve members of the European Communities voted to modernize their own trade and monetary relations. The 1992 Maastricht Treaty consolidated the European Communities into the European Union, opening borders, lowering tariffs, and creating a common currency for its member states.

The larger trading world was moving in an even more ambitious direction. The 1994 Marrakesh agreement formally ended the Uruguay round, the GATT's last. Finally, after nearly fifty years as the lesser sibling of the International Monetary Fund and the World Bank, in 1996 the ad hoc, informal GATT was replaced by the 123-member World Trade Organization (WTO). The United States was a key sponsor of the WTO and almost immediately advocated the addition of its new favorite trading partner, the People's Republic of China, which joined in December 2001 with Washington's imprimatur.

The 1990s was a high point for market-friendly reforms within the United States too. At home, Congress and the Clinton administration cut taxes and financial red tape, most notably the 1929 Glass-Steagall Act separating commercial and investment banking. Unlike Ronald Reagan, Bill Clinton balanced the budget—he even left a surplus—and made good on his promise to "end welfare as we know it" through the 1996 Welfare Reform Act.

The most revolutionary developments were unplanned. Under Reagan, the United States and the Soviet Union entered a so-called second Cold War. No one expected the collapse of communism in eastern Europe between 1989 and 1993, but in postcommunist Russia oligarchic capitalism easily dominated the new trappings of liberal democracy. Even more consequential was China's rise. In 1997, when negotiations to include China in the WTO began, the Clinton administration had all the leverage, and the Chinese had little. The deal that brought China into the WTO looked like an unqualified win for the United States: Beijing had to conform to the standards of the WTO, where Washington was primus inter pares. Overestimating the US economy and underestimating China's, US policymakers bestowed on China the same exemptions and preferences as any other developing country joining the WTO. Today, US politicians and corporations complain that China is cheating at the WTO, but in many cases, the Chinese are simply taking advantage of rules the United States wrote or approved two decades earlier.

Equally unexpected from Washington's perspective was the rise of China's political and economic influence in low-income countries. Previously, the United States worried about the Soviet development model as an inspiration for Third World leaders. Today, China has replaced Russia as the United States' greatest economic and diplomatic challenge, in both real terms (foreign investment and development aid) and model forms (illiberal state capitalism).

Neoliberal Globalization's Winners

Who benefited from the forty years of neoliberal globalization that came in the NIEO's wake? Inequality scholar and former World Bank head economist Branko Milanovic has crunched the numbers, and the results are simpler than one might expect: "[One] of the key issues of the current globalization process [is] the diverging economic trajectories of people in the old rich world versus those in resurgent Asia. In short: the great winners have been the Asian poor and middle classes; the great losers, the lower middle classes of the rich world."[5]

First, consider the "great winners." Market reforms and the removal of barriers to trade and capital in rich and poor countries alike encouraged the growth of a new global middle class, especially in large countries such as India and China. On the whole, this has resulted in a relative convergence of global incomes. From this, one might conclude that neoliberal globalization achieved what the NIEO desired: the reduction of inequality, especially between the rich North and the poor South. Removing China or India from the equation, however, leaves a different impression: "Up to 2000, China was the great income equalizer; after 2000, India joined it in playing this role. These countries first kept the increase in global inequality in check and then contributed to reducing the overall level of inequality."[6] Without these two countries' gains, global inequality in this period actually *increased*; with them, global inequality decreased most significantly after 2008, which means that stagnation in the rich countries since the Great Recession also played an important role (discussed in more detail later). Further, there are few accurate data on top incomes in most poor countries, in part because Northern banks and governments have been such eager facilitators in helping the global rich hide income and assets abroad.[7]

Globalization advocates also point to the success of the so-called Asian Tigers: Hong Kong, Singapore, South Korea, and Taiwan. Despite a regional financial crisis in 1997 caused by overlending and dollar-arbitrage schemes (encouraged through low US interest rates), their export-based economies recovered quickly. For nearly three decades now, the World Bank has considered all four Asian Tigers to be high-income or developed economies. South Korea and Taiwan have strong, liberal democratic systems, while Singapore and Hong Kong are (for different reasons) essentially one-party states with an independent (for the most part) civil service. All, however, have mixed economies, broad social protections for workers, and governments and publics in favor of open global trade.[8]

Using data from India, China, and the United States, Milanovic estimates that inequality between nations "probably reached its highest point" in 1970.[9] Poor countries experienced that inequality acutely and disproportionately during the world food crisis of 1972–74. The 1974 NIEO centered on this injustice in its assertion that "the developing countries, which constitute 70 per cent of the world's population, account for only 30 per cent of the world's income." At the same time inequality between rich and poor countries peaked, inequality *within* the United States and western Europe sank to its lowest point since the beginning of the Great Depression. In 1928 the top 10 percent of US earners (families with annual incomes of at least $135,000) captured half of all national income. During the New Deal and World War II, their share declined to about 32 percent, where it stayed through the 1970s.[10]

This was about to change. In 1982—a banner year for free-market reformers in the United States due to the Kemp-Roth tax bill—income distribution began a steady shift upward. By 2007—one year before the financial crisis and the Great Recession—the top 10 percent (the upper middle class and above) once again claimed half of all national income.[11] (They retain this share today.) Yet even the well-off in the United States have become much more unequal. In a major paper titled "Striking It Richer," economist Emmanuel Saez analyzed income growth and distribution among the lucky top 10 percent of US earners from 1928 to the present. As of 2018, the top 1 percent (income above $480,000) takes in a quarter of all income—another return to pre–New Deal levels. The top 0.01 percent has done even better. From FDR to Jimmy Carter, their share remained at 1 percent, down from about 5 percent in 1928. When Barack Obama took office in 2009, these multimillionaires and billionaires raked in an astonishing 6 percent of all national income, right about where it sits today.[12] (It is worth noting that at least half of that income came from returns on investments, or capital gains, which are taxed at a substantially lower rate than market income.)

Neoliberal Globalization's Losers

Now, consider the "great losers." The economic gains during globalization's high point were, for most Americans, meager. From 1993 to 2018, average real incomes per family in the United States grew by 30 percent—basically, just enough to keep up with consumer prices. However, if one removes the top 1 percent, growth in average real incomes for the other 99 percent drops to 18.3 percent. Meanwhile, the top 1 percent saw their incomes grow by an astonishing 100.5 percent through the Clinton, Bush, and Obama years. Saez writes: "This implies that top 1 percent incomes captured 48% of the overall economic growth of real incomes per family over the period 1993–2018."[13] During this same period, skyrocketing tuition costs made it impossible for most young Americans to earn college degrees without taking on massive loans at usurious rates. Along with strong unions (whose membership has declined precipitously), affordable and accessible higher education was an essential equalizing force in the postwar years. Today, the large majority of young Americans—the best educated and the most indebted in US history—will be the first generation not to outearn their parents.

Since the 1990s, centrist Democrats and Republicans have advocated grants for job retraining and other "trade adjustment assistance" for Americans in sectors affected by outsourcing and automation. Most studies have concluded that the benefits are modest, at best; at worst, such programs insult or alienate the people they are trying to help.[14] Further, US workers' incomes may have stagnated, but the workers themselves have not. In fact, from 1979 to 2018, net productivity among US workers rose by an impressive 69.6 percent. During the same period, average CEO compensation grew by 940 percent, while typical employee compensation (or hourly pay) rose by only 12 percent. Put simply, "although Americans are working more productively than ever, the fruits of their labors have primarily accrued to those at the top and to corporate profits."[15]

Facing low wages, regressive taxes, unresponsive bureaucracies, expensive and employer-dependent health care, and endless war in the Middle East, it is no wonder so many Americans now see themselves—and, to an extent, their country—as victims of globalization rather than its beneficiary and steward. This is the sad irony of US foreign policy's defeat of the global South's NIEO in the 1970s. Again, Milanovic states: "Politicians in the West who pushed for greater reliance on markets in their own economies and the world after the Reagan-Thatcher revolution could hardly have expected that the much vaunted globalization would fail to deliver palpable benefits to the majority of their citizens—that is, precisely to those whom they were trying to convince of the advantages of neoliberal policies compared with more protectionist welfare regimes."[16] The North's reconstitution of the world order along global *and* domestic free-market principles in the 1980s and beyond increased the costs of US primacy abroad while leaving an economy at home where the benefits are overwhelmingly redistributed upward, toward globalization's main beneficiaries. Instead of diffusing global responsibility, US policy made the American household the world's buyer of last resort. The result at home was an unsustainable bargain of cheap consumer goods and credit in lieu of wage increases, universal health care, and affordable housing and higher education. The opportunity costs of these policies would be made apparent in the 2007–10 subprime mortgage crisis, from which the American middle class has yet to recover.

Plus ça Change? The Enduring Inequality of Food

Despite slow growth and rising inequality in rich countries—and, equally important, an impressive reduction of poverty in poor ones (especially in Asia)—we still live in a North-South world. According to Milanovic, "The world where location has the most influence on one's lifetime income is still the world we live in." At its most extreme, just being born in the United States rather than in the Congo multiplies a person's income by ninety-three.[17] Though the difference is smaller for citizens in Mexico, for example, an American whose income is in the bottom tenth is still better off in significant ways than his or her Mexican counterpart. Typically, this has encouraged neoliberal immigration reform in rich countries (here, Canada leads the way), where wealthy foreigners are admitted quickly and legally through real estate and other investments.

Food is another example of how neoliberal globalization has failed the world's poor. During the world food crisis of 1972–74, high oil prices collided with cuts in US foreign aid, rich-country protectionism, and the reorganization of US agriculture to meet the needs of markets rather than people. After falling to less than $150 a bushel in 1977–78 from a high of about $270 at the height of the 1974 crisis, the average price of rice, wheat, and cereals had jumped back to near-crisis levels of $250 by the middle of 1981.[18]

By the mid-1980s, food prices had readjusted and entered another period of relative stability, although the stratification of food production increased in new ways. In the 1980s and 1990s a second Green Revolution in Asia greatly increased agricultural productivity and security there, but most of Africa and the Middle East made no such advances and still relied on imports for more than half their food needs. US dominance in the production of wheat, corn, and soybeans continued unabated, as did poor countries' vulnerability to decisions made by major food and oil exporters. Without the global food strategy promised by Henry Kissinger and others at the World Food Conference, there was a virtual repetition of the 1972–74 crisis in 2007–8 and 2010–12. Once again, a combination of surging energy and fertilizer prices, a falling dollar, and overdependence on US reserves (this time, burnt up as biofuel in gas-guzzling SUVs) caused global food prices to skyrocket, placing the world (in the words of World Bank president Robert Zoellick) "one shock away from a full-blown [food] crisis."[19]

As in 1972–74, the term *world food crisis* was misleading. In the United States, where much of the world's food is grown, grocery store prices hardly budged. Consumers in food-importing developing countries were not so lucky: in 2007 alone, their import bills jumped by 25 percent. The situation was especially dire in Africa and the Middle East, where individuals spend upward of 75 percent of their income on food (more than half of which is imported from abroad).[20] Put simply, many millions of poor people in poor countries could not afford to buy or grow their own food.

Expensive oil was one obvious culprit, but experts agreed that the behavior of rich countries, especially the United States, was decisive in turning a food shortage into a crisis.[21] The jump in oil prices following the US invasion of Iraq in 2003 spurred Western governments' investment in food-based biofuels (especially ethanol, made from corn), and US car companies such as Ford and General Motors promoted new "flex-fuel" versions of their popular but gas-guzzling SUVs as both eco- and wallet-friendly. Given the generous government subsidies and built-in demand, many US farmers ditched less profitable crops to grow corn exclusively for the ethanol market. World cereal stocks sank to lows not seen since 1980, while the global price of corn doubled.[22]

At a United Nations food summit in June 2008, US officials denied responsibility for the consequences of US food and energy policies, insisting that only

2 to 3 percent of the rise in food prices could be attributed to biofuels. Jacques Diouf, head of the UN Food and Agriculture Organization, expressed his frustration at the US government's lack of awareness and accountability: "Nobody understands how $11 to $12 billion a year subsidies [from the US Congress] in 2006 and protective tariff policies have the effect of diverting 100 million tons of cereals from human consumption, mostly to satisfy the thirst for fuel for vehicles."[23]

This time, structural change was not even considered. Instead, the United States preached the ecological benefits of fueling large cars with "renewable" food instead of oil (as if the two could be separated), while Saudi Arabia and other oil-rich Gulf countries continued their appalling land-grabbing practices in poor but fertile countries (especially in Africa). This sorry state of affairs is an enduring legacy of US foreign policy in the 1970s, when the nation failed to use its primacy in the service of world order by relinquishing some of it.

Notes

Abbreviations Used in Notes

CPH   Collected Papers of Theodore Hesburgh
EBP   Earl Butz Papers
FRUS *Foreign Relations of the United States*
GFPL   Gerald Ford Presidential Library
JCPL   Jimmy Carter Presidential Library
memcon memorandum of conversation
PUA   Purdue University Archives
telcon telephone conversation
UNDA   University of Notre Dame Archives
WHCF   White House Central Files

Introduction

1. Jimmy Carter, Address at Commencement Exercises at the University of Notre Dame, May 22, 1977, http://www.presidency.ucsb.edu/ws/?pid=7552.

2. Daniel J. Whelan, "'Under the Aegis of Man': The Right to Development and the Origins of the New International Economic Order," *Humanity: An International Journal of Human Rights, Humanitarianism, and Development* 6, no. 1 (2015): 93–108. For an extended discussion of the relationship between the right to development and the NIEO, see Christopher Dietrich, *Oil Revolution: Anticolonial Elites, Sovereign Rights, and the Economic Culture of Decolonization* (New York: Cambridge University Press, 2017).

3. "A Letter from the President of Venezuela to the Chairman of the World Food Conference Meeting in Rome," November 5, 1974 (Caracas: Oficina Central de Informacion).

4. For the NIEO and Europe, see Giuliano Garavini, *After Empires: European Integration, Decolonization, and the Challenge from the Global South 1957–1986* (Oxford: Oxford University Press, 2012). For the NIEO and OPEC, see Dietrich, *Oil Revolution*; Giuliano Garavini, *The Rise and Fall of OPEC in the Twentieth Century* (New York: Oxford University Press, 2019). For the NIEO's larger role in global South–Third World politics and thought, see Adom Getachew, *Worldmaking after Empire: The Rise and Fall of Self-Determination* (Princeton, NJ: Princeton University Press, 2019), especially chapter 5; Christy Thornton, *Revolution in Development: Mexico and the Governance of the*

202 NOTES TO PAGES 4-7

Global Economy (Oakland: University of California Press, 2021). For prominent European neoliberals' (or "ordoliberals'") opposition to the NIEO, see Quinn Slobodian, *Globalists: The End of Empire and the Rise of Neoliberalism* (Cambridge, MA: Belknap Press/Harvard University Press, 2018), especially chapter 7 and conclusion. For the NIEO and global human rights movements, see Samuel Moyn, *Not Enough: Human Rights in an Unequal World* (Cambridge, MA: Harvard University Press, 2018), especially chapter 5.

5. Those delegations were Bolivia, Brazil, Chile, China, Colombia, Costa Rica, Cuba, Ecuador, Egypt, El Salvador, Ethiopia, Guatemala, Haiti, Honduras, India, Iran, Iraq, Liberia, Mexico, Nicaragua, Panama, Paraguay, Peru, Philippines, Puerto Rico, Uruguay, and Venezuela.

6. Keynes and White quoted in John Toye and Richard Toye, *The UN and Global Political Economy: Trade, Finance, and Development* (Bloomington: Indiana University Press, 2004), 23.

7. The Center for Financial Stability provides an explanation of and access to the transcripts at http://www.centerforfinancialstability.org/brettonwoods_docs.php.

8. Shroff quoted in Michael Franczak, "'Asia' at Bretton Woods: India, China, and Australasia in Comparative Perspective," in *Global Perspectives on the Bretton Woods Conference and the Post-War World Order*, ed. Giles Scott-Smith and J. Simon Rofe (London: Palgrave, 2017), 111–27. For more about the South and development at Bretton Woods, see Eric Helleiner, *Forgotten Foundations of Bretton Woods: International Development and the Making of the Postwar Order* (Ithaca, NY: Cornell University Press, 2014).

9. Two excellent overviews are Nils Gilman, *Mandarins of the Future: Modernization Theory in Cold War America* (Baltimore: Johns Hopkins University Press, 2003), and David Ekbladh, *The Great American Mission: Modernization and the Construction of an American World Order* (Princeton, NJ: Princeton University Press, 2010).

10. W. W. Rostow, *The Stages of Economic Growth: A Non-Communist Manifesto* (London and New York: Cambridge University Press, 1960). For a detailed history of this period, see Michael Latham, *Modernization as Ideology: American Social Science and Nation Building in the Kennedy Era* (Chapel Hill: University of North Carolina Press, 2000).

11. Resolution IV.32, adopted at OPEC's fourth meeting, Geneva, Switzerland, April 1962, quoted in Garavini, *Rise and Fall of OPEC*, 133.

12. "Raúl Prebisch: Latin America's Keynes," *Economist*, March 5, 2009, https://www.economist.com/books-and-arts/2009/03/05/latin-americas-keynes. Like the NIEO itself, most global histories of capitalism either misrepresent Prebisch's ideas or ignore him altogether (the former was common in Prebisch's lifetime, much to his frustration). An excellent corrective is the biography by Edgar J. Dosman, *The Life and Times of Raúl Prebisch, 1901–1986* (Montreal: McGill-Queen's University Press, 2008).

13. B. R. Tomlinson, "What Was the Third World?" *Journal of Contemporary History* 38, no. 2 (2003): 31.

14. See David Engerman, *The Price of Aid: The Economic Cold War in India* (Cambridge, MA: Harvard University Press, 2018).

15. Speech by Deng Xiaoping, chairman of the delegation of the People's Republic of China, at the special session of the UN General Assembly, April 10, 1974, in Barbara Barnouin and Changgen Yu, *Chinese Foreign Policy during the Cultural Revolution* (New York: Routledge, 1998), 214–26.

16. Elizabeth O'Brien Ingleson, *Making Made in China: The Transformation of U.S.-China Trade in the 1970s* (Cambridge, MA: Harvard University Press, forthcoming).

17. Congyan Cai, *The Rise of China and International Law: Taking Chinese Exceptionalism Seriously* (New York: Oxford University Press, 2019), 171.

18. James Mark and Yakov Feygin, "The Soviet Union, Eastern Europe, and Alternative Visions of a Global Economy 1950s–1980s," in *Alternative Globalizations: Eastern Europe and the Postcolonial World*, ed. James Mark, Artemy M. Kalinovsky, and Steffi Marung (Bloomington: Indiana University Press, 2020), 43–44. See also Johanna Bockman, "Socialist Globalization against Capitalist Neocolonialism: The Economic Ideas behind the New International Economic Order," *Humanity: An International Journal of Human Rights, Humanitarianism, and Development* 6, no. 1 (2015): 109–28.

19. Vijay Prashad, *The Poorer Nations: A Possible History of the Global South* (New York: Verso Books, 2012), 66; Marcin Wojciech Solarz, *The Language of Global Development: A Misleading Geography* (London: Routledge, 2014), 120; Bruce Lambert, "Lord Franks, Diplomat Who Led Marshall Plan Effort, Dies at 87," *New York Times*, October 18, 1992, https://www.nytimes.com/1992/10/18/world/lord-franks-diplomat-who-led-marshall-plan-effort-dies-at-87.html.

20. Along with Hermann Abs of Deutsche Bank and Allan Sproul of the New York Federal Reserve, who accompanied him on the trip, Franks filed a lengthy analysis that the World Bank released on April 20, 1960, titled "Bankers' Mission to India and Pakistan," http://documents1.worldbank.org/curated/en/865621594705223686/pdf/Announcement-of-Bankers-Mission-to-India-and-Pakistan-on-April-20–1960.pdf.

21. Franks quoted in Miriam Camps, *Britain and the European Community, 1955–63* (Princeton, NJ: Princeton University Press, 1964), 239–40.

22. Alex Danchev, *Oliver Franks: Founding Father* (New York and Oxford: Oxford University Press, 1993).

23. W. W. Rostow, *Concept and Controversy: Sixty Years of Taking Ideas to Market* (Austin: University of Texas Press, 2003), 241–42.

24. Ball told an audience at the University of North Carolina, "Lord Franks called attention to this division 5 years ago in referring to 'the relationship of the industrialize[d] nations of the North to the under-developed and developing countries that lie to the South of them, whether in Central or South America, in Africa or the Middle East, in South Asia or in the great island archipelagos of the Pacific.'"

25. George C. Ball, "The Open vs. Closed System in North-South Relations," speech at University of North Carolina, April 9, 1964, *Department of State Bulletin* 50, no. 1296 (April 27, 1964): 659–70.

26. See especially Joseph S. Nye, Jr., "UNCTAD: Poor Nations' Pressure Group," in Robert W. Cox and Harold Jacobson, *The Anatomy of Influence: Decision Making in International Organizations* (New Haven, CT: Yale University Press, 1973) and Fred C. Bergsten, Robert Keohane, and Joseph Nye, "International Economics and International Politics: A Framework for Analysis," *International Organization* 29 (Winter 1975): 3–36; Susan Strange, "What Is Economic Power, and Who Has It?" *International Journal* 30, no. 2 (1975): 207–24; Branislav Gosovic and John G. Ruggie, "On the Creation of a New International Economic Order: Issue Linkage and he Seventh Special Session of the UN General Assembly," *International Organization* 30 (Spring 1976): 309–46; G. K. Helleiner, *A World Divided: The Less-Developed Countries in the International Economy* (New York:

Cambridge University Press, 1976) and G. K. Helleiner, *International Economic Disorder: Essays in North-South Relations* (London: Palgrave Macmillan, 1980); Robert W. Cox, "The Crisis of World Order and the Problem of International Organization in the 1980s," *International Journal* 35, no. 2 (1980): 370–95; and Stephen Krasner, *Structural Conflict: The Third World against Global Liberalism* (Berkeley: University of California Press, 1985).

27. Robert W. Cox, "Ideologies and the New International Economic Order: Reflections on Some Recent Literature," *International Organization* 33, no. 2 (1979): 257–302.

28. Richard Nixon, "Address to the Nation Outlining a New Economic Policy: The Challenge of Peace," August 15, 1971, http://www.presidency.ucsb.edu/ws/?pid=3115.

29. Richard E. Moody, "The Economic Scene," *New York Times*, July 20, 1975.

30. UN General Assembly, Resolution 3202, "Programme of Action on the Establishment of a New International Economic Order," May 1, 1974, https://digitallibrary.un.org/record/218451?ln=en.

31. For an overview of works on Kissinger up to 2003, see Jussi M. Hanhimäki, "Kissingerology, Thirty Years and Counting," *Diplomatic History* 27, no. 5 (2003): 637–76.

32. Some recent titles are Joshua Kurlantzick, *A Great Place to Have a War: America in Laos and the Birth of a Military CIA* (New York: Simon and Schuster, 2017); Nancy Mitchell, *Jimmy Carter in Africa: Race and the Cold War* (Palo Alto, CA: Stanford University Press, 2018), especially chapters 1 and 2; Steven O'Sullivan, *Kissinger, Angola and U.S.-African Foreign Policy: The Unintentional Realist* (London: Taylor and Francis, 2020); Stephen G. Rabe, *Kissinger and Latin America: Intervention, Human Rights, and Diplomacy* (Ithaca, NY: Cornell University Press, 2020).

33. Emma Rothschild, "Short Term, Long Term," *New Yorker*, May 26, 1975, 66.

34. For the origins, evolution, and alternative applications of the Washington Consensus, see John Williamson, "The Strange History of the Washington Consensus," *Journal of Post Keynesian Economics* 27, no. 2 (Winter 2004–2005): 195–206.

1. Food Power and Free Markets

1. See Derek Headey and Fan Shengen, *Reflections on the Global Food Crisis: How Did It Happen? How Has It Hurt? And How Can We Prevent the Next One?* (Washington, DC: International Food Policy Research Institute, 2010), especially chapter 4, "Learning from the Past: Comparisons to the 1972–74 World Food Crisis."

2. Clyde H. Farnsworth, "Arabs Vow Money for New Aid Fund," *New York Times*, November 17, 1974.

3. UN General Assembly, Resolution 3201, "Declaration on the Establishment of a New International Economic Order," May 1, 1974, http://www.un-documents.net/s6r3201.htm. On the same day, the General Assembly adopted Resolution 3202, "Programme of Action." The US delegation registered only minor criticisms of the "Programme of Action," which it called a "significant political document." Cited in John Toye and Richard Toye, *The UN and Global Political Economy: Trade, Finance, and Development* (Bloomington: Indiana University Press, 2004), 241–42.

4. Antoine J. Groosman, "World Food Problems and the New International Economic Order," in *Change and the New International Economic Order*, ed. J. A. van Lith (Dordrecht, NL: Springer, 1979), 119.

5. Richard E. Moody, "The Economic Scene," *New York Times*, July 20, 1975.

6. European leaders also argued this point. Helmut Schmidt "repeatedly explained that the so-called third world was now split into rich and poor countries and that the actions of the rich—especially oil-producing—severely affected the poor countries." Rudiger Graf, "Making Use of the 'Oil Weapon: Western Industrialized Countries and Arab Petropolitics in 1973–1974'" *Diplomatic History* 36, no. 1 (January 2012): 199n71.

7. Geoffrey Barraclough, "Wealth and Power: The Politics of Food and Oil," *New York Review of Books*, August 7, 1975. Barraclough attached great importance to the global South's challenge to the postwar world order and went on to write several more essays on the emerging North-South dialogue for the *New York Review of Books*: "The Great World Crisis I," January 23, 1975; "The Haves and the Have Nots," May 13, 1976; "The Struggle for the Third World," November 9, 1978; "Waiting for the New Order," October 26, 1978.

8. Henry Kissinger, *Years of Renewal* (New York: Simon & Schuster, 1999), 699.

9. Barraclough, "Wealth and Power."

10. See Daniel Sargent, *A Superpower Transformed* (Cambridge, MA: Harvard University Press, 2015), for this term.

11. Dale E. Hathaway, *The World Food Crisis—Periodic or Perpetual?* (Washington, DC: International Food Policy Research Group, 1975), 67.

12. Hathaway, 68.

13. Figures from Samuel S. Kim, *China, the United Nations, and World Order* (Princeton, NJ: Princeton University Press, 1979), 243–44, and Tamim Bayoumi, "Changing Patterns of International Trade," a report prepared by the Strategy, Policy, and Review Department of the International Monetary Fund, 8, https://www.imf.org/external /np/pp/eng/2011/061511.pdf.

14. Hathaway, *World Food Crisis*, 68–69.

15. Annual Report of the Council of Economic Advisors, Economic Report of the President (Washington: Government Printing Office, 1967), 173, https://fraser .stlouisfed.org/title/economic-report-president-45/1967-8138.

16. Martha M. Hamilton, *The Great American Grain Robbery and Other Stories* (Washington, DC: Agribusiness Accountability Project, 1972), 313.

17. Hamilton, 313.

18. Jyoti Shankar Singh, *A New International Economic Order: Toward a Fair Redistribution of the World's Resources* (New York: Praeger, 1977), 57.

19. Headey and Shengen, *Reflections on the Global Food Crisis*, 81–84.

20. "Transcript of a Recording of a Meeting between the President and H. R. Haldeman in the Oval Office on June 23, 1972," https://www.nixonlibrary.gov/forresearchers /find/tapes/watergate/wspf/741-002.pdf.

21. Richard Nixon, "Address to the Nation Outlining a New Economic Policy: The Challenge of Peace," August 15, 1971, http://www.presidency.ucsb.edu/ws/?pid=3115.

22. Headey and Shengen, *Reflections on the Global Food Crisis*, 85.

23. The six countries (in order of production magnitude) were Saudi Arabia, Kuwait, Libya, United Arab Emirates, Algeria, and Qatar. Iraq was the sole Arab OPEC member not to join.

24. Quoted in William D. Smith, "Price Quadruples for Iran Crude Oil," *New York Times*, December 12, 1973.

25. Vijay Prashad, *The Poorer Nations: A Possible History* (London: Verso, 2012), 19.

26. Eckart Woertz, *Oil for Food: The Global Food Crisis and the Middle East* (Oxford: Oxford University Press, 2013), 87; Prashad, *Poorer Nations*, 18.

27. Wade Greene, "Triage: Who Shall Be Fed? Who Shall Starve?" *New York Times Magazine*, January 5, 1975, 44.

28. See Jeremi Suri, *Henry Kissinger and the American Century* (Cambridge, MA: Harvard University Press, 2007); Sargent, *Superpower Transformed*; Christopher Dietrich, "Oil Power and Economic Theologies: The United States and the Third World in the Wake of the Energy Crisis," *Diplomatic History* 40, no. 3 (June 2016): 500–29.

29. "Kissinger on Oil, Food, and Trade," *Business Week*, January 13, 1975.

30. *FRUS, 1969–1976*, vol. E-14, pt. 1, *Documents on the United Nations, 1973–1976*, doc. 129, https://history.state.gov/historicaldocuments/frus1969-76ve14p1/d129.

31. *FRUS, 1969–1976*, vol. 31, *Foreign Economic Policy, 1969–76*, doc. 252, https://history.state.gov/historicaldocuments/frus1969-76v31/d252.

32. For a discussion of Orr's World Food Board and its defeat by the US State Department and UK Foreign Office, see Amy L. S. Staples, "To Win the Peace: The Food and Agriculture Organization, Sir John Boyd Orr, and the World Food Board Proposals," *Peace and Change: A Journal of Peace Research* 28, no. 4 (2003): 495–523.

33. D. John Shaw, *World Food Security: A History since 1945* (Basingstroke, UK: Palgrave, 2007), 86–89.

34. In addition to Grant of the ODC, Aziz's collaborators included Mahbub ul-Haq at the World Bank, Amartya Sen at the International Labor Organization, and Barbara Ward at the Society for International Development in the United Kingdom. See Oral History of Richard Jolly, 57, http://www.unhistory.org/CD/PDFs/Jolly.pdf.

35. Shaw, *World Food Security*, 122.

36. Group of 77 refers to a coalition of developing countries (now 134) at the UN, with the goal of increasing their bargaining power in international economic relations. The G-77 acts as the main coordinating body in the UN Conference on Trade and Development (UNCTAD). *FRUS, 1969–1976*, vol. 38, pt. 1, *Foundations of Foreign Policy, 1973–76* doc. 17, https://history.state.gov/historicaldocuments/frus1969-76v38p1/d17. Proposed by Mexican president Luis Echeverria at the April–May 1972 session of the Third World–dominated UNCTAD, CERDS put some basic elements of the NIEO (such as the right to "permanent sovereignty over natural resources") in the form of international law. CERDS would be adopted by the UN General Assembly (against US opposition) in December 1974, one month after the World Food Conference.

37. UN General Assembly, Resolution 3201, "Declaration on the Establishment of a New International Economic Order"; Priya Lal, "African Socialism and the Limits of Global Familyhood: Tanzania and the New International Economic Order in Sub-Saharan Africa," *Humanity: An International Journal of Human Rights, Humanitarianism, and Development* 6, no. 1 (Spring 2015): 22.

38. Giuliano Garavini, "Completing Decolonization: The 1973 'Oil Shock' and the Struggle for Economic Rights" *International History Review* 33, no. 3 (2011): 483.

39. Advertisement, "The President of Venezuela Responds to the President of the United States," *New York Times*, September 25, 1974.

40. *FRUS, 1973–1976*, vol. 31, *Foreign Economic Policy*, doc. 266, http://www.fordlibrarymuseum.gov/library/document/0314/1552792.pdf; emphasis added.

41. James P. Grant to Members of the ODC Board of Directors, "ODC Treatment of Interdependence Themes: Energy and Food," August 7, 1973, in University of Notre Dame Archives, Collected Papers of Theodore Hesburgh, box 93, folder 17.

42. The hearings' conclusions were reprinted in the *New York Times*, September 10, 1974, 7.

43. "Farming and Farm Income," US Department of Agriculture, https://www.ers .usda.gov/data-products/ag-and-food-statistics-charting-the-essentials/farming-and -farm-income/.

44. Bill Peterson, "Earl Butz: Controversial Hoosier," *Louisville Times*, June 9, 1971, in Earl Butz Papers, Purdue University Library (hereafter EBP), Album of News Clippings, binder 1, 1971.

45. Garnett D. Horner, "Nixon Won't Abolish Agriculture Department," *Indianapolis Star*, November 11, 1971, EBP, Album of News Clippings, binder 1, 1971.

46. Nick Kotz, "Butz an Agribusiness Man," and "Butz Denies that He Favors Corporate over Family Farm," *Washington Post*, November [n.d.] 1971, EBP, Album of News Clippings, binder 1, 1971.

47. "Is Butz that Bad?" *Salt Lake City Tribune*, November 21, 1971, EBP, Album of News Clippings, binder 1, 1971.

48. "Farm Group Backs Butz," *Chicago Tribune*, November 20, 1971, EBP, Album of News Clippings, binder 1, 1971.

49. Nick Kotz, "Butz Approved, 51–44, after Price Promise," *Washington Post*, December 3, 1971, EBP, Album of News Clippings, binder 1, 1971.

50. Ralph D. Wennblom, "The Battle over Butz," *Farm Journal*, January 1972, EBP, Album of News Clippings, binder 2, 1972.

51. "Interview with the Secretary of Agriculture: Why Food Prices Are Up," *U.S. News and World Report*, April 10, 1972, EBP, Album of News Clippings, binder 3, 1972.

52. Julius Duscha, "Up, up, up—Butz Makes Hay down on the Farm," *New York Times Magazine*, April 16, 1972, EBP, Album of News Clippings, binder 3, 1972.

53. "Corn Has a Bright Future in Agriculture," *1973 Corn Annual*, EBP, Album of News Clippings, binder 5, 1973.

54. "Corn Has a Bright Future in Agriculture."

55. Butz to Nixon, April 27, 1973, EBP, box 16—Correspondence, 1971–1975, folder 3, Secretary Butz, 1973.

56. Earl Butz, "Agriculture's Potential in World Trade," address to the 26th World Trade Conference, Chicago, March 8, 1973, EBP, box 8, Statements & Speeches, 1973–74, folder 1, Statements & Speeches, Jan. 12, 1973–May 31, 1973.

57. Earl Butz, "Food Power—A Major Weapon," address to the Advertising Council, Mayflower Hotel, Washington, DC, June 24, 1974, EBP, box 8, Statements & Speeches, 1973–74, folder 4, Statements & Speeches, March 12, 1974–June 26, 1974.

58. Bryan L. McDonald, *Food Power: The Rise and Fall of the Postwar American Food System* (New York: Oxford University Press, 2016), 188.

59. Assistant secretary of state for economic affairs Thomas Enders told Kissinger, "This is a major element in the politics of one of the farm groups, the American Farm Bureau. And they are adamantly against government-held stocks, and return to the former system. This is what Butz is responding to." *FRUS, 1969–1976*, vol. 31, doc. 263, https://history.state.gov/historicaldocuments/frus1969-76v31/d263.

60. The NSC was "doubtful" that "such privately held stocks could be counted upon" in a crisis, nor could "private trade . . . be expected to incur the heavy carrying charges (interest and storage) for the stocks required to meet a contingency which occurs only once in six years or so." *FRUS, 1969–1976*, vol. 31, doc. 252.

61. *FRUS, 1969–1976*, vol. 31, doc. 263.

62. *FRUS, 1969–1976*, vol. E-14, pt. 1, doc. 147, https://history.state.gov/historical documents/frus1969-76ve14p1/d147.

63. Scowcroft to the President, "Results of Meeting to Review Issues in World Food Conference Speech," November 2, 1974, Gerald Ford Presidential Library (hereafter GFPL), Files of the National Security Adviser, Presidential Subject File, box 6, Food/ Food Aid/World Food Conference (3).

64. Emma Rothschild, "Short Term, Long Term," *New Yorker*, May 26, 1975, 40.

65. In the months leading up to the Rome conference, secretary-general Sayed Marei asked Ward to convene a group of "eminent persons from all over the world . . . to consider the issues that are likely to arise [at the conference], to examine the proposals that are being put forward and to give guidance and leadership in the search for solutions." The attendees, which included Nobel Prize-winning agronomist and Green Revolution pioneer Norman Borlaug, anthropologist Margaret Mead, and ketchup heir and CEO Henry J. Heinz II, produced a series of essays released as *Hunger, Politics, and Markets: The Real Issues in the Food Crisis* (New York: New York University Press, 1975).

66. Anthony Lewis, "The Politics of Hunger," *New York Times*, October 24, 1974; "The Politics of Hunger: II," *New York Times*, October 30, 1974.

67. Leslie H. Gelb and Anthony Lake, "Washington Dateline: Less Food, More Politics," *Foreign Policy* 17 (Winter 1974–75): 185, 188.

68. *FRUS, 1969–1976*, vol. E-14, pt. 1, doc. 153, https://history.state.gov/historical documents/frus1969-76ve14p1/d153.

69. Shaw, *World Food Security*, 129.

70. Shaw, 129.

71. "Address by Secretary Kissinger," November 5, 1974, *Department of State Bulletin* 71, no. 1851 (December 16, 1974): 821–29. http://www.fordlibrarymuseum.gov /library/document/dosb/1851.pdf#page=3.

72. Leslie Gelb, "Rome Strategy on Food Is Dividing US Officials," *New York Times*, November 3, 1974.

73. Nigel Hawkes, "World Food Conference: Amid Politicking, Some Progress," *Science* 186, no. 4167 (December 6, 1974): 905–8.

74. "Address by Secretary Kissinger," November 5, 1974.

75. Farnsworth, "Arabs Vow Money."

76. Farnsworth.

77. *FRUS, 1969–1976*, vol. E-14, pt. 1, doc. 153.

78. Ross Talbot, "The International Fund for Agricultural Development," *Political Science Quarterly* 95, no. 2 (Summer 1980): 263.

79. Farnsworth, "Arabs Vow Money."

80. Pronk quoted in Thomas G. Weiss, *UN Voices: The Struggle for Development and Social Justice* (Bloomington: Indiana University Press, 2005), 226.

81. Talbot, "International Fund for Agricultural Development," 264.

82. *FRUS, 1969–1976*, vol. E-14, pt. 1, doc. 153.

83. Gelb, "Rome Strategy."

84. "Address by Secretary Butz," November 6, 1974, *Department of State Bulletin* 71, no. 1851 (December 16, 1974): 829–31.

85. *FRUS, 1969–1976*, vol. E-14, pt. 1, doc. 148, https://history.state.gov/historical documents/frus1969-76ve14p1/d148.

86. Rothschild, "Short Term, Long Term," 43.

87. Shaw, *World Food Security*, 133–34.

88. Rothschild, "Short Term, Long Term," 42. Those countries were Bangladesh, Central African Republic, Chad, Dahomey, Democratic Yemen, El Salvador, Ethiopia, Ghana, Guinea, Guyana, Haiti, Honduras, India, Ivory Coast, Kenya, Khmer Republic, Laos, Lesotho, Malagasy Republic, Mali, Mauritania, Niger, Pakistan, Senegal, Sierra Leone, Somalia, Sri Lanka, Sudan, United Republic of Cameroon, United Republic of Tanzania, Upper Volta, and Yemen. *Report on the World Food Conference*, Hearing before the Committee on Foreign Affairs, House of Representatives, Ninety-Third Congress, Second Session, November 26, 1974 (Washington, DC: Government Printing Office, 1974), 22.

89. Farnsworth, "Arabs Vow Money."

90. On October 4 the US government signed an agreement to sell Bangladesh a hundred thousand tons of wheat; the first shipment did not arrive until December 26. Rothschild, "Short Term, Long Term," 42.

91. Rothschild, 41.

92. Mitchell B. Wallerstein, *Food for War, Food for Peace: United States Food Aid in a Global Context* (Cambridge, MA: MIT Press, 1980), 202.

93. Shaw, *World Food Security*, 135.

94. Rothschild, "Short Term, Long Term," 42, 66.

95. Hawkes, "World Food Conference," 905.

96. Statement of Hon. Edwin M. Martin, US coordinator for the World Food Conference, in *Report on the World Food Conference*, 23.

97. *FRUS, 1969–1976*, vol. E-14, pt. 1, doc. 153.

98. "A Letter from the President of Venezuela to the Chairman of the World Food Conference Meeting in Rome," November 5, 1974 (Caracas: Oficina Central de Informacion).

99. US Department of State, "World Food Conference—November 7 Plenary Sessions," November 9, 1974, https://wikileaks.org/plusd/cables/1974ROME15572_b .html.

100. Rothschild, "Short Term, Long Term," 72; Shaw, *World Food Security*, 135.

101. Figures from https://www.macrotrends.net/2534/wheat-prices-historical -chart-data.

102. Statement of Martin McLaughlin, senior fellow, Overseas Development Council, "Implementation of World Food Conference Recommendations," Subcommittee on Foreign Agricultural Policy, US Senate, November 6, 1975 (Washington: GPO, 1975) 79.

103. "The Status of Proposals on Grain Reserves and the Proposed Kissinger Speech," May 7, 1975, GFPL, Seidman Files, EPB Subject Files, box 113.

104. Memo, Butler to Scowcroft, "EPB Meeting on Food Reserves Proposal," May 11, 1975, GFPL, Files of the National Security Advisor, Presidential Subject File, box 6.

105. Shaw, *World Food Security*, 158.

106. The IFAD was finally formed in 1977; unsurprisingly, it was undercapitalized, and Kissinger's September 1975 promise at the UN for a $200 million US contribution never materialized.

107. Examples include the Saudi Arabian Development Fund, the Kuwait Fund for Arab Economic Development, the Islamic Development Bank, the Arab Fund for Economic Social Development, the Special Arab Fund for Africa, the Arab Technical Assistance Fund for Africa, and the Abu Dhabi Development Fund. Prashad, *Poorer Nations*, 21.

2. North-North Dialogues

1. State Department Office of the Historian, "The 1973 Arab-Israeli War," Milestones: 1969–76 https://history.state.gov/milestones/1969-1976/arab-israeli-war-1973.

2. James Cronin, *Global Rule: America, Britain, and a Disordered World* (New Haven, CT: Yale University Press 2014), 33.

3. Henry Kissinger, "1973: The Year of Europe" (Department of State, Bureau of Public Affairs, Office of Media Services, 1973).

4. Craig Daigle, *The Limits of Détente: The United States, the Soviet Union, and the Arab-Israeli Conflict, 1969–1973* (New Haven, CT: Yale University Press, 2012), 323.

5. Jussi Hanhimäki, *The Flawed Architect: Henry Kissinger and American Foreign Policy* (New York: Oxford University Press, 2004), 277.

6. "Organization for European Cooperation and Development," http://www.oecd.org/general/organisationforeuropeaneconomicco-operation.htm.

7. Robert Schumann, speech, May 9, 1950, http://www.schuman.info/9May1950.htm.

8. William Brown, *The EU and Africa: The Restructuring of North-South Relations* (London: I. B. Tauris, 2002), 40.

9. John Peterson and Mark Pollack, *Europe, America, Bush: Transatlantic Relations in the Twenty-First Century* (London: Routledge, 2003), 3.

10. Brown, *EU and Africa*, 42–43.

11. Giuliano Garavini, *After Empires: European Integration, Decolonization, and the Challenge from the Global South 1957–1986* (Oxford: Oxford University Press, 2012), 121.

12. The golden age narrative of postwar capitalism typically dates the period from 1945 to 1973, when economic events in the developed countries seemed to belie the assumptions of the postwar Keynesian consensus. However, some authors refer specifically to a golden age of social democracy in Europe. Garavini (*After Empires*) begins this period in 1969. Stefan Berger places it a little earlier, 1966–69, and notes that it was replaced by a social-liberal coalition in 1969 that lasted until 1982. See Berger, "Democracy and Social Democracy," *European History Quarterly* 32, no. 1 (2002): 13–37

13. Garavini, *After Empires*, 123, 127.

14. Garavini, 142–44.

15. Garavini, 145.

16. US Department of State, *Foreign Relations of the United States* [hereafter *FRUS*], *1969–1976*, vol. 4, *Foreign Assistance, International Development, Trade Policies, 1969–72*, doc. 146, https://history.state.gov/historicaldocuments/frus1969-76v04/d146.

17. Vanya Walker-Leigh, "Was UNCTAD III a Failure?" *World Today* 28, no. 9 (September 1972): 41120.

18. *FRUS, 1969–1976*, vol. 3, *Foreign Economic Policy; International Monetary Policy, 1969–72*, doc. 91, https://history.state.gov/historicaldocuments/frus1969-76v03/d91.

19. Garavini, *After Empires*, 148.

20. *FRUS, 1969–1976*, vol. 3, doc. 91.

21. *FRUS, 1969–1976*, vol. 3, doc. 91.

22. Quoted in David Milne, *Worldmaking: The Art and Science of American Diplomacy* (New York: Farrar, Straus, and Giroux, 2015), 371.

23. Milne, 371.

24. Gian Giancomo Migone, "The Nature of Bipolarity," in *Dealignment: A New Foreign Policy Perspective*, ed. Mary Kaldor, Richard A. Falk, and Gerard Holden (New York: United Nations University Press, 1987), 56–57. European public opinion reacted strongly against the coup, and several European socialist governments adopted special programs extending refugee status to Chilean political prisoners and their families. See Johan Cels, "Refugee Policies of Western Europe," in *Human Rights and Foreign Policy: Principles and Practice*, ed. Dilys M. Hill (New York: St. Martin's Press, 1989), 167.

25. Henry Kissinger, *Years of Renewal* (New York: Touchstone, 1999), 602.

26. *FRUS, 1969–1976*, vol. 31, *Foreign Economic Policy, 1973–76*, doc. 31, https://history.state.gov/historicaldocuments/frus1969-76v31/d31.

27. Jeremi Suri, *Henry Kissinger and the American Century* (Cambridge, MA: Belknap Press of Harvard University, 2007), 171–72.

28. Tony Judt, *Postwar: A History of Europe since 1945* (New York: Penguin Press, 2005), 455.

29. Daniel Sargent, *A Superpower Transformed: The Remaking of American Foreign Relations in the 1970s* (New York: Oxford University Press, 2015), 157.

30. Statement of Federal Reserve Chairman Arthur Burns, in "Kissinger-Simon Proposals for Financing Oil Imports," Hearings before the Joint Economic Committee, Ninety-Third Congress of the United States, Second Session, November 26–29, 1974, http://www.jec.senate.gov/reports/93rd%20Congress/Hearings/Kissinger-Simon%20Proposals%20for%20Financing%20Oil%20Imports%20(679).pdf.

31. Alberto Clo, *Oil Economics and Policy* (New York: Springer Science and Business Media, 2013), 126.

32. *FRUS, 1969–1976*, vol. 36, *Energy Crisis, 1969–74*, doc. 314, https://history.state.gov/historicaldocuments/frus1969-76v36/d314.

33. *FRUS, 1969–1976*, vol. 36, doc. 262, https://history.state.gov/historicaldocuments/frus1969-76v36/d262.

34. *FRUS, 1969–1976*, vol. 36, doc. 299, https://history.state.gov/historicaldocuments/frus1969-76v36/d299.

35. Anthony Lewis, "A Fortress America," *New York Times*, December 3, 1973.

36. *FRUS, 1969–1976*, vol. 36, doc. 256, https://history.state.gov/historicaldocuments/frus1969-76v36/d256.

37. *FRUS, 1969–1976*, vol. 36, doc. 295, https://history.state.gov/historicaldocuments/frus1969-76v36/d295.

38. Memorandum of conversation (hereafter memcon), January 17, 1974, Gerald Ford Presidential Library (hereafter GFPL), http://www.fordlibrarymuseum.gov /library/document/0314/1552652.pdf.

39. Memcon, February 9, 1974, GFPL, http://www.fordlibrarymuseum.gov/library /document/0314/1552661.pdf.

40. "Final Communique of the Washington Energy Conference," http://www.cvce .eu/content/publication/1999/1/1/96e19fad-6aba-4b79-a791-34624e94acf9 /publishable_en.pdf.

41. Emanuele Gazzo, "Conference and Crisis," *European Community* 175 (April 1974): 8, http://aei.pitt.edu/43960/1/A7561.pdf.

42. Sargent, *Superpower Transformed*, 159.

43. Memcon, March 6, 1974, GFPL, http://www.fordlibrarymuseum.gov/library /document/0314/1552666.pdf.

44. Keith Hamilton, "Britain, France, and America's Year of Europe, 1973," *Diplomacy and Statecraft* 17, no. 4 (2016): 890.

45. Thomas George Weiss, *UN Voices: The Struggle for Development and Social Justice* (Bloomington: Indiana University Press, 2005), 227; emphasis added.

46. Kissinger, *Years of Renewal*, 607.

47. Alan Dobson, *Anglo-American Relations in the Twentieth Century* (London: Routledge, 2012), 143.

48. Kissinger, *Years of Renewal*, 608–9.

49. For "idiot," see Memcon, February 9, 1974, GFPL; Kissinger, *Years of Renewal*, 622.

50. Kissinger, *Years of Renewal*, 613.

51. Max Otte and Jürgen Greve, *A Rising Middle Power? German Foreign Policy in Transformation, 1989–1999* (New York: St. Martin's Press, 2000), 38.

52. Memcon, December 17, 1974, GFPL, http://www.fordlibrarymuseum.gov /library/document/0314/1552890.pdf.

53. Memcon, December 15, 1974, GFPL, http://www.fordlibrarymuseum.gov /library/document/0314/1552887.pdf.

54. Memcon, December 17, 1974.

55. *FRUS, 1969–1976*, vol. 31, doc. 34, https://history.state.gov/historicaldocuments /frus1969-76v31/d34.

56. Helmut Schmidt, *Men and Powers: A Political Retrospective* (New York: Random House, 1990).

57. *FRUS, 1969–1976*, vol. 31, doc. 94, https://history.state.gov/historicaldocuments /frus1969-76v31/d94.

58. *FRUS, 1969–1976*, vol. 31, doc. 124, https://history.state.gov/historicaldocuments /frus1969-76v31/d124.

59. Kissinger, *Years of Renewal*, 677.

60. *FRUS, 1969–1976*, vol. 31, doc. 93, https://history.state.gov/historicaldocuments /frus1969-76v31/d93.

61. *FRUS, 1969–1976*, vol. 31, doc. 116, https://history.state.gov/historicaldocuments /frus1969-76v31/d116.

62. Quoted in Sargent, *A Superpower Transformed*, 191.

63. Economic Policy Board, May 1975, GFPL, U.S. Council of Economic Advisers Records, Alan Greenspan Files, box 58, Economic Policy Board Meetings.

64. Simon and Seidman to Ford, [n.d.] 1975, GFPL, William Seidman Files, Foreign Trips File, box 312, International Economic Summit, Nov. 15–17, 1975—Memoranda (1). .

65. Simon and Seidman to Ford, [n.d.] 1975.

66. Gerrit Faber, "The Lomé Conventions and the Causes of Economic Growth" (paper presented at the 5th SUSTRA workshop on European Governance and European Opinions on Trade and Sustainable Development, IFRI, Paris, June 3–4, 2004), http://www.agro-montpellier.fr/sustra/research_themes/ue_governance/papers/Faber.pdf.

67. Briefing book, "Relations with Developing Countries," GFPL, Federal Reserve, Subject File, box B62, International Economic Summit, Rambouillet 1975.

68. E. L. M. Völker, *Euro-Arab Cooperation* (Leiden, the Netherlands: Brill, 1976), 144.

69. Memcon, December 2, 1975, GFPL, http://www.fordlibrarymuseum.gov/library/document/0314/1553299.pdf.

70. Memcon, December 2, 1975.

71. Memcon, December 2, 1975.

72. Memcon, December 2, 1975.

73. Memcon, December 2, 1975.

74. Memcon, February 24, 1976, GFPL, http://www.fordlibrarymuseum.gov/library/document/0314/1553378.pdf.

75. Sargent, *A Superpower Transformed*, 194.

76. Memo, Greenspan and Scowcroft to the President, "Puerto Rico Summit Overview," June 25, 1976, GFPL, Council of Economic Advisers, Alan Greenspan File, box 39, Economic Summit (Puerto Rico) June 1976 (1). .

77. Sargent, *Superpower Transformed*, 194–95.

78. Michael Crozier, Samuel P. Huntington, and Joji Watanuki, *The Crisis of Democracy: Report on the Governability of Democracies to the Trilateral Commission* (New York: NYU Press, 1975), 64.

79. Seidman to EPB Executive Committee Members, June 7, 1976, "Preparation for International Summit," 3, GFPL, Seidman Files, Economic Policy Board, EPB Executive Committee Memoranda, box 33. .

80. Sargent, *Superpower Transformed*, 195.

81. Garavini, *After Empires*, 221.

82. Kissinger, *Years of Renewal*, 693.

83. *FRUS, 1969–1976*, vol. 31, doc. 300, https://history.state.gov/historicaldocuments/frus1969-76v31/d300.

84. *FRUS, 1969–1976*, vol. 31, doc. 301, https://history.state.gov/historicaldocuments/frus1969-76v31/d301.

3. Neoconservatives and the NIEO at the United Nations

1. Frederick A. O. Schwarz Jr., *Democracy in the Dark: The Seduction of Government Secrecy* (New York: New Press, 2015), 177.

2. Quoted in Foreign Policy Association, "Rethinking U.S. Foreign Policy: How Should Our Power Be Used?" *Great Decisions* (1976): 76.

3. Quoted in Irving Kristol, "The 'New Cold War,'" *Wall Street Journal*, July 17, 1975, Gerald Ford Presidential Library (hereafter GFPL), L. William Seidman Files, box 50, Commodities—International.

4. Kristol.

5. Michael Harrington, "The Welfare State and Its Neoconservative Critics," *Dissent*, Fall 1973, https://www.dissentmagazine.org/article/the-welfare-state-and-its-neoconservative-critics.

6. Penn Kemble, "The New Politics and the Democrats," *Commentary*, December 1, 1972, https://www.commentarymagazine.com/articles/the-new-politics-the-democrats/.

7. Justin Vaïsse, *Neoconservatism: The Biography of a Movement* (Cambridge, MA: Belknap, 2010), 4.

8. See Irving Kristol, "Confessions of a True, Self-Confessed 'Neoconservative,'" *Public Opinion*, October/November 1979, and *Neoconservative: The Autobiography of an Idea* (New York: Free Press, 1995) for Kristol's early embrace of the term. For two partisan defenses, see Douglas Murray, *Neoconservatism: Why We Need It* (New York: Encounter Books, 2006); Adam L. Fuller, *Taking the Fight to the Enemy: Neoconservatism and the Age of Ideology* (Lanham, MD: Lexington Books, 2012). For attacks on neoconservatism, see Gary Dorrien, *Imperial Designs: Neoconservatism and the New Pax Americana* (New York: Routledge, 2004); Bruce W. Holsinger, *Neomedievalism, Neoconservatism, and the War on Terror* (Chicago: Prickly Paradigm, 2007); Jean-François Drolet, *American Neoconservatism: The Politics and Culture of a Reactionary Idealism* (London: Hurts, 2011).

9. In *Neoconservatism*, Vaïsse speaks of "Three Ages" of neoconservatism, tracing its history from the leftward drift of the Democratic Party in the 1960s through the turn toward foreign policy concerns in 1972 and finally to the Reagan administration, which gave birth to the contemporary understanding associated primarily with the administration of George W. Bush.

10. John Ehrman, *The Rise of Neoconservatism: Intellectuals and Foreign Affairs, 1945–1994* (New Haven, CT: Yale University Press, 1995), 69–70.

11. Gil Troy, *Moynihan's Moment: America's Fight against Zionism as Racism* (New York: Oxford University Press, 2013), 48.

12. Ehrman, *Rise of Neoconservatism*, 67.

13. Murray Rothbard, "Confessions of a Right-Wing Liberal," *Ramparts* 6, no. 4 (June 1968), https://mises.org/library/confessions-right-wing-liberal; Troy, *Moynihan's Moment*, 49.

14. Vaïsse, *Neoconservatism*, 70, proposes *Commentary*'s 1970 offensive as one of neoconservatism's possible birth dates.

15. Troy, *Moynihan's Moment*, 51–52.

16. Troy, 52.

17. Troy, 55–56.

18. Notable neoconservatives in the coalition included Daniel Bell, Midge Decter, Nathan Glazer, Samuel Huntington, Max Kampleman, Jeane Kirkpatrick, Charles Krauthammer, Irving Kristol, Daniel Patrick Moynihan, Michael Novak, and Norman Podhoretz.

19. Vaïsse, *Neoconservatism*, 136–37; Douglas Schoen, *The Nixon Effect: How His Presidency Has Changed American Politics* (New York: Encounter Books, 2016), 190.

20. Daniel Patrick Moynihan, "Was Woodrow Wilson Right?" *Commentary*, May 1, 1974, https://www.commentarymagazine.com/articles/was-woodrow-wilson-right/.

21. Israel Shanker, "Moynihan Finds UN with Head Lost in Cloud of Ideals," *New York Times*, November 10, 1971.

22. Ehrman, *Rise of Neoconservatism*, 83.

23. Daniel Patrick Moynihan, "The United States in Opposition," *Commentary*, March 1, 1975, https://www.commentarymagazine.com/articles/the-united-states-in-opposition/.

24. Troy, *Moynihan's Moment*, 60.

25. Memorandum of conversation (hereafter memcon), Ford, Moynihan, Kissinger, and Scowcroft, "American Strategy at the UN," April 12, 1975, https://www.fordlibr arymuseum.gov/library/document/0314/1553022.pdf.

26. Troy, *Moynihan's Moment*, 59–61.

27. See Niall Ferguson, *Kissinger*, vol. 1, *1923–1968: The Idealist* (New York: Penguin, 2015). For the argument that Kissinger was actually a neoconservative pioneer, see Greg Grandin, *Kissinger's Shadow: The Long Reach of America's Most Controversial Diplomat* (New York: Metropolitan Books, 2015). I reject both views.

28. Memo, White House, "The Moynihan Article in *Commentary* Magazine," April 15, 1975, GFPL, folder: Moynihan, Daniel (1), box 26, Robert Goldwin Papers.

29. US Department of State, *Foreign Relations of the United States* [hereafter *FRUS*], *1969–1976*, vol. E-14, pt. 1, *Documents on the United Nations, 1973–1976*, ed. William B. McAllister (Washington, DC: Government Printing Office, 2008), doc. 13, https://history.state.gov/historicaldocuments/frus1969-76ve14p1/d13.

30. *FRUS, 1969–1976*, vol. 35, *National Security Policy, 1973–1976*, ed. M. Todd Bennett (Washington, DC: Government Printing Office, 2014), doc. 29, https://history.state.gov/historicaldocuments/frus1969-76v35/d29.

31. Memcon, Ford et al., "American Strategy at the UN"; emphasis added.

32. John Toye and Richard Toye, *The UN and Global Political Economy: Trade, Finance, and Development* (Bloomington: Indiana University Press, 2004), 241; Ash Narain Roy, *The Third World in the Age of Globalization: Requiem or New Agenda?* (New York: Zed Books, 1999), 56.

33. Telephone conversation (hereafter telcon), Kissinger-Ingersoll, "U.N. Vote on Economic Rights Charter," December 6, 1974, in "The Kissinger Telephone Conversations: A Verbatim Record of U.S. Diplomacy, 1969–1977" (hereafter "Kissinger Telcons"), National Security Archive at George Washington University, http://search.proquest.com/dnsa_ka/docview/1679092061/3A02D9DCD17047DCPQ/58?accountid=9673.

34. Memcon, Ford, Kissinger, and Scowcroft, April 15, 1975, https://www.fordlibrarymuseum.gov/library/document/0314/1553028.pdf.

35. Memo, Hormats to Kissinger, "Followup to Consumer/Producer Preparatory Conference," April 25, 1975, GFPL, folder: Utilities, box 4, White House Central Files (hereafter WHCF).

36. *FRUS, 1969–1976*, vol. 31, *Foreign Economic Policy, 1973–76*, doc. 94, https://history.state.gov/historicaldocuments/frus1969-76v31/d94.

37. Memo, Hormats to Kissinger, "Scenario for Dealing with Energy and Raw Materials," May 16, 1975, GFPL, folder: Utilities, box 4, WHCF.

38. Memo, Economic Policy Board, "Kissinger's UN 7th Special Session Speech," August 20, 1975, GFPL, folder: Porter, Roger (2), box 200, Economic Policy Board.

39. Memcon, Ford et al., "American Strategy at the UN."

40. Clipping, "United Nations: Barking Less and Liking It More," *Time*, September 29, 1975, GFPL, folder: Moynihan, Daniel P. (1), box K25, Arthur Burns Papers;

telcon, Kissinger-Moynihan, "U.N. Issue and Treasury Department," September 13, 1975, in "Kissinger Telcons," http://search.proquest.com.proxy.bc.edu/dnsa_ka /docview/1679101022/70D0F486ECD44D35PQ/18?accountid=9673.

41. Clipping, Don Shannon, "Rich, Poor Nations Compromise on Aid," *Los Angeles Times*, September 17, 1975, GFPL, folder: Moynihan, Daniel P. (1), box K25, Arthur Burns Papers.

42. Daniel Patrick Moynihan, *A Dangerous Place* (Boston: Little, Brown, 1978), 131–32.

43. Shannon, "Rich, Poor Nations Compromise."

44. Clipping, Paul Hofmann, "Shift in Third World's Views Shown in U.N. Session," *New York Times*, September 19, 1975, GFPL, folder: Moynihan, Daniel P. (1), box K25, Arthur Burns Papers.

45. Telcon, Kissinger-Moynihan, "U.N. Economic Debate," September 13, 1975, in "Kissinger Telcons," http://search.proquest.com/dnsa_ka/docview/1679104673 /CF5415D9F7E04EB8PQ/11?accountid=9673.

46. Hofmann, "Shift in Third World's Views."

47. "Benign Attention at the U.N.," *Newsweek*, September 22, 1975, GFPL (II), folder: Moynihan, Daniel P. (2), box 26, Robert Goldwin Papers.

48. "Winning the Fourth World," *Wall Street Journal*, September 26, 1975, GFPL, folder: Moynihan, Daniel P. (2), box 26, Robert Goldwin Papers.

49. Moynihan, *Dangerous Place*, 118.

50. Members of the commission were particularly fond of this phrase. See, for example, C. Fred Bergsten, Georges Berthoin, and Kinhide Mushakoji, "The Reform of International Institutions: A Report of the Trilateral Task Force on International Institutions to the Trilateral Commission," *Triangle Papers* no. 11 (1976), v; Richard N. Gardner, "To Make the World Safe for Interdependence," UN 30 (New York: United Nations Association of the USA, 1975).

51. Moynihan, *Dangerous Place*, 118.

52. Moynihan, *Dangerous Place*, 140.

53. Moynihan, 141.

54. Henry Kissinger, "Building International Order," address to the 30th General Assembly of the United Nations, September 22, 1975, https://www.fordlibrarymuseum .gov/library/document/dosb/1894.pdf#page=3.

55. *FRUS, 1969–1976*, vol. 31, doc. 292, https://history.state.gov/historicaldocuments /frus1969-76v31/d292#fn2.

56. See Richard N. Cooper, *The Economics of Interdependence: Economic Policy in the Atlantic Community* (New York: Columbia University Press, 1968); Zbigniew Brzezinski, "U.S. Foreign Policy: The Search for Focus," *Foreign Affairs* 51, no. 4 (July 1973): 708–27.

57. Moynihan, *Dangerous Place*, 148; emphasis in original.

58. Moynihan, 142, 147.

59. Television transcript, *Meet the Press*, GFPL (II), folder: Meet the Press—Sept. 14, 1975, box 70, Ron Nessen Files.

60. Michael Novak, "Twice Chosen," in *The Neoconservative Imagination: Essays in Honor of William Kristol*, ed. Christopher C. Demuth and William Kristol (Washington, DC: AEI Press, 1995), 73–82.

61. Television transcript, *Meet the Press*.

62. Moynihan, *Dangerous Place*, 153–54.

63. Moynihan, 155.

64. Moynihan, 154.

65. Moynihan, 155–56.

66. Joel Peters, *Israel and Africa: The Problematic Friendship* (London: I. B. Tauris Press, 1992), 75–76.

67. "Clearer Days at Turtle Bay," *Wall Street Journal*, October 14, 1975, GFPL, folder: Moynihan, Daniel P. (2), box 26, Robert Goldwin Papers.

68. Poll conducted by Opinion Research Corporation, Princeton, NJ, January 12, 1976, GFPL, folder: Moynihan, Daniel P. (2), box 26, Robert Goldwin Papers.

69. Troy, *Moynihan's Moment*, 104.

70. "Moynihan Criticism of Amin Has U.N. People Buzzing," *New York Times*, October 5, 1975, GFPL, folder: Moynihan, Daniel P. (2), box 26, Robert Goldwin Papers.

71. Troy, *Moynihan's Moment*, 103; "The Moynihan Controversy," *Newsweek*, October 20, 1975.

72. Telcon, Kissinger-Ingersoll, "Daniel Moynihan and Organization of African Unity," October 9, 1975, in "Kissinger Telcons," http://search.proquest.com/dnsa_ka/docview/1679102728/AA93F227380C427FPQ/2?accountid=9673.

73. Troy, *Moynihan's Moment*, 98.

74. Memo, Hal Horan to Scowcroft, "Presidential Statement on Zionism/Racism," October 24, 1975, GFPL, folder: USUN (8), box 21, Presidential Agency Files, National Security Advisor (hereafter NSA).

75. Telcon, Kissinger-Buffum, "Daniel Moynihan's Statement on Zionism," November 10, 1975, in "Kissinger Telcons," http://search.proquest.com/dnsa_ka/docview/1679101778/AC632375A56849A1PQ/3?accountid=9673.

76. "An 'Infamous Act' at the U.N.," *Newsweek*, November 24, 1975.

77. *FRUS, 1969–1976*, vol. E-14, pt. 1, doc. 36, https://history.state.gov/historicaldocuments/frus1969-76ve14p1/d36.

78. "'Infamous Act' at the U.N."

79. Ehrman, *Rise of Neoconservatism*, 85.

80. Clipping, "A Fighting Irishman," *Time*, January 26, 1976, GFPL, folder: USUN (9), box 21, International Economic Affairs Staff, NSA.

81. John F. Burns, "Huge Rally Here Condemns U.N. Anti-Zionism Move," *New York Times*, November 12, 1975.

82. Vaïsse, *Neoconservatism*, 122–24.

83. Telcon, Kissinger-Buffum, "UN Resolution; Includes Follow-up Telephone Conversation at 3:43 pm," November 5, 1975, in "Kissinger Telcons," http://search.proquest.com/dnsa_ka/docview/1679091106/DED11DCFF2A14EADPQ/1?accountid=9673.

84. Daniel J. Sargent, *A Superpower Transformed: The Remaking of American Foreign Relations in the 1970s* (New York: Oxford University Press, 2005), 199.

85. Moynihan, *Dangerous Place*, 162.

86. *FRUS, 1969–1976*, vol. 16, *Soviet Union, August 1974–December 1976*, doc. 299, https://history.state.gov/historicaldocuments/frus1969-76v16/d229.

87. Memcon, "Rambouillet Economic Summit," November 16, 1975, https://www.fordlibrarymuseum.gov/library/document/0314/1553299.pdf.

88. "Fighting Irishman."

89. *FRUS, 1969–1976*, vol. E-14, pt. 1, doc. 38, https://history.state.gov/historical documents/frus1969-76ve14p1/d38.

90. Moynihan, *Dangerous Place*, 275–76.

91. "Fighting Irishman."

92. Ehrman, *Rise of Neoconservatism*, 91–92.

93. Kissinger explained: "We should try to break what the Chancellor [Helmut Schmidt] correctly called the unholy alliance between the LDCs and OPEC. This can happen, and we can achieve our results, if they know that their disruptive actions could stop discussions on commodities or that they will pay a price in terms of cooperation, or military exports. In this way we can combat our dependence with a coherent strategy." *FRUS, 1969–76*, vol. 31, doc. 124, https://history.state.gov/historicaldocuments/frus1969-76v31/d124.

94. Henry Kissinger, *Years of Renewal* (New York: Simon and Schuster, 1999), 677.

95. US State Department, Office of the Historian, "The Panama Canal and the Torrijos-Carter Treaties," https://history.state.gov/milestones/1977-1980/panama-canal.

96. Gerald E. Thomas, "The Black Revolt: The United States and Africa in the 1960s," in *The Diplomacy of the Crucial Decade: American Foreign Relations during the 1960s*, ed. Diane B. Kunz (New York: Columbia University Press, 1994), 346–47.

97. *FRUS, 1969–1976*, vol. E-14, pt. 1, doc. 18, https://history.state.gov/historical documents/frus1969-76ve14p1/d18.

98. Sargent, *Superpower Transformed*, 220–21.

99. *FRUS, 1969–1976*, vol. E-6, *Documents on Africa, 1973–1976*, doc. 34, https://history .state.gov/historicaldocuments/frus1969-76ve06/d34.

100. *FRUS, 1969–1976*, vol. E-6, doc. 31, https://history.state.gov/historicaldocuments /frus1969-76ve06/d31.

101. *FRUS, 1969–1976*, vol. E-6, doc. 44, https://history.state.gov/historicaldocuments /frus1969-76ve06/d44.

102. *FRUS, 1969–1976*, vol. E-6, doc. 44.

103. Memcon, Ford, Kissinger, and congressional leadership, "Report on Secretary's Trip to Africa," May 12, 1976, GFPL, folder: Africa, box 1, International Economic Affairs Staff, NSA.

104. *FRUS, 1969–1976*, vol. E-6, doc. 42, https://history.state.gov/historicaldocuments /frus1969-76ve06/d42.

105. *FRUS, 1969–1976*, vol. 31, doc. 301, https://history.state.gov/historicaldocu ments/frus1969-76v31/d301.

106. Briefing paper, State Department, "Relationship of CIEC and Other International Agencies," n.d., GFPL, folder: State Department (1), box 105, Paul W. MacAvoy Files, Council of Economic Advisors.

107. *FRUS, 1969–1976*, vol. 31, doc. 304, https://history.state.gov/historicaldocu ments/frus1969-76v31/d304.

108. Kissinger, *Years of Renewal*, 925.

109. *FRUS, 1969–1976*, vol. E-6, doc. 44.

110. *FRUS, 1969–1976*, vol. E-6, doc. 39, https://history.state.gov/historicaldocuments /frus1969-76ve06/d39.

111. Henry Kissinger, "America and Africa," April 30, 1976, *Department of State Bulletin* 74, no. 1927 (1976): 679, https://www.fordlibrarymuseum.gov/library/document /dosb/1927.pdf#page=3.

112. Henry Kissinger, "United States Policy on Southern Africa," April 27, 1976, *Department of State Bulletin* 74, no. 1927 (1976): 674.

113. Sargent, *Superpower Transformed*, 206, 225. Kaunda was known for weeping at public events, so this would not have surprised Zambians.

114. "Press Conference by Secretary Kissinger and British Foreign Secretary Crosland," April 24, 1976, *Department of State Bulletin* 74, no. 1927 (1976): 691.

115. Kissinger, "United States Policy on Southern Africa," 677.

116. B. P. Menon, *Global Dialogue: The New International Economic Order* (New York: Pergamon, 1977), 20.

117. Gamani Corea, *Taming Commodity Markets: The Integrated Programme and the Common Fund in UNCTAD* (Manchester, UK: Manchester University Press, 1992). About UNCTAD II, Corea writes, "The ideas and the analysis presented there established the basis of UNCTAD's approach to the commodity problem and UNCTAD's efforts in the subsequent period—right up to UNCTAD IV in 1976—were essentially to win acceptance of this [comprehensive] approach" (24).

118. Menon, *Global Dialogue*, 23–25.

119. Menon, 26.

120. Gwenyth Williams, *Third World Political Organizations: A Review of Developments* (London: Macmillan Press, 1987), 35; Giuliano Garavini, *After Empires: European Integration, Decolonization, and the Challenge from the Global South 1957–1986* (Oxford: Oxford University Press, 2012), 223.

121. "UNCTAD IV: Expanding Cooperation for Global Economic Development," May 6, 1976, *Department of State Bulletin* 74, no. 1927 (1976): 622–23.

122. Ann Crittendom, "Kissinger's Trade-off on Aid," *New York Times*, May 7, 1976, http://www.nytimes.com/1976/05/07/archives/kissingers-tradeoff-on-aid-plan-for-resources-bank-is-viewed-as.html.

123. Garavini, *After Empires*, 202.

124. Paul Hallwood and Stuart Sinclair, *Oil, Debt, and Development: OPEC in the Third World* (London: Routledge, 1981), 84. Those countries, in order of most to least indebted were Mexico, Brazil, India, Israel, Korea, Pakistan, Egypt, Argentina, Turkey, and Chile.

125. Garavini, *After Empires*, 222.

126. "UNCTAD IV," 670.

127. See Corea, *Taming Commodity Markets*, 52–53, for a detailed explanation of this phenomenon.

128. Corea, 52–57.

129. The G-77 leaders were Herbert Walker of Jamaica, Layachi Yaker of Algeria, Manuel Perez-Guerrero of Venezuela, Wijojo Nitisastro of Indonesia, and "certain others." For Group B, they were Charles Robinson of the United States, Frank Judd of Britain, Jean Francois-Poncet of France, Jan Pronk of the Netherlands, Hans Friderichs and Egon Bahr of Germany, C. Lindbom of Sweden, and B. Yoshino of Japan. Corea, 59.

130. Corea, 59–60.

131. Corea, 63.

132. This is the source of an old joke in UN circles regarding UNCTAD's name: Under No Circumstances Take Any Decisions. The General Agreement on Tariffs and Trade was also mocked as the General Agreement to Talk and Talk. For UNCTAD, see Thomas George Weiss, *UN Voices: The Struggle for Development and Social Justice*

(Bloomington: Indiana University Press, 2005), 421. For GATT, see Robert Kuttner, "Another Great Victory of Ideology over Prosperity," *Atlantic*, October 1991.

133. Corea, *Taming Commodity Markets*, 66–68.

134. Menon, *Global Dialogue*, 28.

135. *FRUS, 1969–1976*, vol. 31, doc. 304.

136. *FRUS, 1969–1976*, vol. 31, doc. 304.

137. Memo, Robinson to Kissinger, "Discussion with Giscard on North-South Relations," May 17, 1976, GFPL (II), folder: France (2), box 1, International Economic Affairs Staff, NSA.

138. *FRUS, 1969–1976*, vol. 31, doc. 304.

139. Corea, *Taming Commodity Markets*, 110–14.

140. Robert A. Pastor, ed., *Latin American Debt Crisis: Adjusting for the Past or Planning for the Future* (Boulder, CO: Lynne Rienner, 1987), 9.

141. Donella H. Meadows, *The Global Citizen* (Washington, DC: Island Press, 1991), 77.

142. Corea, *Taming Commodity Markets*, 52.

143. State Department, "Briefing Paper on CIEC," July 26, 1976, GFPL, folder: International Organizations, box 1, International Organizations, WHCF.

144. Menon, *Global Dialogue*, 32.

145. "Brazil, Venezuela, Argentina, India, Indonesia, Zaire, and Zambia," the State Department reported in April 1977, "all indicated that their support for postponement was based on expectations that the new Administration will soften the U.S. position on LDC debt rescheduling and ask Congress for increased U.S. contributions to the World Bank's 'soft loan' facility." Telegram, State to Embassies, April 1977, Jimmy Carter Presidential Library, RAC, NLC-24-59-2-4-4. .

146. Vaïsse, *Neoconservatism*, 125.

147. CDM member Penn Kemple explained, "Carter was not elected with any real ideological views, he was just somebody all people could coalesce around, and this was very uncomfortable for us, because we didn't have much confidence in Carter, we were against him, we were for [Henry] Scoop [Jackson]." Vaïsse, 126.

148. Transcript, "The Second Ford-Carter Presidential Debate, October 6, 1976," http://www.debates.org/index.php?page=october-6-1976-debate-transcript.

4. Interdependence, Development, and Jimmy Carter

1. Robert A. Strong, "Jimmy Carter: Campaigns and Elections," http://millercenter.org/president/biography/carter-campaigns-and-elections.

2. Zbigniew Brzezinski, *Power and Principle: Memoirs of the National Security Advisor, 1977–1981* (New York: Farrar, Straus, and Giroux, 1983), 7.

3. Second Debate—Carter on Foreign Policy—Briefing Book (1), October 6, 1975, Gerald Ford Presidential Library (hereafter GFPL), White House Special Files Unit, box 2, https://www.fordlibrarymuseum.gov/library/document/0010/1554419.pdf.

4. Gardner to Eizenstat, October 12, 1976, Jimmy Carter Presidential Library (hereafter JCPL), Carter-Mondale Campaign Committee, Eizenstat Subject Files, box 3, Commodities, 6/74–10/76; Strong, "Jimmy Carter."

5. Richard N. Cooper, *The Economics of Interdependence: Economic Policy in the Atlantic Community* (New York: Columbia University Press, 1968).

6. Address by President Nixon to the UN General Assembly, September 18, 1969, http://www.state.gov/p/io/potusunga/207305.htm.

7. US Department of State, *Foreign Relations of the United States* [hereafter *FRUS*], *1969–1976*, vol. E-14, pt. 1, *Documents on the United Nations, 1973–1976*, doc. 129, https://history.state.gov/historicaldocuments/frus1969-76ve14p1/d129.

8. Henry Kissinger, "An Age of Interdependence: Common Disaster or Common Community," speech before the 29th UN General Assembly, September 23, 1974, https://www.fordlibrarymuseum.gov/library/document/dosb/1842.pdf#page=8.

9. Greg Grandin, *Kissinger's Shadow: The Long Reach of America's Most Controversial Statesman* (New York: Metropolitan Books, 2015), 130.

10. Stephen McGlinchey, "Review—Brzezinski's Technetronic Era," July 22, 2011, E-International Relations, http://www.e-ir.info/2011/07/22/review-between-two -ages-america%E2%80%99s-role-in-the-technetronic-era/; Andrew Gavin Marshall, "Controlling the Global Economy," August 3, 2009, Center for Research on Global- ization, http://www.globalresearch.ca/controlling-the-global-economy-bilderberg-the -trilateral-commission-and-the-federal-reserve/14614.

11. Richard Ullman, "Trilateralism: Partnership for What?" *Foreign Affairs*, Octo- ber 1976, 3–4.

12. "Meeting on Proposed Trilateral Commission," July 23–24, 1972, JCPL, Zbig- niew Brzezinski Collection, Gerard Smith Subject Files, box 1, Gerard Smith File— Chron File, 5/11/72–2/28/73.

13. Richard N. Gardner, Saburo Okita, and B. J. Udink, *A Turning Point in North- South Economic Relations: A Report of the Trilateral Task Force on Relations with Develop- ing Countries to the Executive Commission of the Trilateral Commission*, Triangle Papers no. 3 (1974), 11, http://trilateral.org//download/doc/economic_relations_19741.pdf.

14. Gardner et al., 9, 15.

15. Scowcroft to the President, "Results of Meeting to Review Issues in World Food Conference Speech," November 2, 1974, GFPL, Files of the National Security Adviser, Presidential Subject File, box 6, Food/Food Aid/World Food Conference (3). .)

16. Richard N. Gardner, Saburo Okita, and B. J. Udink, *OPEC, the Trilateral Countries, and the Developing Countries: New Arrangements for Cooperation 1976–1980*, Triangle Papers no. 7 (1975), 9–12, http://trilateral.org//download/doc/OPEC_new_arrangements _cooperation_1976_1980.pdf.

17. Gardner et al., 13–14.

18. A. van de Laar, *The World Bank and the Poor*, vol. 6 of Institute of Social Studies Series on the Development of Societies (Boston: Martinus Nijhoff, 1980), 30–31.

19. Bergsten advised: "Politicization of issues is better avoided in functionally spe- cific institutions [such as the IMF and GATT] simply because of the consensus that such institutions are the best, perhaps only, places where serious business could be done. The same countries which will indulge in fanciful rhetoric in a broad, multipur- pose organization (such as various UN agencies) will often be negotiating seriously and cooperatively in another organization (such as GATT) on the same issue at the very same time. The more technical focus, and lesser public awareness, of such organizations promotes such a result." C. Fred Bergsten, Georges Berthoin, Kinhide Mushakoji, and John Pinder, *The Reform of International Institutions*, 6, http://trilateral.org//download /doc/reform_of_internatioal_institutions.pdf.

20. Bergsten et al., 2.

21. Jimmy Carter, *Keeping Faith: Memoirs of a President* (New York: Bantam Books, 1982), 51.

22. Brzezinski, *Power and Principle*, 5.

23. Carter, *Keeping Faith*, 51.

24. *FRUS, 1969–1976*, vol. E-14, pt. 1, doc. 147, https://history.state.gov/historical documents/frus1969-76ve14p1/d147.

25. Brzezinski, *Power and Principle*, 5.

26. Carter, *Keeping Faith*, 51–52.

27. Jimmy Carter, *Why Not the Best? The First 50 Years* (New York: Bantam Books, 1976), 141–42. Historian Douglas Brinkley explains in the introduction to a 1996 reprint of this book: "Almost as a matter of policy Carter would ask reporters about to interview him if they had read his book." When a reporter asked whether Carter had a "master plan" for his presidency, Carter "snapped, 'It's in the book . . . how I decided to run for the presidency, and the plans are in the book. There's no point in talking about these things when they're in the book.'"

28. Brzezinski is referring to the Conference on International Economic Cooperation, which first met in Paris on December 16–19, 1975.

29. Brzezinski, *Power and Principle*, 7.

30. Brzezinski, 7.

31. Jimmy Carter, "Relations between the World's Democracies," speech to the New York Foreign Policy Association, in *FRUS, 1977–1980*, vol. 1, *Foundations of Foreign Policy*, doc. 6, https://history.state.gov/historicaldocuments/frus1977-80v01/d6.

32. "'Ask President Carter': Remarks during a Telephone Call-in Program on the CBS Radio Network," March 5, 1977, in *Public Papers of the Presidents of the United States: Jimmy Carter, 1977* (Washington, DC: Federal Register Division, National Archives and Records Service, General Services Administration, 1977), 313.

33. Edward S. Berman, *The Influence of the Ford, Rockefeller, and Carnegie Foundations on American Foreign Policy: The Ideology of Philanthropy* (Albany, NY: SUNY Press, 1983), 140.

34. Javier A. Reyes and W. Charles Sawyer, *Latin American Economic Development* (New York: Routledge, 2016), 281.

35. John Toye and Richard Toye, *The UN and Global Political Economy: Trade, Finance, and Development* (Bloomington: Indiana University Press), 13; "Raul Prebisch: Latin America's Keynes," *Economist*, March 5, 2009, http://www.economist.com/node/1322 6316.

36. Colm Foy and Henry Helmich, *Public Support for International Development* (Development Centre of the OECD, 1996), 71.

37. David Ekbladh, *The Great American Mission: Modernization and the Construction of an American World Order* (Princeton, NJ: Princeton University Press, 2010), 190.

38. Bauer collected many of his earlier critiques in a book published in 1971. See P. T. Bauer, *Dissent on Development: Studies and Debates in Development Economics* (London: Weidenfeld and Nicolson, 1971). He was also active in neoconservative circles and penned many criticisms of US development and North-South policy in *Commentary* throughout the 1970s. Bauer's relationship with and influence on Margaret Thatcher is well known, but his influence was also felt in the Reagan administration, where, a top

official recalled receiving "'many position papers of the P. T. Bauer variety'" on foreign aid. See Steven G. Livingston, "The Politics of International Agenda-Setting: Reagan and North-South Relations" *International Studies Quarterly* 36, no. 3 (Sept. 1992): 319.

39. Ekbladh, *Great American Mission*, 244.

40. Devesh Kapur and John P. Louis, *The World Bank: Its First Half Century; History*(Washington, DC: Brookings Institution Press, 1997), 233.

41. Edward Ramsamy, *World Bank and Urban Development: From Projects to Policy* (New York: Routledge, 2006), 61–63.

42. "World Banking McNamara-Style," *Business Week*, September 27, 1969, 100.

43. Ekbladh, *Great American Mission*, 245.

44. Berman, *Influence of the Ford, Rockefeller, and Carnegie Foundations*, 140; Ekbladh, *Great American Mission*, 245.

45. Michael O'Brien, *Hesburgh: A Biograph* (Washington, D.C.: Catholic University Press of America, 1998), 145.

46. "World Banking McNamara-Style," 100.

47. Berman, *Influence of the Ford, Rockefeller, and Carnegie Foundations*, 140.

48. Kapur and Louis, *World Bank*, 227–28.

49. Thomas G. Weiss, Tatiana Carayannis, Louis Emmerij, and Richard Jolly, *UN Voices: The Struggle for Development and Social Justice* (Bloomington: Indiana University Press, 2005), 240–42; Louis Emmerij, "The Basic Human Needs Development Strategy," background paper, UN World Economic and Social Survey 2010, http://www.un.org/en/development/desa/policy/wess/wess_bg_papers/bp_wess2010_emmerij.pdf.

50. Ekbladh, *Great American Mission*, 245.

51. Kapur and Louis, *World Bank*, 229.

52. James P. Grant, "Growth from Below: A People-Oriented Development Strategy," ODC Development Paper 16, December 1973, 5–6.

53. Donald Mackay Fraser, inventory of his papers at the Minnesota Historical Society, http://www2.mnhs.org/library/findaids/00290.xml.

54. Arvonne Fraser and Hudson Perdita, eds., *Third World Women Speak Out: Interviews in Six Countries on Change, Development, and Basic Human Needs* (New York: Praeger for the Overseas Development Council, 1979).

55. Brian H. Smith, *More than Altruism: The Politics of Private Foreign Aid* (Princeton, NJ: Princeton University Press, 1990), 67–68.

56. Mark F. McGuire and Vernon W. Ruttan, "Lost Directions: U.S. Foreign Assistance Policy since New Directions," Economic Development Center, University of Minnesota, August 1989, 2, http://ageconsearch.umn.edu/bitstream/7465/1/edc89-05.pdf.

57. James W. Howe, *The United States and the Developing World: Agenda for Action, 1974* (New York: Praeger for the Overseas Development Council, 1974), v.

58. James W. Howe, *The United States and the Developing World: Agenda for Action, 1975* (New York: Praeger for the Overseas Development Council, 1975), v.

59. Quoted in Howe, *Agenda for Action, 1975*, v–vii; emphasis in original.

60. "Stuart Eizenstat Exit Interview," January 10, 1981, JCPL,https://www.jimmycarterlibrary.gov/assets/documents/oral_histories/exit_interviews/Eizenstat.pdf.

61. Owen to Eizenstat, April 17, 1974, JCPL, Carter-Mondale Campaign Committee, Eizenstat Subject Files, box 16, Foreign Policy, 10/73–8/74.

62. Hesburgh to Ford, November 22, 1974; Ford to Hesburgh, December 9, 1974; Hesburgh to Ford, December 14, 1974; Ford to Hesburgh, January 21, 1975; Hesburgh to Ford, February 13, 1975; Ford to Hesburgh, March 18, 1975, JCPL, Carter-Mondale Campaign Committee, Eizenstat Subject Files, box 3, Commodities, 11/74–3/75.

63. O'Brien, 144–45.

64. O'Brien, 148.

65. Gardner to Eizenstat, October 12, 1976.

66. Transcript, "The Second Ford-Carter Presidential Debate, October 6, 1976," http://www.debates.org/index.php?page=october-6-1976-debate-transcript.

67. O'Brien, *Hesburgh*, 148.

68. Jimmy Carter, Address at Commencement Exercises at the University of Notre Dame, May 22, 1977, https://www.presidency.ucsb.edu/documents/address-comme ncement-exercises-the-university-notre-dame.

69. Second Debate—Carter on Foreign Policy—Briefing Book (1).

70. Second Debate—Carter on Foreign Policy—Briefing Book (1).

71. Guy Erb to Brzezinski, "North-South Policies: Assessment and Recommenda-tions," February 11, 1978, JCPL, NLC-15-108-2-1-3.

72. Lars Schoultz, *Human Rights and United States Policy toward Latin America* (Prince-ton, NJ: Princeton University Press, 1981), 122.

73. Arthur Schlesinger Jr., "Human Rights and the American Tradition," *Foreign Af-fairs*, Fall 1978, 512.

74. Lucy Komisar, "Kissinger Covered up Torture," *Guardian* (Manchester), Febru-ary 28, 1999, http://www.theguardian.com/world/1999/feb/28/theobserver3.

75. Second Debate—Carter on Foreign Policy—Briefing Book (1).

76. Schoultz, *Human Rights*, 118.

77. General Assembly resolution 29/3281, *Charter of Economic Rights and Duties of States*, A/RES/29/3281 (December 12, 1974), http://www.un-documents.net/a29r32 81.htm.

78. Roland Burke, "Competing for the Last Utopia? The NIEO, Human Rights, and the World Conference for the International Women's Year, Mexico City, June 1975," *Humanity: An International Journal of Human Rights* 6, no. 1 (Spring 2015): 1, 50–53.

79. Roger D. Hansen, "North-South Policy—What's the Problem?" *Foreign Affairs*, Summer 1980, 1111.

5. Debt, Development, and Human Rights

1. Henry Kissinger, *Years of Renewal* (New York: Simon and Schuster, 1999), 707–9.

2. Kissinger, 709.

3. US Department of State, *Foreign Relations of the United States* [hereafter *FRUS*], *1969–1976*, vol. 36, *Energy Crisis, 1969–74*, doc. 299, https://history.state.gov/historical documents/frus1969-76v36/d299.

4. Kissinger, *Years of Renewal*, 710.

5. Christopher Dietrich, *Oil Revolution: Anticolonial Elites, Sovereign Rights, and the Eco-nomic Culture of Decolonization* (New York: Cambridge University Press, 2017), 277–78.

6. Kissinger, *Years of Renewal*, 710.

7. Henry Kissinger, "A Just Consensus: A Stable Order, a Durable Peace," speech to the 28th session of the UN General Assembly, September 24, 1973, *Department of State Bulletin* 69, no. 1790 (October 15, 1973): 469–73.

8. Henry Kissinger, "A Western Hemisphere Relationship of Cooperation," October 5, 1973, *Department of State Bulletin* 69, no. 1792 (October 29, 1973): 543.

9. *FRUS, 1969–1976*, vol. 38, pt. 1, *Foundations of Foreign Policy*, doc. 18, https://history.state.gov/historicaldocuments/frus1969-76v38p1/d18.

10. See Zbigniew Brzezinski, *Between Two Ages: America's Role in the Technetronic Era* (New York: Viking Press, 1970).

11. *FRUS, 1969–1976*, vol. 38, pt. 1, doc. 18.

12. Abraham Lowenthal, "The United States and Latin America: Ending the Hegemonic Presumption," *Foreign Affairs* 55, no. 199 (1976–77): 202.

13. Odd Arne Westad, *The Cold War: A Global History* (New York: Basic Books, 2017), 344.

14. Hal Brands, *Latin America's Cold War* (Cambridge, MA: Harvard University Press, 2012), 13, 58–59.

15. Westad, *Cold War*, 349–51.

16. John W. Young and John Kent, *International Relations since 1945: A Global History* (Oxford: Oxford University Press, 2013), 149.

17. Ronald W. Cox, *Power and Profits: U.S. Policy in Central America* (Lexington: University Press of Kentucky, 1994), 83–85.

18. Peter H. Smith, *Talons of the Eagle: Dynamics of U.S.–Latin American Relations* (Oxford: Oxford University Press, 1999), 150–52.

19. International Commission for Central American Recovery and Development, *Central American Recovery and Development Task Force Report* (Durham, NC: Duke University Press, 1989), 352–53.

20. Quoted in John Toye and Richard Toye, *The UN and Global Political Economy: Trade, Finance, and Development* (Bloomington: Indiana University Press, 2004), 143–44.

21. Robert D. Bond, "Regionalism in Latin America: Prospects for the Latin American Economic System (SELA)," *International Organization* 32, no. 2 (Spring 1978): 402.

22. "Special Latin American Coordinating Committee (CECLA)—European Communities: Declaration Establishing Machinery for Dialogue on System of Cooperation," *International Legal Materials* 10, no. 4 (1971): 873–76.

23. Judith Ewell, *Venezuela and the United States: From Monroe's Hemisphere to Petroleum's Empire* (Athens: University of Georgia Press, 1996), 219.

24. Bond, "Regionalism in Latin America," 402.

25. Ewell, *Venezuela and the United States*, 204–5.

26. "The President of Venezuela Responds to the President of the United States," *New York Times*, September 25, 1974.

27. David Binder, "20 Latin Countries Condemn U.S. Trade Act," *New York Times*, January 24, 1975, 3.

28. Arthur S. Banks et al., *Political Handbook of the World 1998* (London: Palgrave, 1998), 1120, s.v. "SELA."

29. Kissinger, *Years of Renewal*, 730.

30. Kissinger, 724.

31. *FRUS, 1969–1976*, vol. 38, pt. 1, doc. 63, fn. 3, https://history.state.gov/historical documents/frus1969-76v38p1/d63#fn3.

32. *FRUS, 1969–1976*, vol. 38, pt. 1, doc. 63.

33. Russel Crandall, *Gunboat Diplomacy: U.S. Interventions in the Dominican Republic, Grenada, and Panama* (Lanham, MD: Rowman and Littlefield, 2006), 184.

34. Kissinger, *Years of Renewal*, 716.

35. US Department of State, "The Panama Canal and the Torrijos-Carter Treaties," https://history.state.gov/milestones/1977-1980/panama-canal.

36. Kissinger, *Years of Renewal*, 716.

37. Transcript, "The Second Carter-Ford Presidential Debate," October 6, 1976, http://www.debates.org/index.php?page=october-6-1976-debate-transcript.

38. Zbigniew Brzezinski, *Power and Principle: Memoirs of a National Security Advisor* (New York: Farrar, Straus, and Giroux, 1983), 51.

39. Abraham Lowenthal, "Latin America—A Not so Special Relationship," *Foreign Policy* no. 32 (Autumn 1978): 110.

40. "Review of U.S. Policy toward Latin America," n.d. (but matches other documents from February–March 1977), Jimmy Carter Presidential Library (hereafter JCPL), RAC, NLC-24-65-3-8-9.

41. Robert A. Pastor, "The Carter Administration and Latin America: A Test of Principle," July 1992, 12–13, http://www.cartercenter.org/documents/1243.pdf.

42. Commission on United States–Latin American Relations, "The United States and Latin America, Next Steps: A Second Report," Center for Inter-American Relations, December 20, 1976.

43. Commission on United States–Latin American Relations, 3–5.

44. Pastor, "Carter Administration and Latin America," 9–10.

45. National Security Council, "Presidential Review Memorandum/NSC 1," January 21, 1977, JCPL, http://www.jimmycarterlibrary.gov/documents/prmemorandums/prm01.pdf.

46. "The Panama Canal Treaties: The Terms of the Treaties," JCPL, http://www.jimmycarterlibrary.gov/education/panama/terms.phtml.

47. Pastor, "Carter Administration and Latin America," 14–15.

48. "Statement on the Panama Canal Treaty Signing," September 7, 1977, http://millercenter.org/president/carter/speeches/speech-3928. Panamanians ratified the treaties in October 1977 through a national plebiscite, with two-thirds in favor. The US Congress took longer—a resolution from a freshman congressman threatened to derail the entire effort—but the Senate approved the second treaty on March 16, 1978, and the first treaty on April 18.

49. Pastor, "Carter Administration and Latin America," 17–19.

50. Memo, Pastor to Brzezinski, "'Do We Need a Latin American Policy?'" March 14, 1977, JCPL, RAC, NLC-24-60-9-1-9; emphasis added.

51. *FRUS, 1969–1976*, vol. 38, pt. 1, doc. 63; emphasis in original.

52. Pastor to Brzezinski, "'Do We Need a Latin American Policy?'"; emphasis in original.

53. Jimmy Carter, "Organization of the American States Address before the Permanent Council," April 14, 1977, http://www.presidency.ucsb.edu/ws/?pid=7347.

54. Pastor, "Carter Administration and Latin America," 22.

55. Arthur M. Schlesinger, Jr., "Human Rights and the American Tradition," *Foreign Affairs* 57, no. 3 (1978): 503.

56. Tony Smith, *America's Mission: The United States and the Worldwide Struggle for Democracy in the 20th Century* (Princeton, NJ: Princeton University Press, 1994). For a historiographic overview of recent scholarship on the Carter administration's post–Cold War foreign policy, see David F. Schmitz and Vanessa Walker, "Jimmy Carter and the Foreign Policy of Human Rights," *Diplomatic History* 28, no. 1 (January 2004): 113–43.

57. Brzezinski, *Power and Principle*, 49.

58. Brzezinski, 124.

59. "Presidential Review Memorandum/NSC-28: Human Rights," August 15, 1977, 2–3, JCPL, RAC, NLC-28-10-10-4-5.

60. "Presidential Review Memorandum/NSC-28," 3.

61. "Mrs. Carter's Trip: The Western Hemisphere in Creative Flux," May 23, 1977, JCPL, RAC, NLC-24-49-6-2-3.

62. Pastor, "Carter Administration and Latin America," 23.

63. Memorandum for Dr. Zbigniew Brzezinski, "Follow-up to President Carter's Pan-American Day Speech and Mrs. Carter's Trip," July 19, 1977, 2–3, JCPL, RAC, NLC-24-61-3-5-9.

64. "Review of U.S. Policy toward Latin America."

65. Ewell, *Venezuela and the United States*, 209–17.

66. Ewell, 209.

67. See the chapter "Disarmament and Development" in the Brandt Report, officially titled *North-South: A Programme for Survival* (London: Pan Books, 1980), 117.

68. Westad, *Cold War*, 573–74.

69. John Dinges and Saul Landau, *Assassination on Embassy Row* (New York: Pantheon, 1980), 139.

70. Pastor, "Carter Administration and Latin America," 24.

71. Memorandum of conversation, "President Carter's First Meeting with the President of Venezuela during His State Visit," June 28, 1977, JCPL, RAC, NLC-24-61-3-5-9.

72. Memo, Christopher to Carter, "Visit by Venezuelan President Carlos Andres Perez," June 23, 1977, JCPL, RAC, NLC-5-15-1-1-8.

73. "North/South Dialogue, Resource Transfer," n.d., JCPL, RAC, NLC-24-63-8-2-5.

74. Kissinger's speech at UNCTAD IV, which met in May 1976 in Nairobi, is covered in chapter 3.

75. Jahangir Amuzegar, "A Requiem for the North-South Conference," *Foreign Affairs*, October 1977, 136–37.

76. Memo, Christopher to Carter, June 4, 1977, JCPL, RAC, NLC-128-12-9-3.

77. Telegram, State to Embassies, April 1977, JCPL, RAC, NLC-24-59-2-4-4.

78. "Carlos Andres Perez," *Economist*, January 6, 2011, http://www.economist.com/node/17848513.

79. "New Strains Ahead as North-South Dialogue Resumes?" n.d., JCPL, RAC, NLC-24-59-2-2-7.

80. Telegram, State to Embassies, April 1977.

81. Jimmy Carter, "Remarks before the Venezuelan Congress," March 29, 1978, in *Public Papers of the Presidents of the United States: Jimmy Carter, 1978* (Washington, D.C.: Government Printing Office, 1979), 619–23. Upon his return, Carter tapped Father

Hesburgh as his special ambassador to the UN Conference on Science and Technology for Development. This conference is covered in chapter 6.

82. Memorandum of conversation, President Carter and President Perez of Venezuela, March 29, 1978, JCPL, RAC, NLC-24-47-2-11-9.

83. Memcon, Carter and Perez.

84. In early 1974 the State Department commented that "never in history has such a transfer of resources occurred without a war." Ewell, *Venezuela and the United States*, 204.

85. Terry Lynn Karl, *The Paradox of Plenty: Oil Booms and Petro-states* (Berkeley and Los Angeles, CA: The University of California Press, 1997), 120

86. Judith Ewell, *Venezuela: A Century of Change* (Stanford, CA: Stanford University Press, 202–3.

87. Ewell, *Venezuela*, 200.

88. H. Micheal Tarver and Julia C. Frederick, *The History of Venezuela* (Westport, CT: Greenwood Press, 2005), 133.

89. US Congress, Joint Economic Committee, *Outlook on Venezuela's Petroleum Policy* (Washington, DC: Government Printing Office, 1980), http://www.jec.senate.gov /reports/96th%20Congress/Outlook%20on%20Venezuela's%20Petroleum%20Policy%20(959).pdf.

90. "President Carter's Talks with Lopez-Portillo: North/South Relations," n.d. (probably September 1979), JCPL, NLC-15-89-6-26-4.

91. See Gaddis Smith, *Morality, Reason, and Power: American Diplomacy in the Carter Years* (New York: Hill and Wang, 1986); David Skidmore, *Reversing Course: Carter's Foreign Policy, Domestic Politics, and the Failure of Reform* (Nashville, TN: Vanderbilt University Press, 1996); Jerel Rosati, "The Rise and Fall of America's First Post–Cold War Foreign Policy," in *Jimmy Carter: Foreign Policy and Post-Presidential Years*, ed. Herbert D. Rosebaum and Alexej Ugrinsky (Westport, CT: Greenwood Press, 1994), 44–47.

92. Michael Hunt makes this point in his classic *Ideology and U.S. Foreign Policy* (New Haven, CT: Yale University Press, 1987). One notable iteration of this persistent theme is Betty Glad, *An Outsider in the White House: Jimmy Carter, His Advisors, and the Making of American Foreign Policy* (Ithaca, NY: Cornell University Press, 2009).

93. Robert Pastor, "The Caricature and the Man," in *Zbig: The Strategy and Statecraft of Zbigniew Brzezinski*, ed. Charles Gati (Baltimore: Johns Hopkins University Press, 2013), 108–9.

94. Pastor, "Carter Administration and Latin America," 38–39.

95. Pastor, 43–44.

96. Memo, Brzezinski to Carter, "The Caribbean Group," September 13, 1980, JCPL, NLC-126-22-25-1-9.

97. Memo, Pastor to Brzezinski, "Beyond Panama: A PRC on Latin America/Caribbean?" May 8, 1978, JCPL, NSA, Staff Material—North/South Files, Robert Pastor Files (Latin America and the Caribbean), box 27, Latin America, 10/77–12/78.

98. Jaime Suchlicki, *Mexico: From Montezuma to NAFTA and Beyond* (New Brunswick, NJ: Transaction Publishers, 2000), 145.

99. Pastor, "Carter Administration and Latin America," 31–32.

100. In a lengthy North-South policy retrospective written in late 1980, the NSC's Thomas Thornton wrote:

Many of us believe that this sacrifice [on foreign aid] should be made for humanitarian or other reasons but we are probably a very small minority. Americans resist this kind of thinking within their own borders and no doubt have still less sympathy for it when applied to distant parts. Nevertheless, the administration failed to test the proposition since the President was never mobilized to argue the foreign assistance case to the American public in the opening months of the Administration when he had his best chance to make a decisive impact. By the time he recognized the need himself it was too late and there were other priorities. Vance's speech [in 1979] was a case of too little and too late.

FRUS, 1977–1980, vol. 3, *Foreign Economic Policy*, doc. 354, https://history.state.gov /historicaldocuments/frus1977-80v03/d354.

101. Quotes and figures from Pastor, "Carter Administration and Latin America," 46, 49.

102. *FRUS, 1977–1980*, vol. 3, doc. 354, fn. 2, https://history.state.gov/historical documents/frus1977-80v03/d354#fn2.

103. *FRUS, 1977–1980*, vol. 3, doc. 295, https://history.state.gov/historicaldocuments /frus1977-80v03/d295. Erb described the US approach at the CIEC and UNCTAD "as one word: containment. We seek to contain first those developed countries that wish to adopt more forthcoming approaches to negotiations with developing countries; and second, the leading developing countries, whose proposals are seen as a challenge to an economic system that has served our interests well and could also serve the interests of developing countries if given a chance."

104. *FRUS, 1977–1980*, vol. 3, doc. 295.

105. *FRUS, 1977–1980*, vol. 3, doc. 295.

106. *FRUS, 1977–1980*, vol. 3, doc. 295.

107. *FRUS, 1977–1980*, vol. 3, doc. 296, https://history.state.gov/historicaldocuments /frus1977-80v03/d296.

108. *FRUS, 1977–1980*, vol. 3, doc. 295.

6. Basic Needs and Appropriate Technology

1. Brzezinski quoted in Stanley Hoffman, "The Hell of Good Intentions," *Foreign Policy* 29 (1977): 4.

2. Memo, Brzezinski to Carter, "Four-Year Goals," April 29, 1977, Jimmy Carter Presidential Library (hereafter JCPL), RAC, NLC-12-26-6-2-2.

3. US Department of State, *Foreign Relation of the United States* [hereafter *FRUS*], *1977–1980*, vol. 2, *Human Rights and Humanitarian Affairs*, doc. 313, https://history.state .gov/historicaldocuments/frus1977-80v02/d313.

4. G-7, London Summit, Session 2, May 7, 1977, http://www.margaretthatcher.org /document/111491.

5. William Glen Grey, "Commercial Liberties and Nuclear Anxieties: The U.S.-German Feud over Brazil, 1975–7," *International History Review* 34, no. 3 (2012): 450.

6. Thornton to Brzezinski, "Annual Report—North-South," December 8, 1977, JCPL, RAC, NLC-24-101-8-3-1.

7. "Anatomy of PRM-8," *CIA Studies in Intelligence* 21, no. 4 (Winter 1977), JCPL, RAC, NLC-29-42-4-10-9. .

8. NSC memorandum, Hansen to Aaron, "My 'Resignation,'" April 11, 1977, JCPL, RAC, NLC-133-225-2-4-8. Although few of his colleagues knew it, Hansen suffered from severe depression. After his tragic suicide in 1991 at age fifty-five, his college friend Calvin Trillin wrote a moving and insightful book on Hansen's life, his struggles, and their meaning. See Calvin Trillin, *Remembering Denny* (New York: Farrar, Straus and Giroux, 1994).

9. NSC memorandum, Pastor to Aaron, April 11, 1977, JCPL, RAC, NLC-24-59-2-3-5.

10. *FRUS, 1977–1980*, vol. 3, *Foreign Economic Policy*, doc. 271, https://history.state.gov/historicaldocuments/frus1977-80v03/d271.

11. Presidential Directive/NSC, "U.S. Policies toward Developing Countries," n.d., JCPL, RAC, NLC-24-101-8-2-2.

12. The expectation that the Carter administration would "soften the U.S. position on LDC debt" was the main reason Brazil, Venezuela, Argentina, Nigeria, and others postponed reconvening the CIEC in the second half of 1976. Telegram, State to Embassies, April 1977, JCPL, RAC, NLC-24-101-8-2-2.

13. Memorandum of conversation (hereafter memcon), President Carter and President Pérez of Venezuela, March 29, 1978, JCPL, RAC, NLC-24-47-2-11-9.

14. *FRUS, 1977–1980*, vol. 3, doc. 306, https://history.state.gov/historicaldocuments/frus1977-80v03/d306.

15. *FRUS, 1977–1980*, vol. 3, doc. 315, https://history.state.gov/historicaldocuments/frus1977-80v03/d315.

16. *FRUS, 1977–1980*, vol. 3, doc. 295, https://history.state.gov/historicaldocuments/frus1977-80v03/d295.

17. *FRUS, 1977–1980*, vol. 3, doc. 320, https://history.state.gov/historicaldocuments/frus1977-80v03/d320.

18. *FRUS, 1977–1980*, vol. 3, doc. 314, https://history.state.gov/historicaldocuments/frus1977-80v03/d314.

19. *FRUS, 1977–1980*, vol. 3, doc. 313, https://history.state.gov/historicaldocuments/frus1977-80v03/d313; emphasis added.

20. *FRUS, 1977–1980*, vol. 3, doc. 315.

21. Cyrus Vance, "Human Rights Policy," April 30, 1977, http://digitalcommons.law.uga.edu/cgi/viewcontent.cgi?article=1015&context=lectures_pre_arch_lectures_lawday.

22. *FRUS, 1977–1980*, vol. 3, doc. 315.

23. Robert K. Olson, *U.S. Foreign Policy and the New International Economic Order: Negotiating Global Problems, 1974–1981* (Boulder, CO: Westview Press, 1981), 36n12.

24. The framework proposed eight negotiating groups to address the following topics: 1. Structural changes and the way UNCTAD could be strengthened; 2. Abolishing Group B protectionism; 3. Revisiting North-South terms of trade; 4. More debt relief and fewer conditionalities for loans; 5. Technology transfer; 6. Special treatment for least developed countries; 7. Trade between developing and socialist countries; 8. Economic cooperation among developing countries. Stephen Taylor, "Note of the Month," *World Today* 35, no. 8 (1979): 311–15.

25. The action plan included a global system of exclusionary trade preferences among developing countries, cooperation among state trading organizations, establish-

ment of multinational enterprises, strengthening of existing regional and subregional groups such as the Latin American Economic System (SELA), and technology sharing.

26. I. S. Gulati, "UNCTAD Yes, Structural Reform No," *Economic and Political Weekly* 14, no. 36 (1979): 1547.

27. In a 1985 interview, Raul Prebisch, the "father" of UNCTAD, summarized the results of Latin American regional economic integration with characteristic ambivalence and wit: "It was not a failure. It was not a success. It was a mediocrity. A typical Latin American mediocrity." Raul Prebisch, interview with David Pollock, http://www .cepal.org/publicaciones/xml/7/20097/lcg2150i_Pollock.pdf.

28. Commonwealth secretary-general Shridath S. Ramphal said at Arusha, "We had high hopes when [US undersecretary of state for economic affairs] Dick Cooper joined the administration, but nothing changed. What happens to people when they get into office?" Quoted in Olson, *U.S. Foreign Policy*, 34.

29. Olson, 33.

30. *FRUS, 1977–1980*, vol. 3, doc. 321, https://history.state.gov/historicaldocuments /frus1977-80v03/d321.

31. *FRUS, 1977–1980*, vol. 3, doc. 321.

32. Carter himself submitted plans for the IDCA to Congress, which approved the new agency in July 1979. The idea, which initially came from senator Hubert Humphrey, was to depoliticize foreign aid by removing USAID from the State Department and placing it under the IDCA's control. Guy Erb, an ODC senior fellow and NSC North-South cluster member, was its first deputy director. However, according to one scholar, "President Carter did not support IDCA . . . [and] USAID programs were not immediately transferred from the State Department to IDCA. The end result was that the State Department co-opted IDCA." In any case, the Reagan administration quickly brought the IDCA—and with it, USAID—back under State Department control. With no permanent staff or clear purpose, it was disbanded in 1998. Rachel M. McCleary, *Global Compassion: Private Voluntary Organizations and U.S. Foreign Policy* (New York: Oxford University Press, 2009), 130.

33. *FRUS, 1977–1980*, vol. 1, *Foundations of Foreign Policy*, doc. 115, https://history .state.gov/historicaldocuments/frus1977-80v01/d115.

34. Gamani Corea described UNCTAD's conundrum:

> On the one hand, you have UNCTAD as an organization which takes various strong positions on various issues but is really a debating house in which certain views are expressed and goals are defined. It passes resolutions, but does not get on to implement them. You then have an institution which serves a purpose but after a while . . . begins to lose credibility because then the countries, including developing countries, will say that UNCTAD does not produce results. A point can be reached where developing countries themselves feel that it is not UNCTAD where they can do business. Thus UNCTAD should be not only a generator of new ideas but should also supplement this role by becoming a place where you can do business.

"Interview with Gamani Corea," *Third World Quarterly* 1, no. 3 (1979): 10.

35. Gamani Corea, *Need for Change: Towards the New International Economic Order* (London: Pergamon, 1980), 28.

36. Olson, *U.S. Foreign Policy*, 47, 65, 71.

37. *FRUS, 1977–1980*, vol. 3, doc. 330, https://history.state.gov/historicaldocuments/frus1977-80v03/d330.

38. Olson, *U.S. Foreign Policy*, 74–75.

39. Paul Hallwood and Stuart Sinclair, *Oil, Debt, and Development: OPEC in the Third World* (London: George Allen and Unwin, 1981), 182–83.

40. *FRUS, 1969–1976*, vol. E-14, pt. 1, *Documents on the United Nations*, doc. 36, https://history.state.gov/historicaldocuments/frus1969-76ve14p1/d36.

41. Olson, *U.S. Foreign Policy*, 74–75.

42. Charles A. Jones, *The North-South Dialogue: A Brief History* (New York: St. Martin's Press, 1983), 91.

43. *FRUS, 1977–1980*, vol. 3, doc. 330.

44. *FRUS, 1977–1980*, vol. 3, doc. 330.

45. *FRUS, 1977–1980*, vol. 3, doc. 315.

46. Janet Raloff, "Vienna: Where North Meets South," *Science News* 116, no. 7 (1979): 126.

47. Stephen J. Macekura, *Of Limits and Growth: The Rise of Sustainable Development in the Twentieth Century* (New York: Cambridge University Press, 2015), 143.

48. "Declaration on the Establishment of a New International Economic Order," May 1, 1974, http://www.un-documents.net/s6r3201.htm.

49. *FRUS, 1977–1980*, vol. 3, doc. 315.

50. Thomas P. Thornton, "The Regional Influentials: Perception and Reality," *SAIS Review* 9, no. 2 (1989): 247.

51. *FRUS, 1977–1980*, vol. 3, doc. 315.

52. David Dickson, *The New Politics of Science* (New York: Pantheon Books, 1984), 125, 183.

53. Zbigniew Brzezinski, *Between Two Ages: America's Role in the Technetronic Era* (New York: Viking Press, 1970).

54. Dickson, *New Politics of Science*, 182–84.

55. See chapter 4 for more on the ODC and its relationship to the Carter campaign.

56. James P. Grant, "Growth from Below: A People-Oriented Development Strategy," ODC Development Paper 16, December 1973, 5–6.

57. "'Have' Nations Scored on Aid to 'Have-Nots,'" *Christian Science Monitor*, April 22, 1972, University of Notre Dame Archives (hereafter UNDA), Collected Papers of Theodore Hesburgh (hereafter CPH) 93/13, folder ODC—Executive Committee and Board of Directors—1972. .

58. Letter, Martin Bordelon to Hesburgh, UNDA, CPH 93/02, folder ODC Correspondence, July–October 1971.

59. Michael O'Brien, interview with James Grant, 1989/1104, UNDA, Michael O'Brien Interviews, AMOB 29855-CT.

60. Hesburgh on *Today Show*, UNDA, CPH 93/24, folder ODC—Agenda for Action—1974.

61. Memo, James Grant to ODC Board Members, "Food Assistance Appeal to President Ford," November 27, 1974, UNDA, CPH 94/05, folder ODC—Gerald Ford and World Famine—1974.

62. "What Is the ODC?" UNDA, CPH 93/01, folder ODC—Programs and Projects—1971.

63. *FRUS, 1977–1980*, vol. 3, doc. 271, https://history.state.gov/historicaldocuments/frus1977-80v03/d271.

64. *FRUS, 1977–1980*, vol. 3, doc. 273, https://history.state.gov/historicaldocuments/frus1977-80v03/d273.

65. Memo, Department of State, "North-South Relations—Status, Plans, and Prospects," April 14, 1977, JCPL, RAC, NLC-24-101-5-1-6.

66. Olson, *U.S. Foreign Policy*, 84.

67. Dickson, *New Politics of Science*, 199, 201.

68. Macekura, *Of Limits and Growth*, 168–69.

69. Hesburgh passed away in February 2015. One year later, I received a research grant from Notre Dame's Cushwa Center to view his files on the ODC and UNCSTD.

70. Letter, Andrew Young to Cyrus Vance, October 21, 1977, UNDA, CPH 108/01, folder UNCSTD—Correspondence—1977.

71. Letter, Jean Wilkowski to James Grant, September 20, 1977, UNDA, CPH 108/02, folder UNCSTD—Correspondence—1977.

72. Letter, James Grant to Jean Wilkowski, October 11, 1977, UNDA, CPH 108/02, folder UNCSTD—Correspondence—1977.

73. Macekura, *Of Limits and Growth*, 161–63.

74. Report, JW to Hesburgh, "Visiting Scientists' Views on UNCSTD," December 15, 1977, UNDA, CPH 108/03, folder UNCSTD—Correspondence—1977.

75. JW to Hesburgh, "Visiting Scientists' Views on UNCSTD."

76. "UNCTAD IV: Expanding Cooperation for Global Economic Development," Fourth Ministerial Meeting of the United Nations Conference on Trade and Development, Nairobi, Kenya, May 6, 1976, https://www.fordlibrarymuseum.gov/library/document/dosb/1927.pdf#page=3.

77. Dickson, *New Politics of Science*, 185–90.

78. Dickson, 192.

79. Letter, Grant to Wilkowski, July 17, 1978, UNDA, CPH 108/06, folder UNCSTD—Correspondence—1978.

80. *FRUS, 1977–1980*, vol. 3, doc. 331, https://history.state.gov/historicaldocuments/frus1977-80v03/d331.

81. These dollar amounts were the range of expected capitalization by 1985 and 1990, respectively.

82. Dickson, *New Politics of Science*, 198. UNCSTD documents actually put the Third World's share of the global research and development budget at 3 percent.

83. *FRUS, 1977–1980*, vol. 3, doc. 334, https://history.state.gov/historicaldocuments/frus1977-80v03/d334.

84. Letter, Owen to Hesburgh, January 30, 1979, UNDA, CPH 108/07, folder UNCSTD—Correspondence—1979.

85. Memcon, Hesburgh and Blumenthal, October 17, 1978, UNDA, CPH 108/12, folder UNCSTD—Memoranda—1978.

86. Memcon, Hesburgh and Vance, August 14, 1979, UNDA, CPH 108/14, folder UNCSTD—Memoranda—1979–1980.

87. Memcon, Hesburgh and Vance, August 14, 1979.

88. Zbigniew Brzezinski, *Power and Principle: Memoirs of the National Security Advisor, 1977–1981* (New York: Farrar, Straus, and Giroux), 432, 429, 444.

89. Tokyo Economic Summit Conference Declaration, June 29, 1979, http://www.presidency.ucsb.edu/ws/?pid=32562.

90. Dickson, *New Politics of Science*, 199.

91. Anne C. Roark, "To Many, the United States Was the Biggest Culprit at the U.N.'s Conference on Science and Technology," *Chronicle of Higher Education*, September 10, 1979, UNDA, CPH 108/10, folder UNCSTD—Correspondence—1979.

92. Eric Bourne, "Technology Is Still a 'Have-Not' for Third World," *Christian Science Monitor*, August 31, 1979.

93. *FRUS, 1977–1980*, vol. 3, doc. 333, https://history.state.gov/historicaldocuments/frus1977-80v03/d333.

94. Roark, "To Many, United States Was Biggest Culprit."

95. Dickson, *New Politics of Science*, 200.

96. Memo, Brzezinski to Carter, "Foreign Policy Overview and the Summit," April 29, 1977, JCPL, RAC, NLC-12-26-6-2-2.

97. Jimmy Carter, Address at Commencement Exercises of Notre Dame University, May 22, 1977, http://www.presidency.ucsb.edu/ws/?pid=7552.

98. *FRUS, 1977–1980*, vol. 3, doc. 336, https://history.state.gov/historicaldocuments/frus1977-80v03/d336.

99. Memo, Thornton to North-South Meeting Group, "North-South Matters," October 27, 1978, JCPL, RAC, NLC-24-98-2-2-3.

100. Memo, Thornton to Brzezisnki, "Annual Report," December 8, 1977, JCPL, RAC, NLC-24-101-8-3-1.

101. US Department of State, "North/South Dialogue and CIEC Strategy," February 1977, JCPL, RAC, NLC-133-157-1-9-0.

102. Stephen S. Rosenfeld, "Carter's Grandest Idea," *Washington Post*, n.d., UNDA, CPH 108/11, folder UNCSTD—Memoranda—1977.

103. Martin Schram, "Carter Commission Renews the War against Hunger," *Washington Post*, June 3, 1979.

104. *FRUS, 1977–1980*, vol. 3, doc. 337, https://history.state.gov/historicaldocuments/frus1977-80v03/d337.

105. *FRUS, 1977–1980*, vol. 3, doc. 336.

106. Samuel Moyn, *Not Enough: Human Rights in an Unequal World* (Cambridge, MA: Harvard University Press, 2018), 130.

107. UNCTAD V, "Arusha Programme for Collective Self-Reliance and Framework for Negotiations," Manila, May 1979, 80–81.

108. *FRUS, 1977–1980*, vol. 3, doc. 354, https://history.state.gov/historicaldocuments/frus1977-80v03/d354.

109. *FRUS, 1977–1980*, vol. 3, doc. 295.

110. *FRUS, 1977–1980*, vol. 3, doc. 327, https://history.state.gov/historicaldocuments/frus1977-80v03/d327.

111. Memcon, Carter and Pérez, March 29, 1978.

112. Alexis Rieffel, *Restructuring Sovereign Debt: The Case for Ad-Hoc Machinery* (Washington, DC: Brookings Institution Press, 2003), 143–44.

113. Cable, State Department to U.S. Delegation, "U.S. Positions on Key UNCTAD V Issues," June 2, 1979, JCPL, RAC, NLC-16-116-4-21-9.

114. Memcon, Hesburgh and Vance, August 14, 1979.

115. Henry Kissinger, "United States Policy on Southern Africa," speech in Lusaka, Zambia, *Department of State Bulletin* 74, no. 1927 (1976): 677.

116. *FRUS, 1977–1980*, vol. 3, doc. 295.

117. Olson, *U.S. Foreign Policy*, 95.

118. *FRUS, 1977–1980*, vol. 3, doc. 354.

119. *FRUS, 1977–1980*, vol. 3, doc. 354.

7. The Reagan Revolution and the End of the North-South Dialogue

1. Republican Party Platform of 1980, Address by the Republican National Convention, July 15, 1980, http://www.presidency.ucsb.edu/ws/?pid=25844.

2. Al Haig, "Peaceful Profess in Developing Nations," *Department of State Bulletin* 81, no. 2052 (July 1981).

3. Tamar Jacoby, "The Reagan Turnaround on Human Rights," *Foreign Affairs*, Summer 1986, https://www.foreignaffairs.com/articles/1986-06-01/reagan-turnaround -human-rights.

4. Mary Stuckey, *Human Rights and the National Agenda* (College Station: Texas A&M Press, 2008), 23.

5. William F. Buckley Jr., "Elliott Abrams Is on the Right Track: Assistant Secretary of State for Human Rights and Humanitarian Affairs, He Monitors International Morality," *Esquire*, December 1984.

6. Jacoby, "Reagan Turnaround on Human Rights."

7. Elliott Abrams, "United States Human Rights Policy," speech before the Council on Foreign Relations, February 10, 1982, http://www.disam.dsca.mil/Pubs/Indexes /Vol%204-4/Abrams.pdf.

8. "Ernest W. LeFever Dies at 89; Founder of Conservative Policy Organization," *Los Angeles Times*, July 31, 2009, http://www.latimes.com/local/obituaries/la-me -ernest-lefever31-2009jul31-story.html.

9. "Hearing before the Committee on Foreign Relations, United States Senate, Ninety-Seventh Congress, First Session, on Nomination of Elliott Abrams, of the District of Columbia, to Be Assistant Secretary of State for Human Rights and Humanitarian Affairs," November 17, 1981, https://catalog.hathitrust.org/Record/01133 8487.

10. David Johnston, "Elliott Abrams Admits His Guilt on 2 Counts in Contra Cover-up," *New York Times*, October 8, 1991, http://www.nytimes.com/1991/10/08 /us/elliott-abrams-admits-his-guilt-on-2-counts-in-contra-cover-up.html?pagewanted =all.

11. William Greider, "The Education of David Stockman," *Atlantic*, December 1981, https://www.theatlantic.com/magazine/archive/1981/12/the-education-of-david -stockman/305760/.

12. Sarah Babb, *Behind the Development Banks: Washington Politics, World Poverty, and the Wealth of Nations* (Chicago: University of Chicago Press, 2009), 73.

13. Henry Nau, "Where Reaganomics Works," *Foreign Policy* 57 (1984): 14.

14. Babb, *Behind the Development Banks*, 75.

15. Nau, "Where Reaganomics Works," 14.

16. Nau, 15, 23.

17. Nau, 24.

18. In an interview, Nau told me that the "magic" line was Reagan's own: "We took it out! Not we, but the State Department, they took it out, and we kept putting it back in, take it out, put it back in. And when it got to Reagan at the last stage, he always insisted, "Where's my phrase? I want magic of the 'marketplace in there.'" That was *his* wording! Nobody knew about all of his transcripts from radio, they thought someone gave him a script and he read it. No! He thought through all those scripts, they made a mountain of a book out of all those, his thinking, as it evolved in the 1960s." Author interview with Henry Nau, Washington, D.C., December 5, 2008.

19. Ronald Reagan, "Remarks at the Annual Meeting of the Board of Governors of the World Bank Group and International Monetary Fund," September 29, 1981, http://www.presidency.ucsb.edu/ws/?pid=44311.

20. Vassilis K. Fouskas, *The Politics of International Political Economy* (New York: Routledge, 2013), 153.

21. Steven G. Livingston, "The Politics of International Agenda-Setting: Reagan and North-South Relations," *International Studies Quarterly* 36, no. 3 (September 1992): 322.

22. Reagan, "Remarks at Annual Meeting."

23. Gary H. Sampliner, "The 1981 OPIC Amendments and Reagan's Newer Directions in Third World Development Policy," *Law and Policy in International Business* 14, no. 181 (1982): 186–87.

24. "My Global Life: A Conversation with Raymond Malley," interview by Charles Stuart Kennedy for the Diplomatic Oral History Series, Association for Diplomatic Studies and Training, 131.

25. Ramesh Ramsaran, "The US Caribbean Basin Initiative," *World Today* 38, no. 11 (1982): 431.

26. David Stockman, *The Triumph of Politics: How the Reagan Revolution Failed* (New York: Harper and Row, 1986), 116.

27. Stockman, 117; Livingston, "Politics of International Agenda-Setting," 320.

28. Livingston, "Politics of International Agenda Setting," 319; Liam Downey, *Inequality, Democracy, and the Environment* (New York: NYU Press, 2015), 93.

29. Gregory D. Moffett III, "Reagan's Imprint on Foreign Aid," *Christian Science Monitor*, May 23, 1985, https://www.csmonitor.com/1985/0523/zaid1-f1.html.

30. Richard E. Feinberg, "American Power and Third World Economies," in *Eagle Resurgent: The Reagan Era in American Foreign Policy*, ed. Kenneth A. Oye, Robert J. Leiber, and Donald Rothchild (Boston: Little, Brown, 1983), 147.

31. John W. Sewell, Richard E. Feinberg, and Valeriana Kallab, eds., *U.S. Foreign Policy and the Third World: Agenda 1985–86* (Washington, DC: Overseas Development Council, 1985), 11.

32. "Editorial: From Venice to Cancun" *Third World Quarterly* 3, no. 4 (1981): xxiii.

33. Livingston, "Politics of International Agenda-Setting," 317.

34. Author interview with Henry Nau, Washington, D.C., December 5, 2008.

35. John English, *Just Watch Me: The Life of Pierre Elliott Trudeau: 1968–2000* (Toronto: Random House Canada, 2010), 563.

36. Colin McCullough and Robert Teigrob, eds., *Canada and the United Nations: Legacies, Limits, Prospects* (Montreal: McGill-Queens University Press, 2016).

37. Robert McNamara, "To the Board of Governors," September 26, 1977, in *The McNamara Years at the World Bank* (Baltimore: Johns Hopkins University Press, 1981).

38. Giuliano Garavini, *After Empires: European Integration, Decolonization, and the Challenge from the Global South, 1957–1986* (Oxford: Oxford University Press, 2012), 234.

39. The Dutch government paid for about half of the commission's costs; a coalition of countries (Denmark, Finland, India, Japan, Norway, Saudi Arabia, South Korea, and the United Kingdom), the European Commission, OPEC, and a number of foundations and research centers provided the remaining funds. Ramesh Thakur, Andrew F. Cooper, and John English, eds., *International Commissions and the Power of Ideas* (New York: United Nations University Press, 2006), 31.

40. Independent Commission on International Development Issues, *North-South: A Programme for Survival* (London: Pan Books, 1980).

41. John Toye and Richard Toye, *The UN and Global Political Economy: Trade, Finance, and Development* (Bloomington: Indiana University Press, 2004), 255–56.

42. Speech by Lord Carrington, Caracas, Venezuela, August 4, 1980, https://opendocs.ids.ac.uk/opendocs/ds2/stream/?#/documents/43767/page/1.

43. Toye and Toye, *UN and Global Political Economy*, 256.

44. Margaret Thatcher, *The Downing Street Years* (London: HarperCollins, 1993), 168–69.

45. "But Will It Play in Bangladesh?" *National Journal*, July 1981, www.nationaljournal.com/s/240265/focuses-will-play=bangladesh.

46. Livingston, "Politics of International Agenda-Setting," 321.

47. Babb, *Behind the Development Banks*, 78.

48. "Concluding Statements of the Ottawa G-7 Economic Summit Conference Participants," July 21, 1981, http://www.presidency.ucsb.edu/ws/index.php?pid=44103.

49. Helen Thomas, "President Reagan Arrived Today . . . ," https://www.upi.com/Archives/1981/10/21/President-Reagan-arrived-today-at-the-22-nation-Cancun-summit/4201372484800/. Those twenty-two heads of state represented Algeria, Austria, Bangladesh, Brazil, Britain, Canada, China, France, Guyana, India, Ivory Coast, Japan, Mexico, Nigeria, Philippines, Saudi Arabia, Sweden, Tanzania, United States, Venezuela, West Germany, and Yugoslavia.

50. "U.S. Agrees Gingerly to a Cancun Followup," *National Journal*, September 1981, https://www.nationaljournal.com/s/241381/washington-update-policy-politics-brief-u-s-agrees-gingerly-cancun-followup?mref=search-result.

51. Thatcher, *Downing Street Years*, 169.

52. Stephen Buzdugan and Anthony Payne, *The Long Battle for Global Governance* (New York: Routledge, 2016), 102.

53. Thatcher, *Downing Street Years*, 170.

54. Toye and Toye, *UN and Global Political Economy*, 257.

55. Daniel P. Moynihan, "The United States in Opposition," *Commentary*, March 1, 1975, https://www.commentarymagazine.com/articles/the-united-states-in-opposition/.

56. US Department of Treasury, "Cancun Summit," August 5, 1981, https://www .cia.gov/library/readingroom/docs/CIA-RDP84B00049R001700030006-0.pdf.

57. "The Third World appears ready to compromise utopian plans for restructuring the world economy and accept negotiations that would provide procedural protection for the competence of the World Bank and International Monetary Fund. Global Negotiations in the UN will provide the Third World political leverage to accelerate evolutionary change in the international financial institutions but *will not damage their independent legal status or autonomous decisionmaking*." National Foreign Assessment Center, memorandum for Jeane K. Kirkpatrick, "The Impact of Global Negotiations on International Financial Institutions," December 3, 1981, https://www.cia.gov/library/readingroom/docs/CIA-RDP95B00915R000500110019 -5.pdf.

58. Sebastian Edwards, "Forty Years of Latin America's Economic Development: From the Alliance for Progress to the Washington Consensus," NBER Working Paper 15190, July 2009, http://www.nber.org/papers/w15190.pdf.

59. James Cronin, *Global Rules: America, Britain, and a Disordered World* (New Haven, CT: Yale University Press, 2015), 142–43.

60. Toye and Toye, *UN and Global Political Economy*, 258–59.

61. Sarah Hsu, *Financial Crises, 1929 to the Present*, 2nd ed. (Northampton, MA: Edward Elgar Publishing, 2017), 61.

62. Cronin, *Global Rules*, 145.

63. Livingston, "Politics of International Agenda-Setting," 524.

64. Toye and Toye, *UN and Global Political Economy*, 260.

65. John Williamson, the "author" of the Washington Consensus, expressed his ambivalence toward the concept years later. See Williamson, "The Washington Consensus as a Policy Prescription for Development," World Bank, January 13, 2004, https://piie .com/publications/papers/williamson0204.pdf.

66. Cronin, *Global Rules*, 145; Livingston, "Politics of International Agenda-Setting," 324.

67. Quotes by Paul Volcker and Jacque de Larosiere (managing director of the IMF), respectively, in C. Roe Goddard, *U.S. Foreign Policy and the Latin American Debt Issue* (London: Routledge, 1993), 20.

68. L. Ronald Scheman, *Greater America: A New Partnership for the Americas in the Twenty-First Century* (New York: NYU Press, 2003), 99.

69. Ross P. Buckley and Douglas W. Arner, eds., *From Crisis to Crisis: The Global Financial System and Regulatory Failure* (New York: Kluwer Law International, 2011), 273.

70. Toye and Toye, *UN and Global Political Economy*, 258.

71. Quoted in Toye and Toye, 266–70.

72. "Briefing Paper on CIEC," July 26, 1976, Gerald Ford Presidential Library, State Department, folder: International Organizations, box 1, International Organizations, White House Central Files.

73. Presidential Directive/NSC, "U.S. Policies toward Developing Countries," n.d., Jimmy Carter Presidential Library, RAC, NLC-24-101-8-2-2.

Epilogue

1. Independent Commission on International Development Issues, *Common Crisis North-South: Cooperation for World Recovery* (London: Pan Books, 1983), 11–12.

2. Independent Commission, 12–13.

3. Independent Commission on International Development Issues, *North-South: A Programme for Survival* (London: Pan Books, 1980), 31.

4. Sinah Theres Kloß, "The Global South as Subversive Practice: Challenges and Potentials of a Heuristic Concept," *Global South* 11, no. 2 (2017): 6.

5. Branko Milanovic, *Global Inequality: A New Approach for the Age of Globalization* (Cambridge, MA: Belknap/Harvard University Press, 2016), 20.

6. Milanovic, 122.

7. For the postwar origins of this system, see Vanessa Ogle, "Archipelago Capitalism: Tax Havens, Offshore Money, and the State, 1950s–1970s," *American Historical Review* 122, no. 5 (December 2017): 1431–58. A practical and vibrant guide to contemporary North-South money laundering is "Undue Diligence: How Banks Do Business with Corrupt Regimes," a report by Global Witness (March 2009). I had the good fortune to discover this report in a pile of free books while wandering around a basement hallway of the World Bank.

8. The governments of Hong Kong, Singapore, South Korea, and Taiwan have also had notable success in controlling COVID-19, especially when compared with the United States and western Europe. Singaporean diplomat and scholar Kishore Mahbubani predicts that this contrast in responses and outcomes "will hasten the [global] power-shift to the east." "Kishore Mahbubani on the Dawn of the Asian Century," *Economist*, April 20, 2020, https://www.economist.com/by-invitation/2020/04/20/kishore-mahbubani-on-the-dawn-of-the-asian-century.

9. Milanovic, *Global Inequality*, 130.

10. Emmanuel Saez, "Striking It Richer: The Evolution of Top Incomes in the United States (Updated with 2018 Estimates)," https://eml.berkeley.edu/~saez/saez-UStopincomes-2018.pdf. The article was first published by the Stanford Center for the Study of Poverty and Inequality in *Pathways Magazine*, Winter 2008, 6–7.

11. Saez.

12. Saez.

13. Saez.

14. A comprehensive study from the International Labor Organization concluded: "From an economic perspective, generally-available adjustment measures should be preferred over targeted trade adjustment assistance. Apart from the moral concerns as to why those affected by trade liberalization should be treated differently than those affected by other shocks, including those stemming from globalization as a whole, targeted assistance appears to have had rather mixed success in facilitating structural adjustment." Marion Jansen, Ralf Peters, and José Manuel Salazar-Xirinachs, eds., *Trade and Employment: From Myths to Facts* (Geneva: International Labour Office, 2011), 26.

15. Economic Policy Institute, "The Productivity-Pay Gap," updated July 2019, https://www.epi.org/productivity-pay-gap/.

16. Milanovic, *Global Inequality*, 20.

17. Milanovic, 131, 133.

18. Derek Headey and Fan Shengen, *Reflections on the Global Food Crisis: How Did It Happen? How Has It Hurt? And How Can We Prevent the Next One?* (Washington, DC: International Food Policy Research Institute, 2010), 83, fig. 4.1 (from data constructed by the authors).

19. "World Bank head warns of food price crisis," *BBC News*, April 17, 2011, https://www.bbc.com/news/av/business-13110449/world-bank-head-warns-of-food-price -crisis.

20. "The World Food Crisis," editorial, *New York Times*, April 10, 2008, https://www .nytimes.com/2008/04/10/opinion/10thu1.html. The editorial quoted World Bank president Robert Zoellick (formerly George W. Bush's US trade representative), who warned that thirty-three nations were at risk of social unrest because of the rising prices of food: "For countries where food comprises from half to three-quarters of consumption [of income], there is no margin for survival."

21. In May 2008 the *New York Times* ran a special feature on the food crisis and asked Columbia University development economists Jeffrey Sachs and Jagdish Bhagwati— both thoroughly mainstream voices—to diagnose the problem. For one, Sachs explained, African farmers lacked financing to buy critical inputs such as fertilizers and high-yield seeds. This has only exacerbated African countries' dependence on food imports despite arable land and robust local demand. "The donor countries would do Africa and the world a load of good by focusing less on shipping expensive food aid from Europe and the United States and focusing much more on helping African farmers gain access to the inputs they need for higher productivity. Most important for the current crisis, however, was the direct link between the biofuel craze in rich countries and the food crisis in poor ones: "[The] rich countries should stop diverting their food crops, such as maize in the United States and wheat in Europe, and their food-growing land (such as the shift in Europe from wheat and maize to rapeseed) for biofuel production. Using food for biofuels is actually bad for the environment (through the high-energy inputs used to grow the crops and to convert them to biofuels) and is disastrous for global food balances." In his opening statement, Bhagwati put it even more bluntly: "The current crisis is less a result of droughts (except for Australia) and more a result of diversion of crops [by rich countries] such as corn to biofuels production." Daniel Altman, "Dealing with the Global Food Crisis," *New York Times*, May 6, 2008, https://www .nytimes.com/2008/05/06/business/worldbusiness/06iht-glob07.1.12604305.html.

22. According to the International Monetary Fund, ethanol production in the United States *alone* accounted for at least half the rise in world corn demand in 2005, 2006, and 2007.

23. Quoted in Elisabeth Rosenthal and Andrew Martin, "UN Says Solving Food Crisis Could Cost $30 Billion," *New York Times*, June 4, 2008, https://www.nytimes.com /2008/05/06/business/worldbusiness/06iht-glob07.1.12604305.html.

INDEX